THE BOOK OF

# SECOND CORINTHIANS

## GRACE UNDER SIEGE

Advancing the Ministries of the Gospel
**AMG** *Publishers*

*God's Word to you is our highest calling.*

## TWENTY-FIRST CENTURY
### BIBLICAL COMMENTARY SERIES®

THE  OF

# SECOND CORINTHIANS

## GRACE UNDER SIEGE

DAN
# MITCHELL

GENERAL EDITORS

## MAL COUCH &
## ED HINDSON

**The Book of Second Corinthians: Grace Under Siege**
By Dan Mitchell
Copyright © 2008 by Scofield Ministries
Twenty-First Century Biblical Commentary Series®
Published by AMG Publishers
6815 Shallowford Road
Chattanooga, TN 37421

ISBN–13: 978-0-89957-824-8
ISBN–10: 0-89957-824-1

First Published: July 2009

Cover Design by Indoor Graphics Corp.
Editing and Text Design by Warren Baker
Editorial assistance provided by Weller Editorial Services, Chippewa Lake, MI

Printed in Canada
14 13 12 11 10 09 –T– 7 6 5 4 3 2 1

*To my dad, Burton C Mitchell,*
*noted Bible teacher,*
*whose love for the Word of God was exceeded only by*
*his love for the God of the Word*

# Twenty-First Century Biblical Commentary Series®

## Mal Couch, Th.D., and Ed Hindson, D.Phil.

The New Testament has guided the Christian church for over two thousand years. This one testament is made up of twenty-seven books, penned by godly men through the inspiration of the Holy Spirit. It tells us of the life of Jesus Christ, His atoning death for our sins, His miraculous resurrection, His ascension back to heaven, and the promise of His second coming. It also tells the story of the birth and growth of the church and the people and principles that shaped it in its earliest days. The New Testament concludes with the book of Revelation pointing ahead to the glorious return of Jesus Christ.

Without the New Testament, the message of the Bible would be incomplete. The Old Testament emphasizes the promise of a coming Messiah. It constantly points us ahead to the one who is coming to be the King of Israel and the Savior of the world. But the Old Testament ends with this event still unfulfilled. All of its ceremonies, pictures, types, and prophecies are left awaiting the arrival of the "Lamb of God who takes away the sin of the world" (John 1:29).

The message of the New Testament represents the timeless truth of God. As each generation seeks to apply that truth to its specific context, an up-to-date commentary needs to be created just for them. The editors and authors of the Twenty-First Century Biblical Commentary Series have endeavored to do just that. This team of scholars represents conservative, evangelical, and dispensational scholarship at its best. The individual authors may differ on minor points of interpretation, but all are convinced that the Old and New Testaments teach a dispensational framework for biblical history. They also hold to a pretribulational and premillennial understanding of biblical prophecy.

The French scholar René Pache reminded each succeeding generation, "If the power of the Holy Spirit is to be made manifest anew among us, it is of primary importance that His message should regain its due place. Then we shall be able to put the enemy to flight by the sword of the Spirit which is the Word of God."

It has long been observed that 2 Corinthians is Paul's most personal and passionate letter. Erasmus compares it to a river that sometimes flows in a gentle stream and other times rushes down as a torrent sweeping all before it. Charles Hodge said, "It is the most interesting of Paul's letters as bringing out the man before the reader and revealing his intimate relations to the people to whom he wrote." Philip E. Hughes adds, "Indeed, of all the epistles in the New Testament none is, in style and temperament, more characteristic of the great apostle."

F. F. Bruce has observed, "This epistle, more than any other, poses problems to those who attempt to reconstruct the sequence of events or circumstances to which the apostle alludes from time to time." In none of Paul's other letters do we find so much autobiographical information relating to persons, events, problems and situations in the apostle's life and ministry. It is, in fact, these specific details that shout to us of the authenticity of this powerful letter, which expresses both Paul's sincere love and serious concerns for the Corinthian church and, indeed, for the church today as well.

# Abbreviations

| | |
|---|---|
| *AJPS* | *American Journal of Political Science* |
| ATANT | Abhandlungen zur Theologie des Alten und Neuen Testaments |
| *Bib Sac* | *Bibliotheca Sacra* |
| *BZ* | *Biblische Zeitschrift* |
| BZNW | Beihefte zur Zeitschrift für die neutestamentliche Wissenschaft |
| *CBQ* | *Catholic Biblical Quarterly* |
| *EvQ* | *Evangelical Quarterly* |
| *ExpT* | *The Expository Times* |
| ICC | International Critical Commentary |
| *ISBE* | *International Standard Bible Encyclopedia* |
| *JBL* | *Journal of Biblical Literature* |
| *JSNT* | *Journal for the Study of the New Testament* |
| MNTC | Moffatt New Testament Commentary |
| NICNT | New International Commentary on the New Testament |
| NIGTC | New International Greek Testament Commentary |
| *NovT* | *Novum Testamentum* |
| *RB* | *Revue Biblique* |
| SCHNT | Studia ad Corpus Hellenisticum Novi Testamenti (Leiden: Brill) |
| SNTSMS | Society for New Testament Studies Monograph Series |
| *TDNT* | *Theological Dictionary of the New Testament*, G. Kittel and G. Friedrich, eds. |

# Contents

   *2 Corinthians 5:11–6:10*

10. Perfecting Holiness in the Fear of God                   115
    *2 Corinthians 6:11–7:1*

11. Repentance without Regret                                121
    *2 Corinthians 7:2–16*

**Second Trajectory: Practical Needs**

12. We Are in This Together                                  131
    *2 Corinthians 8:1–8:15*

13. Seek Ye First the Kingdom                                143
    *2 Corinthians 8:16–9:15*

**Third Trajectory: Authority Demands Respect**

14. Weapons of Our Warfare                                   157
    *2 Corinthians 10:1–18*

15. Fools Talk                                               169
    *2 Corinthians 11:1–15*

16. Playing the Fool for Jesus' Sake                         181
    *2 Corinthians 11:16–12:21*

17. Examine Yourselves                                       201
    *2 Corinthians 13:1–10*

18. Peace, the Gift of God's Love                            207
    *2 Corinthians 13:11–14*

    Bibliography                                             213

    Notes                                                    215

# Background of 2 Corinthians

Preparation and concern regarding the apostle Paul's third visit to the city of Corinth occasioned the writing of the New Testament letter known as 2 Corinthians. It may well be the fourth written correspondence that he sent to this city.[1] It appears that a "previous epistle" was written prior to 1 Corinthians, and then another "sorrowful letter" was written between 1 Corinthians and 2 Corinthians. This book, the second canonical epistle, has several features that distinguish it. Paul's first epistle is both practical and instructional, but this epistle is intensely personal and autobiographical. In fact, its style appears so spontaneous and emotional that some have questioned its internal consistency. For this reason, a word needs to be said about the unity and authorial integrity of the epistle.[2]

## Authorship, Style, and Literary Unity

Since the late eighteenth century, higher critical analysis has led many to speculate that this epistle may actually constitute a collection of writings rather than one single letter.[3] Dispute is generally focused on whether 1:1–2:13 is connected with what follows. The passage, 6:14–7:1, seems to many to be entirely out of place in its present setting. Chapters 8 and 9, regarding the offering, are thought to be an independent unit likely inserted by a later redactor. And most of chapters 10–13 (excluding 13:11–14 [13]) are thought to have been very possibly the "sorrowful letter" to which the writer makes frequent reference.[4] More recent scholars rarely question the Pauline authorship, even when they question whether it was written all at once.

While each of the various partition theories is unique and deserves careful study on its own terms, all of them seem to have several problems in common.

Placing the burden of proof on the traditional view, they begin with an assumption that the putative writer Paul could not have written the letter in its present constructed form. In their effort to *fix* this problem, redactors are said to do things that are difficult if not unthinkable given the high regard the early believers had for the writings of the apostles. Reconstructions by critics require cutting and pasting introductions and/or conclusions to various individual letters (as they are supposed to be) and placing them somewhere else in order to create compositional unity. It is extremely doubtful that this was a liberty that would have been taken by those responsible for the early collections of the New Testament. One can hardly imagine, for example, Onesimus doing anything like this. After his release from slavery to Philemon, he is reputed to have dedicated much of his life to collecting and arranging the letters of Paul. If this tradition is correct, the placement of his own letter at the bottom of the collection would give mute testimony to the high regard he had for Paul's writings and his own indebtedness to him.

Garland also raises the question of the "physical difficulty involved."[5] The people of Paul's day did not have word processors as we do today. They had scrolls. The difficulty of this procedure is generally not considered. "For example, the hypothetical letter fragment of 6:4–7:1 would have taken up 'approximately one narrow column.' Much of the letter it supposedly came from would have had to be deleted, and this column would have been inserted in the middle of another letter."[6] Why and how this would have been done is largely ignored. It if does not make sense to a would-be editor today, why would an ancient redactor think otherwise?

Those who call in question the unity of 2 Corinthians include Alford, Lake, Moffatt, Kummel, Plummer, and more recently Betz, Koester, Furnish, and Davies.[7] However, their arguments are adequately rebutted by others, such as Thiselton, Fee, Barrett, Wallace, Carson, Barnett, and the earlier work by P. E. Hughes. There is no external evidence to support the contention that 2 Corinthians was ever more than one unit. The arguments rest entirely upon internal evidence, such as the change of tone in chapters 10–13, certain supposed inconsistencies in 1–9 compared with 10–13, and the reconciling of some statements with Paul's geographical location at the time of writing (10:16). Some look for the "severe letter" mentioned above to have been inserted.[8] None of the arguments in support of this carry much weight. No extant manuscripts suggest a patchwork of units. No patristic writers suggest the possibility of multiple documents. Furthermore, other internal arguments support the continuity rather than the discontinuity of the text. The epistle is less formal than others of Paul's epistles. It is much more emotional, and hence, there are more abrupt changes in the writer's thought. Yet the main divisions are clearly visible. Beyond this, Paul refers to a visit by Titus to Corinth in 2 Corinthians 12:18. This could not have been to deliver the severe letter unless these chapters are not the letter. Thiessen is probably correct to suggest that the changes in tone between chapters 1–9 and 10–13 are likely due to the particular group Paul is addressing in each of these sections.[9] This peculiarity in style can be demonstrated, not only in other biblical literature, but in secular literature as well.

A strong case can be made for the unity of the epistle sufficient to resist any attempt to break it up. The writer calls himself Paul (1:1; 10:1). Conservative scholarship is unanimous in its agreement that the Pauline authorship of this epistle is unmistakable, not only in content but in style and vocabulary. Furthermore, it is unlikely Paul would be defending his apostolic authority if the text was not authentic. A pseudo-Pauline author or redactor would not be expected to insert material that would reflect negatively on the apostolic author.

Given what is known of Paul's rhetorical style, his complex situation in Corinth, and his general emotional state attested to in his own words throughout this letter, there seem to be no necessary or sufficient reasons to question that (a) Paul can very well be imagined to have written this just as it is and (b) there is no unambiguous evidence to the contrary. In this study these "units" will be examined as they occur in the text. Not all of the questions will be addressed, but the story presented here will suggest why the unity of the text has the better internal support.

Although the historical evidence is not as early as that of 1 Corinthians, it is almost equally as strong. External evidence suggests that the second epistle of the Corinthians had not yet reached Rome by the end of the first century (AD 96) since Clement of Rome does not quote it (but does quote from the first epistle). However, it is cited in the Letters of Ignatius, and it was known to Polycarp of Smyrna (ca. AD 70–155) who quotes, along with several citations of 1 Corinthians, several passages from 2 Corinthians in his letter to the Philippians, including 4:14; 6:7; 8:21; and 10:1. Second Corinthians is further attested in the letter to Diognetus, Athenagoras, Theophilus of Antioch, Tertullian, Clement of Alexandria, Irenaeus, the Muratorian Canon, and Marcion's *Apostolocon*. It is also found in the old Syriac and the old Latin, along with the first epistle. By the end of the second century, there is little questioning that 2 Corinthians is an authentic writing of Paul and that it carries with it his apostolic authority.

Some have noted the apocalyptic[10] element in the book.[11] Throughout the epistle the use of apocalyptic and eschatological imagery is evident. For example, the comfort of 1:3–11 is from the "God who raises the dead" and against the "end . . . in the day of our Lord" (1:13–14). Chapters 3 and 4 contrast "key revelatory moments in Israel's history"[12] with the surpassing "glory of the Lord" (cf. 3:7–18; 4:3–18). There is, of course, the important section in chapter 5 dealing with the resurrection body (vv. 1–10). Even the collection for Jerusalem is discussed in relation to God's "indescribable gift" of Jesus Christ. Concerning the apocalyptic element in the New Testament compared with similar Jewish materials of the period, it is important to compare and contrast them.

It is certainly true that the ethos and atmosphere of the New Testament are different from that of the Jewish apocalyptic literature. However, it is different not because Jesus and his disciples rejected apocalyptic but because they took it for granted. . . . Jesus accepted the basic expectations of apocalyptic literature—especially the coming from heaven of the Son of Man and the resurrection of the dead, in the context of the two ages—modified or transformed them, and at the same time began to fulfill them (e.g., in his own resurrection). The apostles continued this process of development and fulfillment. Thus apocalyptic teaching forms a bridge from the Old Testament to the New Testament. It helps us to see how God began to act in Jesus in a decisive, eschatological way.[13]

| *Apocalyptic Portions of the Corinthian Letters* | |
| --- | --- |
| Security of the believer | 1 Cor. 1:4–7 |
| Power of the cross | 1 Cor. 1:17–19 |
| Bema Seat judgment | 1 Cor. 3:10–15; 2 Cor. 5:10, 11 |
| Judgment of the lost | 1 Cor. 5:13 |
| Destiny of the righteous and the unrighteous | 1 Cor. 6:9–11 |
| Future prize for service to Christ | 1 Cor. 9:24–27 |
| Future revelation of full knowledge | 1 Cor. 13:9–13 |
| Promise of the bodily resurrection | 1 Cor. 15:12–19; 35–50 |
| Order of the resurrection | 1 Cor. 15:20–28 |
| Resurrection and the Rapture | 1 Cor. 15:51–58; 2 Cor. 4:14–18; 5:1–9 |
| Day of the Lord Jesus | 2 Cor. 1:14[15] |

Much of this apocalyptic speculation was drawn from Daniel's "One like a Son of Man" who "came up to the Ancient of Days" and "was given dominion, glory and a kingdom, that all the peoples, nations, and men of every language might serve Him. His dominion is an everlasting dominion which will not pass away; and His kingdom is one which will not be destroyed" (Dan. 7:13–14). The apocalyptic writers explored the implications of such a promise. It was in its fulfillment in Christ that the New Testament writers began to understand the wonder and the specifics of this promise that was to become the "blessed hope" of all who long for "the appearing of the glory of our great God and Savior, Christ Jesus" (Titus 2:13).[14]

## Background, Purpose, and Argument

Victor Furnish observes that together with the first canonical epistle to this ancient city of Corinth we have "as vivid and informative a snapshot as we are ever likely to have of the apostle's ministry."[16] He elaborates:

> This is in part because his letters to Corinth provide considerable detail about the Corinthian congregation and his continuing relationship to it. Paul mentions the names of several members of that church, answers its letter to him, responds to reports he has received about it, and addresses matters of importance both for its congregational life and for his mission overall. Beyond this, because of the political and economic significance of Corinth in the apostle's day and a full century of careful archaeological excavation at the site, we are able to know a fair amount about the social context of his ministry there. This lends both color and context to the snapshot of Paul's Corinthian ministry. Finally, the letters to Corinth, more than any other Pauline letters, show the apostle engaged in the twofold task to which he was most passionately committed: proclaiming the truth of the gospel and guiding believers in discerning the gospel's impact on their daily lives.[17]

Second Corinthians is written to the assembly that was founded during Paul's first visit to the city. Since his departure and subsequent ministry in Ephesus, he has learned of problems afflicting them and enemies attempting to sabotage his work. Problems continue to fester in spite of his efforts in the first epistle.[18]

Opposition to Paul's ministry continued to mount, probably coming from the party that associated itself with "Christ" (cf. 1 Cor. 1:12; 2 Cor. 10:7; 11:3, 4, 13, 23). The leader of this group seems to have been especially obnoxious to the writer (10:7–11). When news of these conditions reached him at

Ephesus, he made a brief visit to the city in order to deal with them (cf. 2:1; 12:14, 21; 13:1, 2). At this time the personal vendetta against the apostle Paul himself was shown. Upon his return to Ephesus, Paul was so distressed that he penned a letter to the church of such a severe nature that he later regretted having written it (2 Cor. 7:8). This he sent to them by Titus (2:3, 4, 9; 7:8–12). This letter seems to have been lost in its entirety. While some, as noted above, have suggested that this letter is preserved in 2 Corinthians 10–13,[19] the theory is unlikely.[20] The charges leveled against him by this group are indicated in a number of passages in the epistle.

## Accusations Found in Second Corinthians

### Accusations of the Corinthians Against Paul

| | |
|---|---|
| fickle | 2 Corinthians 1:17 |
| authoritarian | 2 Corinthians 1:24 |
| ministering without proper credentials | 2 Corinthians 3:1 |
| cowardice | 2 Corinthians 10:1, 10 |
| failure to maintain proper clerical dignity | 2 Corinthians 11:7 |
| presumption | 2 Corinthians 10:13–17 |
| fleshliness | 2 Corinthians 10:2 |

### Accusations of Paul Against the Corinthians

| | |
|---|---|
| corrupted the word | 2 Corinthians 2:17 |
| deceptive | 2 Corinthians 3:1 |
| Jews masquerading as ministers of Christ | 2 Corinthians 11:23–27 |
| domineering | 2 Corinthians 11:20 |
| bold | 2 Corinthians 11:21 |
| lacked spiritual courage to step out on their own and start their own ministry | 2 Corinthians 11:23–27 |

The epistle is personal and autobiographical throughout. However, the reader cannot help but be amazed at the terms Paul finds necessary to describe his situation and circumstances. These include, "affliction," "anguish," "beatings," "distresses," "fastings," "fightings," "labors," "perils," "persecutions," "sorrows," "stripes," "sufferings," "tears," "tumult," "weak" and "weakness."[21] In expressing his concerns, state of mind, and overwhelming heartbreak for these people to whom God had called him as the undershepherd, he exposes his heart, giving convicting witness to that which may be expected of any pastor who stands to extend God's saving grace to sometimes ungrateful, fickle, and immature people. Few could claim, with Paul, that they endured as much. Nevertheless, it is for this reason that these letters have become so instructive and helpful to churches of every culture and every age since they were first written.

Titus was to deliver a "sorrowful letter" then return to Paul with a report of the response of the Corinthians and subsequent development. However, Paul had to leave Ephesus earlier than scheduled because of the uprising of the silversmiths (cf. Acts 20:1). He stopped at Troas and apparently was engaging in a very fruitful evangelistic effort in that city. However, Titus tarried longer than the overstrained and impetuous apostle could stand. He discontinued his ministry in Troas and crossed over to Macedonia, expecting to meet him somewhere along the *Via Ignatia*, the great highway that connected the chief Macedonian towns along the coast. It was, therefore, with great relief that he received Titus's report that they had been genuinely grieved by the painful letter (7:9), they had dealt with the offending person (2:6–8), the great majority of the Corinthians were really loyal to the apostle as he had suspected all along (7:14), and Titus himself had developed a new appreciation for this assembly (7:15). It is not surprising, then, in the first seven chapters of 2 Corinthians, to see the writer pouring out his thanksgiving to God and encouragement at the progress the church was making. Thus, he sat down immediately and penned 2 Corinthians from Macedonia (2:3; 7:5–7; 8:1; 9:2–4), probably from the city of Philippi.

The identity of Paul's opponents against whom he had so much to say in this epistle is important in terms of understanding the background of the epistle but also in terms of understanding its argument. Concerning the identity of these antagonists, scholars have proposed a number of possibilities, including Jewish Gnostics, Hellenistic Jews who claimed, falsely, to be servants of Christ, or Palestinian Judaizers who were claiming to be more faithful to the teachings of Christ and the apostles (especially Peter) than this alleged interloper, the "apostle to the Gentiles."[22] In spite of some of the difficulties with the traditional view (that his chief antagonists were Palestinian Judaizers), this seems to be supported most by the evidence of the text itself. The reference to "Hebrews" (11:22; cf. Phil. 3:5) refers to ethnic Jews from Palestine. The insinuation of 5:16 is that there were some who were making something of their prior personal knowledge of Jesus Himself (cf. also 11:23). They claimed to be Israelites, descended from Abraham (11:22). Their "gospel" was not the same as that preached by Paul (11:4; cf. Gal. 1:6–9). While they cannot exactly be identified with those cited in Galatians and Colossians (Gal. 6:12–13; Col. 2:16), it is evident that they were attempting to bring the believers of Corinth under the Mosaic Law (3:1–11) and as such would be considered "Judaizers" in Paul's view. Nor should we forget that Paul's problems with the Jewish community began when he "shook out his garments" against them and declared, "Your blood be upon your own heads!" (Acts 18:6). Their former leader, Crispus, then offered his home as a place of meeting, right next door to the synagogue! Many were likely furious at this turn of events. Later when they attempted to bring Paul before Gallio at the *bēma* seat, Gallio threw them all out of court for bringing what he deemed a frivolous religious squabble before him, turning a blind eye to the subsequent abuse of the Jews by the crowd. Their new leader, Sosthenes, who took the place of Crispus in the synagogue was singled out on that occasion for an especially vicious flogging. To make matters worse, even he was later brought to Christ and became Paul's secretary. No wonder they had issues with Paul! It would be only in his absence that they could hope to score against their indomitable foe.

Gleason summarizes the case for how they insinuated themselves into the already dysfunctional assembly at Corinth, laying siege to the gospel of grace.

> Their reception by the Corinthian church can be understood as the "Christ" party, whom they as "servants of Christ" (10:7; 11:2–4; 23) fostered and perpetuated. Their depreciation of Paul's apostolic authority and insistence on the Mosaic Law would also have been welcomed by the "Cephas" party (1 Cor. 1:12; 3:22; 9:5) who extolled Peter as the foremost of the apostles and who like Peter may have been inclined to conform to the Jewish Law (Gal. 2:11–14). Also they would have been impressed by the commendation letters from Jerusalem, the center of Peter's ministry.[23]

The issue he confronts is much more than a question of leadership. It had to do with "whether the churches would evolve as a bizarre Jewish sect with a deviant theology centered on the man Jesus, a community necessarily doomed to oblivion. Otherwise expressed, would the gospel of the grace of God, essentially the key to liberty from sin, death, hell—and the shackles of the old covenant—be hijacked by a stale synagogue format consisting of externals only?"[24]

As Bible expositors have recognized for centuries, the argument of 2 Corinthians flows along three trajectories—sometimes mingled together. The writer presents these as multiple coordinates of a singular concern to bring his readers along in their understanding of what God has directed of him (the apostle) and of them (the church) in terms of the gospel of grace. These "trajectories" represent three "directions" toward which the writer aims his thoughts—sometimes "guns." While these are variously clustered in the three main divisions of the text, they should not be viewed as the exclusive "property" of different constituencies or audiences. The entire letter is a composite whole just as it stands. It might be helpful if the interpreter would imagine Paul more as a coach challenging his players than as an orator preparing a well-polished speech—or as some have it, several speeches. He has called a "time-out," and the team is standing before him. He has a game plan to win, but it will take each of them to come together as a team to achieve victory. As with the first letter, he will exhort, rebuke, correct, and instruct them—but each in turn. Thus the "shape" of the letter is not directed so much by a single proposition as it is by the circumstances and individuals to whom, in turn, the writer directs his thoughts.

| *Honoring Those Who Minister the Gospel* | |
|---|---|
| **Reference** | **Respect to Be Given** |
| Luke 10:7; 1 Tim. 5:18 | Laborer worthy of his support |
| Acts 28:10 | Give marks of honor and provision for their needs. |
| 1 Cor. 9:2 | Honor those who have helped you grow spiritually. |
| 1 Cor. 9:11 | Those who spiritually feed us are worthy of material support. |
| 1 Cor. 9:14 | Those who proclaim the gospel to get their living from this work. |
| 2 Cor. 12:11 | It is a shame to those who do not commend one worthy of respect. |
| Gal. 6:6 | Called to share all good things with them. |
| Phil. 2:20–22, 29 | Uphold and support those who care for your spiritual estate. |
| 1 Thess. 5:12, 13 | Observe those who labor among you and honor and love them. |
| 1 Tim. 5:17 | Those who rule well are worthy of double honor. |
| Heb. 13:7 | Honor them by imitating good behavior. |

These include (1) the first trajectory; Paul greets the church and gives a personal defense of his intentions and actions. He offers an explanation of his conduct (1:1–2:17), his calling (3:1–6:10), and finally, his challenge (6:11–7:16). (2) The second trajectory relates to the generosity of the

Macedonian church and the collection for Jerusalem (8:1–9:15). This is not so much about collecting money. Someone has well said that two books will reveal where a person's heart is—their date book and their checkbook. So this is a test of his readers' hearts. Their response to his appeal will reveal their true commitment to both Paul and the church. (3) Finally, Paul reiterates his apostolic authority (10:1–13:10). Lest any think that his authority is usurped, the apostle makes clear that his gifts and callings were not of his own making, but that he was only being obedient to the heavenly vision (cf. Acts 26:9–20; Phil. 3:3–14). If they would be obedient to God, they must repent, recognize, and respect those whom God sends (cf. 12:12; 13:5), and then the outcome will be to edification and not destruction (13:10). This final section is one of the most unusual to be found in any of Paul's writings. In it he "plays the fool" in order to answer fools. In what can only be described as an extended parody (of himself) he shows up his enemies to be the impostors they really are.

Thus the three sections of the epistle deal respectively with, first, the immediate *past*, together with the writer's defense of his ministry in Corinth. Then there is the matter of the *present* need to participate in assisting with the practical needs of the Jerusalem church. Finally, there is the look to the near *future* when Paul anticipates his personal follow-up visit to Corinth—a visit that is fraught with uncertainties, as chapters 10–13 reveal. However, while his appeal to the church and defense of his own ministry there is personal, what is at stake is the truth of the gospel. As Paul fights to defend his integrity, he does so in order to silence his enemies and to put to rest any doubts about his message concerning the saving grace of God in the finished work of Jesus Christ. Chapter 3 could well be considered Paul's manifesto concerning the superiority of the new covenant over the old. It rivals Hebrews 8–10 in importance regarding the relationship of the work of Christ to the promises of the new covenant to Jeremiah and Ezekiel. Paul will have to come back to this theme again—for example, in his letter to the Galatians, but it is here that he throws down the gauntlet to those who would lay siege to the gospel of grace.

# SECTION I

# First Trajectory:
# Personal Defense

## 2 Corinthians 1–7

# CHAPTER 1

# Greetings from Paul and Timothy
# 2 Corinthians 1:1–2

### Preview:

*In his salutation to the Corinthian church, Paul establishes his authority as their "apostle" but does more than that. He makes it clear that he does not stand alone. He stands with others, such as Timothy, whom they have come to love and respect. But neither do they stand alone. They are not an independently owned and operated ecclesia. They belong to the church of God together with all the saints. It is to these he extends God's continuing grace and peace.*

Good news! Paul leaned forward to hear every word from his protégé. Titus had just returned from Corinth, and while they had planned to meet at Troas, his mentor and friend just could not wait for him to arrive. The riot in Ephesus had forced Paul to leave Ephesus (Acts 19:21–41), and he had made his way to Troas to await Titus's boat from Neapolis. Yet, in spite of the fruitfulness of the work there, Paul was unable to get his mind off the Corinthian situation. He knew he would intersect Titus along the way, and so it was that he crossed the Aegean and headed south through Macedonia along the *Via Ignatia*. They likely met near Philippi. "Tell me everything!" The impatient apostle must have given Titus barely enough time to catch his breath (2 Cor. 7:5–7). As he began, Paul seemed tense—his jaw was set. His head tilted to meet his companion's excited gaze. His fists were clenched. Paul had relived his "sorrowful letter" over and over as he had waited impatiently for his return. Had he been too stern? Would it make matters worse? What would he do if they had not responded as he hoped? It made him feel foolish that they were making such demands on him. How could they? How, indeed, could he show them that he was for real?

The news was encouraging. Paul's bronzed head flashed in the late summer sun as he nodded approvingly. Intermittently flashes of anger were also seen. Titus knew the look and was thankful he never had to be on the receiving end of it. But then the old man seemed to melt. He clapped his hands and waved his arms excitedly. "Titus, fetch the parchments and my quill!" At last he sat down to write. But unlike his previous letters to Corinth, this one began on a positive note. His work with them had finally begun to pay off. So, he began.

## Commissioned and Called

It was against Paul's authority as one called of God and sent by Christ that he had been denounced as an impostor. He began characteristically by establishing his authority and his commission: "Paul, an apostle" (v. 1; cf. Eph. 1:1; Col. 1:1; 1 Tim. 1:1; 2 Tim. 1:1; Gal. 1:1). This ministry was assigned to him "of Christ Jesus by the will of God" (v. 1). Paul takes for granted that he fulfills any requisites for the "office" of apostleship. This is not a usurpation, but obedience to the call of God. These people needed to be reminded of this fact. What is important to note regarding the term "apostle" is that it signifies more than a title of honor (although that is clearly a nuance present in the New Testament and not entirely absent here either), but it is his mission he wishes to underscore in this letter. In earlier classical usage, *apostolos*, as "delegate," and *aggelos*, as "messenger," were distinguished. *Apostolos* as Paul uses it here is already conditioned by its relation to the term in the early church. The twelve who were with the Lord had been commissioned to go to the entire world and preach the gospel to every creature (Matt. 28:19–20). When Paul employs it in relation to himself, he has in mind this command of his Lord— and it certainly should not be lost on his readers who only know this gospel because he was obedient to that calling. Furthermore, it is on this point that he returns again and again in this letter, since there were those who were challenging his right to speak thus.[1]

Much is made in recent studies of the place of "power" in the early church. Doubtless, in these two letters to the Corinthians, the issue is more prevalent than it is in any other of Paul's writings.[2] It would be a mistake, however, to suggest that this was as much about his "right" to exercise authority[3] as it was his "obligation" to do so in obedience to the divine calling (1:21–22; cf. 2:17; 3:4).

Many a church has dismissed a dedicated and obedient pastor, thinking that it was they who called him to the pulpit. Many a weary pastor has fallen prey to the unrealistic demands of such people. Both need to take note of this first-century pastor when the question is raised of "whose" calling is prior.

Paul understood that it was for the sake of the lost souls of Corinth that he was called, but it was not they who called him. It was God. So they had no right to call the shots. Paul was obliged to be obedient to the One who issued the call. Of course one cannot forget that amazing call in Acts 16:9 when Paul had the vision of a man from Macedonia calling upon him to "come over and help us." It was in obedience to this heavenly vision that Paul was the first apostolic missionary to bring the gospel to Europe.

| The Great Commission in the Pauline Epistles | |
| --- | --- |
| **Reference** | **Specific Commission** |
| 1 Cor. 4:16 | Exhorted to follow Paul's example in fulfilling it |
| Phil. 3:17 | Called to imitate Christ before others |
| 1 Thess. 2:11, 12 | Implored to walk worthy of the calling of God |
| 2 Tim. 2:2 | Entrusted to pass on this commission to others |

A second critical point should be added. When we think about Paul's ministry and calling, we must also include his letters. Inspired by the Holy Spirit, they offer instruction that modern readers defy or ignore to their own peril. Today it is commonplace to challenge the biblical writers (Paul especially) as if their writings reflect little more than personal opinion, bias, or the distorted cultures of which they were a part. When writing under the inspiration of the Holy Spirit, that which the writer pens is "normative." That is, it represents timeless truth that must be believed even when it is not fully understood or accepted by the culture at large. Truth, it has been rightly said, is discovered. It is not created. On the matter of truth and community, Paul will have much more to say later.

"Timothy" (v. 1). This companion of Paul is not mentioned in the introduction to 1 Corinthians as he is here. Presumably this is because Timothy had already been sent to Corinth (1 Cor. 4:17; 16:10). That mention of him appears here indicates that he has since rejoined the apostle, given his report concerning the affairs at Corinth, and traveled with him from Ephesus to Macedonia. The writer introduces himself as "the apostle." He introduces his companion and friend, known to his readers, as the "brother." This rather deftly and diplomatically places full responsibility for what follows with Paul—not Timothy. At the same time, by including their friend and his in the opening greeting, Paul is encouraging his readers to grant to Paul's young son in the faith much the same respect they would show to him.

## Holy Ones of Corinth

The epistle is addressed primarily to "the church of God which is at Corinth" (v. 1). This addresses the local assembly directly. That it was intended also as a circular letter to be read by other assemblies "indirectly"[4] is implied by the fact that he also addresses "all the saints who are throughout Achaia" (v. 1). This would embrace at least the Christians that were in Athens (cf. Acts 17:34) and in Cenchrea, the eastern port of Corinth (cf. Rom. 16:1). "Saints" (v. 1) calls to mind all who have been set apart by God and walk in newness of life (cf. Rom. 1:7; 1 Cor. 1:2; 6:11; 2 Cor. 5:17). *Hagioi*, "saints," is a common expression in the New Testament to speak of God's people—not so much as individuals as to the people of God in general. In the New Testament this is characterized by their association with Christ. What is important to note here is that the use of this term does not so much speak of the moral attainment(s) or holy character of the individuals to which the term is applied. Rather, it has in mind God's sovereign claim upon them. This is true of the use of *qadhosh* in the Old Testament as well, but it is an important point often lost on those who are given to "performance-based" Christianity. When Scripture speaks of God's people as "holy" or as "saints," it is speaking of God's initiative in claiming and consecrating them to His use. It is not speaking of a certain level of attainment accomplished by a select few who now have a special place in the church or in heaven. It is also important to note that persons so consecrated by God are expected to demonstrate their holy estate with works "worthy of the saints" and to abstain from works that are not "proper among saints" (Rom. 16:2; Eph. 5:3).

It is important to pay attention to how the writer makes use of the term *ekklēsia*. In Paul's letters the term can refer to a group of Christians meeting for worship (1 Cor. 11:18; 14:19, 28, 35). It can refer to the totality of believers in a given region (Rom. 16:1; Col. 4:16; Gal. 1:2, 22). It can be used to speak of the universal body of believers (1 Cor. 12:28; 15:9; Gal. 1:13; Eph. 1:22; 3:10; cf. Acts 9:31; 20:28). What is especially important to note here is that when Paul uses the term *ekklēsia* for the Corinthian assembly, he implies that in this city the totality of the church is represented. Citing Schmidt, Ladd agrees that "the church universal is not thought of as the totality of all the local churches; rather, 'each community, however small, represents the total community, the Church.'"[5] Barrett also notes: "In 2 Corinthians the word church (*ekklēsia*) does not occur so frequently: nine times in all. In the other eight passages (8:1, 18, 19, 23, 24; 11:8, 28; 12:13) it is used in the plural—a clear indication that, at least at this stage in his career, the primary meaning of the word for Paul was that of a local Christian community, though it is also evident that the local groups belong together (e.g., 'all the churches,' 11:28)."[6]

Paul's expression, "of God," anticipates verse 3. When the early Christians worshipped, they gave equal honor to both God (the Father, *Yahweh*) and the Lord Jesus Christ. These are not given separate identities: "yet for us there is but one God, the Father, from whom are all things, and we exist for Him; and one Lord, Jesus Christ, by whom are all things, and we exist through Him" (1 Cor. 8:6). So it is that the "churches of Christ" (found only in Rom. 16:16) are the churches "of God" (here and in all other references in Paul; cf. Gal. 1:13; 1 Thess. 2:14; 2 Thess. 1:4). Concerning the significance of this, Sabourin notes: "While there is no personal identification between Christ and Yahweh, [neither] is there any dispersion of the faith."[7] The implications are important for those who represented themselves as the "Christ" party (cf. 1 Cor. 1:12, 13) and who continue to foment dissent in this church. Those who worship Christ do not abandon the God of the Old Testament. It is precisely such texts as this that caused Christians to ponder the mystery of the Trinitarian relationship.

The reference to God as "Father" is characteristic of the New Testament portrayal. Jesus taught believers to pray to "Our Father who art in heaven" (Matt. 6:9). And He told His disciples not to worry about having food to eat, clothes to wear, or a place to sleep, because their heavenly Father provides all these needs for the birds of the air and surely has greater concern for people (Matt. 6:26).

## Grace and Peace

"Perceived spiritual growth in the lives of not a few of these people was, at best, minimal. How significant then to note that the author assumes that, notwithstanding their problems, the Corinthians will not fail to experience grace and peace from God the Father and God the Son!"[8] The greeting in verse 2 is characteristic. At least since Tertullian the standard greeting "grace" in the Greco-Roman world has been recognized as correlated with a standard Jewish greeting, *shalom*, "peace."[9] Whether intentioned or not, this certainly links the God of the Old Testament with that of the New Testament Christians (see comment above on "Father"). For Paul's Gentile converts this is a crucial link. It is not accidental that he concludes this letter with a similar reference again to God's grace, love, and peace (cf. 13:11–14). In Paul's soteriology it is also true that grace always precedes peace. Until we have received the grace of God, we can know nothing of His peace. Grace is the love of God that enables Him to pour out infinite favor on those loved without receiving anything in return. It demands no merit and incurs no obligation. It has been extended to all of humanity by the work of Jesus Christ on the cross, which alone makes God's love available to all (1 John 2:2). Anything that might be placed between the *provision* of God's grace and the *power* of God's grace is blasphemy (cf. Paul's treatment of legalism in Galatians). Peace is subsequent and comes because God's grace has been received by faith. There is nothing that brings this peace as much as the undiluted gospel of God's grace (cf. Eph. 2:14; Phil. 4:7; Col. 1:20; 3:15) "from God our Father and the Lord Jesus Christ" (v. 2). The single preposition (Gr. *apo*) links the Father and the Son in an inviolable union, thus, affirming unequivocally the deity of Christ. The reference is to the eternal Father and the incarnate Son (cf. also 13:14).

Those who bring with great agonizing of heart the names of recalcitrant loved ones, wayward church members, and carnal leaders before the throne of grace may be reminded in this text that if those they intercede for are truly born again, "the Lord still loves them and will keep them. They can never be alienated from heavenly peace. Grace abounds."[10]

## Study Questions

1. What is it about the style of 2 Corinthians that leads so many commentators to consider that the "sorrowful letter" is imbedded in it? (See introduction.)

2. In relation to the question of authorship, how does the internal evidence compare with the external evidence? Which is stronger? Why? (See introduction.)

3. Suggest several themes that appear in this epistle that elaborate on Paul's eschatology. Give the references. How do these compare with other letters of Paul?

4. Locate a map of Paul's missionary journeys and trace his travels from Ephesus to Troas, and then across the Aegean to where he likely encountered Titus along the way.

5. Explain the relationship between Paul and his traveling companions, Titus, Timothy, and the other brothers.

6. What is the meaning of the term *apostle*? How does Paul understand this term in relation to the Twelve and to himself?

7. Explain the significance of the term *hagioi* in relation to the church members at Corinth. Why is this so important?

8. Of the various ways the term *ekklēsia* is used of the church, what is especially noteworthy of Paul's employment of this term in 2 Corinthians?

9. How is Paul's soteriology reflected in his characteristic greeting in his letters?

# CHAPTER 2

# Comfort in Conflict
# 2 Corinthians 1:3–11

### Preview:

*In response to the good report he received from Titus, Paul launches into a doxology of praise to the "God of all mercies" to whom this turn of events is credited. In this short text he is so excited at the evidence he had seen of their trust and obedience, he employs the term "comfort" ten times. This exultation is also related to his own experience of deliverance from an unknown circumstance. He likens his experience and their response to the work of God raising the dead. He concludes with a reflection on the power of prayer.*

As discussed in the previous chapter, the writer opens this second letter with ebullience and joy concerning the good report he has received from Titus. It is with this report in mind that he launches into an apostolic benediction of praise to the "Father of mercies" from whom all blessings flow—and especially from whom *this* blessing has come.

## Sing Praise to God

"Blessed" (v. 3; Gr. *eulogētos*, "well spoken of"). In a characteristically Jewish pattern of benediction,[1] Paul begins with a term of adoration and praise. In consideration of God's grace and peace (v. 2) and in anticipation of his mercies and comforts (v. 3b), such a pronouncement from the apostle is understood, for he contemplates both who God is and what God does. While "praise" can be offered to objects or persons who are unworthy of it (Matt. 6:1–4; John 5:44), in the New Testament the term is particularly associated with the adoration of the saints toward God and Jesus Christ (cf. Rev. 4:11; 5:12). Sometimes God is given praise for His attributes (Ps. 104:1; Isa. 6:3). At other times it is for His works, such as His creation, providence, wisdom, power, and redemptive work on behalf of sinners. Certainly, it is this latter point that the writer is extolling as he reflects on the spiritual victories that he is beginning to see in the Corinthian believers. Such worship can be in word or song or prayer. Here the writer essentially breaks out in a prayer of thanksgiving while we, the readers, are privileged to listen in as he worships God with his whole heart.

Since the issue of worship has become such a point of controversy in contemporary Christian circles it is helpful to review briefly the biblical significance of the practice. Lambert notes:

> True praise of God, as distinguished from false praise (Isaiah 29:13; Matthew 15:8), is first of all an inward emotion—a gladness and rejoicing of the heart (Ps. 4:7; 33:21), a music of the soul and spirit (Ps. 103:1; Luke 1:46f) which no language can adequately express (Ps. 106:2; 2 Corinthians 9:15). But utterance is natural to strong emotion, and the mouth instinctively strives to express the praises of the heart (Ps. 51:15 and *passim*). Many of the most moving passages in Scripture come from the inspiration of the spirit of praise awakened by the contemplation of the divine majesty or power or wisdom or kindness, but above all by the revelation of redeeming love. Again, the spirit of praise is a social spirit calling for social utterance. The man who praises God desires to praise Him in the hearing of other men (Ps. 40:10), and desires also that their praises should be joined with his own (Ps. 34:3). Further, the spirit of praise is a spirit of song. It may find expression in other ways—in sacrifice (Leviticus 7:13), or testimony (Ps. 66:16), or prayer (Colossians 1:3); but it finds its most natural and its fullest utterance in lyrical and musical forms. When God fills the heart with praise, he puts a new song into the mouth (Ps. 40:3).[2]

In the present context, it is important to recognize that praise is not so much distinguished by preferential style as it is by the divine object toward which it is directed. Beyond this, praise is understood as a duty as well as it is a natural response to the majestic glory of God's person and presence. Lambert adds:

> Praise is everywhere represented in the Bible as a duty no less than a natural impulse and delight. To fail in this duty is to withhold from God's glory that which belongs to Him (Ps. 50:23; Romans 1:20f); it is to shut one's eyes to the signs of His presence (Isaiah 40:26ff), to be forgetful of

His mercies (Deuteronomy 6:12), and unthankful for His kindness (Luke 6:35). If we are not to fall into these sins, but are to give to God the honor and glory and gratitude we owe Him, we must earnestly cultivate the spirit and habit of praise. From holy men of old we learn that this may be done by arousing the soul from its slothfulness and sluggishness (Ps. 57:8; 103:1), by fixing the heart upon God (Ps. 57:7; 108:1), by meditation on His works and ways (Ps. 77:11 ff.), by recounting His benefits (Ps. 103:2), above all, for those to whom He has spoken in His Son, by dwelling upon His unspeakable gift (2 Corinthians 9:15; compare Romans 8:31ff; I John 3:1).[3]

Actually, in this instance, Paul's praise is with reference to his original readers. One is caused to think of the child who accidentally stumbles upon her devout mother or dad in prayer and is startled to hear her name being brought before the throne of grace with words of gratitude and loving appreciation for the great joy this child has brought to their home. Indeed, it is with reference to and through these very people that Paul has received such encouragement from the Lord.

## God's Mercies Are Ever New

After weeks of worry, Paul is unable to contain his exultation of this One who is also "Father of our Lord Jesus Christ, the Father of mercies and God of all comfort" (v. 3). As noted above, Paul takes a characteristically Jewish blessing and adapts it to a Christian understanding (and doxology) of the relationship between God the Father and God the Son. See this also in Ephesians 1:3 and 1 Peter 1:3. "This is not surprising since it expresses the fundamental conviction that Jesus signifies not the contradiction but the fulfillment of the faith of the Old Testament and of Judaism; the reference to Jesus Christ determines both the way in which God is God and the way in which God is Father."[4]

The new revelation of God as "Father" is one of the ways that Jesus *exegetes* the Father (cf. John 1:18, *exēgeomai*, "explained"). The revelation of God in the Old Testament was that of the Creator God, the Holy One, Yahweh, unapproachable—to be propitiated and whose "day" was a day of wrath and judgment. When Jesus explains or reveals God, He manifests Him with contours of glory, grace, and love that had never been explored by the prophets of old. So grand was the contrast that John declares of the old dispensation, "For of his fulness we have all received, and grace upon grace. For the Law was given through Moses; grace and truth were realized through Jesus Christ" (John 1:16–17). Obviously it is a mistake to imagine that there is no grace in the old—just as we do not imagine that there is no "law" in the new. What John enlarges on in the prolegomenon to his gospel is that since Jesus came, we can now "see" God through His Son. What we see of Him is beyond anything imaginable. In Christ it is God's "nearness" that is most striking. However, the fact that He identifies with humanity in its weakness and suffering more than in its greatness is most instructive. So it is that in Paul's painful experiences with this young church and its immature converts, he is caused to reflect on Psalm 103:13–14, "Just as a father has compassion on his children, So the LORD has compassion on those who fear Him. For He Himself knows our frame; He is mindful that we are but dust." Again, Lamentations 3:22–23, "The LORD's lovingkindnesses indeed never cease, for His compassions never fail. They are new every morning; great is Thy faithfulness."

| *Relationship of God the Father and God the Son* | |
|---|---|
| The Father sent the Son to be the savior of the world | John 3:17; Galatians 4:4; 1 John 4:14 |
| The Son reveals the Father to us | Matthew 11:27; Luke 10:22 |
| The Son has powers like the Father to raise the dead | John 5:21 |
| All judgment is given to the Son | Matthew 11:27; 16:27; John 3:35; 5:22, 27 |
| The Father is pleased with the Son | Matthew 3:17; 17:5; Mark 1:11; 9:7; Luke 3:22; 20:13; 2 Peter 1:17 |
| The Father glorifies the Son so that the Son might glorify the Father | John 13:31; 14:13; 17:1 |
| The Father alone knows the hour the Son will return | Matthew 24:36; Mark 13:32 |

The "mercies" in view here no doubt include such great benefits of the cross as deliverance from the world, sin, death, and the Devil to participation in sonship, light, and life. But what Paul has in mind here is more personal and domestic (if you please) than the grander themes of God's soteriological grace. He has in mind a simpler pleasure that has overflowed to comfort him in the moment.

In Scripture the Father is characterized by mercy (cf. Ps. 86:5; Dan. 9:9; Mic. 7:18). He is "rich in mercy" (Eph. 2:4), "full of compassion and is merciful" (James 5:11). In the New Testament the Greek word *oiktirmos* is used primarily by Paul, and it is, with only one exception, always in the plural (Rom. 12:1; 2 Cor. 1:3; Phil. 2:1, "compassion"; Heb. 10:28, "mercy" though Greek is plural; cf. Col. 3:12, "compassion," here singular in Greek). Again, there are echoes of the Jewish liturgy here, but the writer has something much more personal for which to offer up his praise. This God who is a boundless resource of mercy has, in the midst of his afflictions (v. 4), showered those mercies upon him—not because He was obligated to do so, but out of sheer pity.[5] In the New Testament "mercy" is associated with "grace." It has been noted that when Scripture speaks of God's grace, it has in mind the freeness of God's love. When it speaks of mercy, it has in view relief from misery. Paul has many reasons to extol God's mercy here in terms of the wonderful news just received from Titus concerning the situation at Corinth.

Many a weary pastor has come away from a long and tedious counseling session overflowing with joy, despite the lateness of the hour and difficulty of the situation. When sin has had its day and Satan has done his best to destroy another saint, God steps in with mercy. Confession is followed by forgiveness, cleansing, and reconciliation. The power of the gospel is once again aglow on the faces of those whose lives have been transformed by His grace. The pastor is so weary he can hardly stay awake to drive home. Yet he is thinking, *It doesn't get much better than this!* In this story the weary pastor is Paul.

## A Balm in Gilead

Paul's enthusiasm concerning the good news of his companion is reflected in the fact that in the next four short verses (vv. 3–7) he employs the term "comfort" no fewer than ten times. (cf. "the Helper" John 16:7). The term does not connote "sympathy" as much as "empathy." It has the idea of someone coming alongside to provide support. Since the Comforter abides within (cf. John 14:16–17), a twofold process is implied: strength for the soul and encouragement for the work. Deliverance from grief comes through the impartation of strength. Paul now turns his thoughts to the everyday problems of life. The "God of all comfort . . . comforts us in all our affliction" (vv. 3–4). In the general scope of life, God's comfort extends to every area. The purpose emphasized here is not just for our own good, but "that we may be able to comfort those who are in any (Gr. *pasē*) affliction" (v. 4). God's comfort is transferable and intended to be shared. What, of course, is meant here is that there is a special relation shared between the crucified and resurrected Christ and those who follow Him.

On the other hand, while the writer is communicating the idea that the life of an apostle reflects what every follower of Christ might expect, in this case there is much more going on. From the report given by Titus, it would seem that the majority of the assembly suffers with Paul under the weight of a strong but minority party of opposition. The comfort received from this "Father of mercies" is for "us." The writer pulls those who support him into the inner circle of those who (with him) share the "sufferings of Christ," which are "ours in abundance" (v. 5). In doing this he also offers the same comfort that is "our comfort . . . abundant through Christ." "Abundance" (*perisseuō*, "to be over and above") also has the idea of "overflow." The idea is that the sufferings (and the comfort) of *Christ* overflow to us. When, for the cause of Christ, believers endure suffering and persecution, it is His suffering that we share. With it is the promise that His consolation will also "overflow" to us.[6] That Paul is emboldened to address his audience in this way suggests that by and large they agree and share his pain with respect to those who have opposed Paul's ministry in their city.

Much can be said here for the apostle's pastoral skills. Many a pastor has struggled with the problems created by a strong and vocal minority who would rather terrorize a church and destroy it than see it healed. When examining the character qualities of leadership in the New Testament church (see, e.g., 1 Tim. 3:1–13; Titus 1:5–11), it is evident that those who are appointed to lead the church must be strong. As such they will be capable of great good—wise and able to instruct the weak in the faith. They can also do great harm if they are not given to godliness. This is why their "character" is of such importance. Paul shows great wisdom in his approach here. He is rhetorically gathering the sheep into a protected area—a place where the "comfort" of Christ abounds to the same degree as the "sufferings" they share. When they are safely in the fold, he will turn his attention to the wolves (cf. Matt. 7:15; Acts 20:29).[7]

## Shared Affliction Yields Common Consolation

As the problems increase, so does the consolation. Both, in this case, are measured by the experience of Christ (cf. Luke 24:26, 46; Phil. 3:10; Col. 1:24; 1 Pet. 1:11). Paul's use of the Greek verb *perisseuō* ("to abound; to overflow") is significant throughout this epistle (cf. 2 Cor. 3:9; 4:15; 8:2, 7). Suffering belongs to all those who would follow Him who said, "If anyone wishes to come after Me, let him deny himself, and take up his cross, and follow Me" (Matt. 16:24).

Many ancient manuscripts differ in the order of the clauses in the following verses. The sense in every case is basically the same: "if we are afflicted, it is for your comfort and salvation; or if we are comforted, it is for your comfort" (v. 6). Everything else in these verses is subordinated to these two main ideas. Paul does not glory in suffering *per se*. He knows that the fact of suffering identifies believers with Christ and with His church (1 Cor. 4:12; 15:9;

2 Cor. 4:9; cf. also Rom. 8:17). He also knows "that as you are sharers of our sufferings, so also you are sharers of our comfort" (v. 7). Those who share mutual suffering and affliction share also in the joy of consolation. This relationship of intimacy implied by the apostle's terminology stands in stark contrast to the divisive spirit of his enemies in Corinth. Again, see verses 4, 5. The writer makes it clear that the reason he is able to take comfort in adversity is because he knows that in the end it is for the benefit of (*huper*) those who have come to share his faith in Jesus Christ.

Paul draws upon his recent experience to do two things: to share with his readers his needs and concerns, and also, to explain his change of plans. "We despaired even of life" (v. 8) and the expression, "we had the sentence of death within ourselves" (v. 9) are parallel concepts. Paul's condition, due to external pressures and physical limitations, reached the point where the only way out, visible to him, was death. Yet God's purpose, even in this, was being fulfilled so that Paul would come to the end of himself and trust in "God who raises the dead" (v. 9). It is not insignificant that as Paul is considering examples in his life that correspond in significance to the turn-about of the Corinthian church, he thinks of God's power to "raise the dead." Here we have a small insight into how much he had despaired of their spiritual welfare.

The specifics of the suffering to which he alludes here are strikingly absent. With Harris, I concur that there are several things that may be deduced about it. (1) It happened in Asia but probably not in Ephesus; otherwise it would likely have been mentioned in Acts. (2) It happened since the writing of his first letter to Corinth. (3) It caused Paul to fear for his life. (4) While it is possible that this is an allusion to Acts 14:19, it is unlikely. Perhaps his note of praise for God's mercies in the previous verses are also, at least, in part due to his own deliverance as well as the positive report from Corinth. (5) Paul seems to expect this to happen again (v. 10).[8]

While we may not be able to identify the specifics of what exactly happened to Paul in this instance, the lesson he learned is what he wants readers to take from it. For Paul this provision of God initiated a process of faith that is viewed in a threefold sense: "who delivered us" (v. 10, past), "will deliver us" (v. 10), and now in this present situation "will yet deliver us" (v. 10; indeterminate future). Faith liberated Paul from bondage to his circumstances and the fear of death (cf. Heb. 2:14, 15). Whether it was from enemies without or enemies within, Paul was convinced that God would deliver him—and them.

Against the legalism and attempts by Paul's detractors at Corinth to place these Gentile Christians back under the law, this is crucial. John Piper's phrase by which he entitles his book *Future Grace*, captures the import of this text exactly. Too many people imagine that they are called to live the Christian life from the gratitude of the "debtor's ethic."[9] That is to say, Christians are thought to be empowered out of thanksgiving to live up to God's expectations of us out of sheer appreciation for what He has done for us on Calvary. Not only is such thinking preposterous; it is heresy. It insinuates that the life of the Spirit can be supported in the strength of the flesh. How could we ever expect to live up to God's standards in our own strength now if we could never do it in the first place. Worse, such thinking robs the believer of the "grace" that is in reserve when obedience to God's directives stretches our resources to the breaking point. Paul put it this way: "He who did not spare His own Son, but delivered Him up for us all, how will He not also with Him freely give us all things? Who will bring a charge against God's elect? God is the one who justifies; who is the one who condemns? Christ Jesus is He who died, yes, rather who was raised, who is at the right hand of God, who also intercedes for us" (Rom. 8:32–34). Paul understood with Jeremiah that God's mercies "are new every morning" (Lam. 3:23). The saving grace of God is applied past, present, and future. It saves from the penalty of sin. It delivers from the power of sin. It will yet save from the very presence of sin. To that end the army of the *forgiven* continue as Paul later wrote: "looking for the blessed hope and the appearing of the glory of our great God and Savior, Christ Jesus; who gave Himself for us, that He might redeem us from every lawless deed and purify for Himself a people for His own possession, zealous for good deeds" (Tit. 2:13).

| *Encouraged to Walk after the Spirit* | |
|---|---|
| Matthew 26:41 | "'Keep watching and praying, that you may not enter into temptation; the spirit is willing, but the flesh is weak.'" |
| John 6:63 | "It is the Spirit who gives life; the flesh profits nothing; the words that I have spoken to you are spirit and are life." |
| Romans 8:6 | "For the mind set on the flesh is death, but the mind set on the Spirit is life and peace," |
| Galatians 5:16 | "But I say, walk by the Spirit, and you will not carry out the desire of the flesh." |
| Galatians 6:8 | "For the one who sows to his own flesh shall from the flesh reap corruption, but the one who sows to the Spirit shall from the Spirit reap eternal life." |

"Joining in helping" (v. 11) probably has reference to their cooperation in interceding on his behalf with the other churches. Paul's thinking in this verse is very much like that in verses 6–7. Paul notes that since there were many who where sharing together in prayer for them, his deliverance is also cause for "thanks . . . by many persons on our behalf" (v. 11). The preposition *dia*, "by" (v. 11) is best rendered "by means of." Thus the sense of the verse is: as health was rendered by means of prayer, so also thanksgiving to God is rendered by means of many who shared in that prayer. Does prayer change things? Indeed, it does. And while the divine "power" is His, the divine command to pray is given to us. When Elijah prayed, God sent fire from heaven to consume the sacrifice. Make no mistake; it was also because Elijah prayed! This is a wonderful mystery. The fact that we cannot comprehend how this happens should never discourage us from taking advantage of the thrilling privilege of participating with God in the accomplishment of His work.

## Study Questions

1. For what does Paul give praise in verse 3 and following? How does this relate to the biblical teaching on the purpose and exercise of praise in worship?

2. How does Paul's doxology of praise give support to the biblical doctrine of the Trinity? How is this "new" to the New Testament?

3. Why does Paul extol the "mercies" of God? How does this also reflect Paul's "Jewish" roots?

4. In Paul's thought, how is it that affliction serves to prepare a person for ministry?

5. Explain the significance of Paul's reference to "God who raises the dead" in relation to his circumstances (v. 9).

6. Explain Paul's threefold sense of the process of faith. How is this important to remember in the practical outworking of the Christian life?

# CHAPTER 3

# Answering Critics
# 2 Corinthians 1:12–2:4

### Preview:

*Facing problems is not every pastor's strong suit. Paul, however, does not hesitate to get right to it. First, he makes it clear that when he speaks he speaks the truth. Then, since they and he are sealed by the Spirit, he makes no imposition upon their liberty in Christ. He has resisted coming right away because he does not wish another "sorrowful" visit. Nevertheless, be assured, he is coming. He just wants to give them all the time they need to get their act together.*

Paul finds it necessary to explain his change of plans. In the opening section, he alludes to his desire to come again to Corinth. It was on this matter that he had been criticized by his enemies in the assembly. Apparently some had accused him of promising them a visit with no intention of ever coming. Paul must answer their charges. The practical importance of the text is that it gives a candid example of how commonplace such criticism is and how important it is to deal with it as quickly as possible.

Politics in America has become noticeably nasty in recent years. Many have learned through bitter experience that when negative charges are brought, the candidate will do well to respond as fully and as quickly as possible. Otherwise, the charge (whether true or false) will remain in the public consciousness. It will inevitably cost the candidate at the polls.

Many pastors make the mistake of imagining that problems and criticisms will just go away if they ignore them. In fact, they will emphatically *not* go away. They will fester and in time give birth to a whole course of problems that will hamstring the initiatives of the leadership and bring great harm to the testimony of Christ in the community. Good leaders *go to the problems;* they do not *run from* them. Paul shows himself to be a good leader. He faces these criticisms head-on.

## Face the Problem

"The testimony of our conscience" (v. 12) may suggest the "ground" of Paul's rejoicing or the "substance" of his rejoicing. The latter idea seems to fit best with what follows. Paul was able to rejoice in a ministry of "holiness and godly sincerity" (v. 12). Someone has said that "conscience" is the worm that never dies. It is that moral faculty within every heart that discriminates between good and evil, right and wrong. As he begins to address the misunderstanding of some, Paul takes the time to examine his own heart. How many times do people fail in this vital exercise? Did not our Lord teach us that when we come with our gift to the altar and there is a brother who has something against us, that we should first "be reconciled" to our brother and then bring our offering (Matt. 5:23–24)? Conflicts sometimes arise (as here) through misunderstandings. Many times there is no misunderstanding at all. We have, in fact, sinned against a brother or sister, and that person understands all too well that we have caused an offense that needs to be addressed. Paul understood this too. He knew that he was fully capable of being the one at fault, and so he acknowledges that his first step was to examine his own conscience. Those in spiritual leadership especially need to practice the art of asking for forgiveness from those we offend by some careless remark or deed. When leaders practice this regularly, the people learn a vital skill as well—they learn that it is acceptable to own up to one's faults, because when they do, a culture of forgiveness is created that facilitates reconciliation. Of course, in this case, upon examination, Paul's conscience was clear, but the example of transparency he gives is vital to the health of the church.

"For we write nothing else to you than what you read and understand" (v. 13). Paul's epistles are characterized by the same degree of honesty and integrity that characterized his life. "You also partially did understand us" (v. 14). This is not given to indicate that the Corinthians understood only part of what he said. Probably most understood perfectly well what he said, but some (for whatever reason—perhaps selective hearing) did not. Many in Corinth stood with the apostle in affirming his integrity. A vocal minority, however, did not.

Using the editorial "we" (v. 14), the writer made it clear that there was good "reason to be proud" (v. 14). He was speaking specifically to those who appreciated his ministry and to emphasize to them that there was good reason to place their confidence in him. The feeling was mutual, "as you also are ours" (v. 14). Likewise, he felt the same way about them. It must have been especially gratifying to this faithful evangelist to see the sheer power of the gospel in transforming the lives of those who received it. The expression "In the day of our Lord Jesus" (v. 14) has a double-edge. First, Paul was confident that in the day when all the secrets of people are revealed, these believers would know that their faith in him was not misplaced. Second, he was equally confident that they would share that "day" together. The consummation of their faith would be manifest in the fact that they would be with Jesus together. As the old hymn says, "What a day of rejoicing that will be."

---

### The Art of Asking for Forgiveness

1. Understand specifically what you did to offend the other person(s).

2. Clearly confess what you did without making excuses.

3. Offer the other person a chance to express their woundedness.

4. Validate the wounded feelings of the offended person(s).

5. Ask for forgiveness.

6. Be open to any reasonable request to restore the relationship

---

"In this confidence" (v. 15). The mutual confidence Paul shared with the Corinthian believers suggests the reason why he was so eager to visit and why he "intended at first to come" (v. 15). In Paul's initial itinerary, he intended to go immediately from Ephesus to Corinth (see 1 Cor. 16:5–9). The comment "twice receive a blessing" (v. 15) must not be misconstrued as a reference to Paul's second visit to them, since he had already visited them twice (cf. 12:14). His point is that in his trip he would be seeing them twice, as he explains: "to pass your way into Macedonia, and again from Macedonia to come to you" (v. 16). Thus he would be visiting with them twice before he went on his way to Judea. "And by you to be helped on my journey" (v. 16, *propemphthēnai*, "to be brought on my way," "to be aided in my journey"). Following the custom of ancient times, since Paul would be traveling immediately to Judea from Corinth, it would be appropriate for one of the assembly to escort him on his way. It is likely that he also has in mind that their assistance would include participation in the collection—a matter to which he will attend directly (chaps. 8–9).

# Truth Telling

"Therefore, I was not vacillating when I intended to do this, was I?" (v. 17). Here Paul emphasizes the sincerity of his purpose. Nor did he intend any hidden advantage to himself "according to the flesh," as he goes on to say, "so that with me there will be yes, yes and no, no" (v. 17). The allusion is to Matthew 5:37, "But let your statement be, 'Yes, yes' or 'No, no'; and anything beyond these is of evil" (cf. also Acts 5:8–9). The apostle cannot be charged with inconsistency. That which he affirmed he affirms still. That which he denied he denies still. Hence, "as God is faithful, our word to you is not yes and no" (v. 18). As the truth of God stands, so does the word of the apostle (cf. also Gal. 1:8; 1 John 5:10). The trustworthiness of Paul's words is seen in the nature of his gospel.

People who are given to telling the truth—all the time—do not have to worry about what to say when the question comes up again later. They just say the same thing they said before. Detectives are trained to watch the eyes of those who are giving testimony to circumstances or crimes being investigated. If a person has to "create" a response, the eyes will veer to the creative side of the brain—searching as it were for a believable story. Paul is not making this up as he goes. He is obviously the victim of circumstances over which he has no control and which have caused him to alter some of his original plans. At no point has he intentionally deceived them.

"Paul's developing argument is that a preacher's faithfulness in what he declares will be validated by the way he lives: the sanctity of the good news of Christ irradiates the man who loves and announces it."[1] "Jesus Christ, who was preached among you by us . . . was not yes and no" (v. 19). Those who truly knew the Lord as Savior in the Corinthian assembly could hardly doubt the veracity of this statement. They had received and experienced the reality of saving faith and knew that Paul's words were true.

"For as many as may be the promises of God, in Him they are yes" (v. 20). The thrust of this expression is that the promises of God find their affirmation and fulfillment in Christ. "Amen" (v. 20) is equivalent to "yes." Whether one is a Gentile (yes) or a Hebrew (amen), the promises of God are sure. We say with him, "Yes! Jesus is the answer!" To this, John G. Stackhouse Jr. exults:

> More than this, Christians have an underlying conviction of the point of it all that makes sense of both our aspirations and our fears. "Our hearts are restless, until they find their rest in thee," Augustine prayed. Blaise Pascal recognized the "God-shaped vacuum" in every person's heart, a vacuum that sucks in everything we use to stop it and remains unfilled. Christianity says "Yes!" to our desire to live forever, "Yes!" to our recogni-

tion that we are currently unfit to live forever, "Yes!" to our need for forgiveness and restoration, "Yes!" to our permanent attachment to loved ones, "Yes!" to our fundamental feeling that we are, in fact, utterly dependent upon God and that this is right. The Bible says, "In [Jesus] every one of God's promises is a 'Yes'" (2 Corinthians 1:20). At the heart's core, Christianity makes sense.[2]

The force of Paul's analogy is that *his* word is as good as the gospel because "He which establishes us with you in Christ . . . is God" (v. 21). The same God who conceived and consummated the redemption of lost humanity energized and undergirded the apostolic ministry. Once again Paul stands out as a powerful example of integrity and faithfulness in ministry.

## Sealed by the Spirit

Together with the reference to "sealing" in the next clause, we should not miss the Trinitarian language used here. The plan of redemption is from "God." The Savior through which that plan was executed is "Christ." The Agent by which the benefits of that plan are applied is the Holy Spirit "who also sealed us" (v. 22). *Sphragizō* and (less frequently) *sphragis* are used in Paul's writings to convey essentially the same idea—that of a legal possession or authority. In Romans 15:28 the verb is used in the only occurrence of the mundane sense to speak of Paul putting a seal on the "fruit," that is, the "financial gift" that the churches of Macedonia are sending to Jerusalem. The other six times convey the owner-slave relationship between God and the believer. The term had a fairly common usage in the language of commerce, in the Septuagint, and in the papyri to speak of seals stamped on legal documents, sacks of merchandise, etc. (cf. Dan. 6:17; 1 Kings 21:18). The term emphasizes the idea of "certified ownership" to be noted by those who receive such documents or materials. Much as with the term *election*, the "seal" denotes that the object sealed belongs to God and (more important to this context) is sent and authorized by God. This sealing has a threefold significance in the New Testament: (1) to indicate ownership; (2) to indicate genuineness; and (3) to preserve and keep safe (cf. Eph. 1:13; 4:30; 2 Tim. 2:19; Rev. 7:2). This last idea is amplified with "the Spirit in our hearts as a pledge" (v. 22). Paul uses the term *arrabōn* only three times and always with reference to the Holy Spirit as a down payment. In Ephesians 1 this is clarified as a down payment on the believer's future inheritance as a child of God. The Holy Spirit Himself is the down payment, or pledge, of redemption. The indwelling Spirit is the surety and the "security" of all that is to follow in the final salvation of the believer (cf. Rom. 8:9–11, 23; Eph. 1:14; 2 Cor. 5:5).

No wonder Paul began this with "He which establishes us." For all those who have participated with Paul in the divine affirmation of their relationship with Him, there is no vacillation between yes and no. There is only God's eternal "yes," confirmed by Calvary and sealed by the Holy Spirit. Few texts are more enlightening and confidence-building than this for those who wonder from day to day if they are still saved. One day it is "yes," and the next it is a "maybe," and on an especially dark day they are certain it must be "no." The security of God's child is in God's hands, not in their wavering emotions or inconsistent walk. He owns us and preserves us, and through the sealing of His Spirit, He has marked each of us. It is that Spirit who "bears witness with our spirit" (Rom. 8:16). The Corinthian believers resonate with the truth of God concerning their own salvation; they will also resonate with the truth concerning Paul's character.

## Authority, Not Authoritarian

"To spare you I came no more" (v. 23). The apostle was eagerly desirous of seeing the Corinthian assembly again. But even more than that, he was concerned when he got there to be able to have a positive ministry among them. He did not wish to come there with a heavy hand.

"Not that we lord it over your faith" (v. 24). Authority and authoritarianism are not the same. Authority may be veracious or intrinsic. Intrinsic authority is *inherent* in a person or thing, often by virtue of his, her, or its relation to others. A mother has intrinsic authority over her children. Paul is a spiritual father to the Corinthian believers (cf. 1 Cor. 4:15—"you would not have many fathers; for in Christ Jesus I became your father through the gospel"). He is obviously not afraid to remind them of this. Veracious authority is authority that a person or thing has by virtue of his, her, or its relation to another authority. A police officer or a military person has authority granted by the state. A book, such as the Bible, has authority because it is inspired by God. Properly understood, authority needs to be distinguished from power. A person who leads or rules obviously needs both. A king who has the "right" to the throne but no power over the military would be unable to rule. A dictator with military might to usurp the throne would have the power to rule but not necessarily the right. Sometimes people confuse power and authority as if they were the same thing. This tendency is "authoritarianism." Many in positions of authority will use their position to "Lord it over" the people. This often results in a repressive culture where people either give up or revolt. Paul has both intrinsic and veracious authority. As their spiritual father, he has intrinsic authority. As an apostle of Jesus Christ, he has veracious authority. He also has the "power" of will to deal

with the troublemakers himself. But he does not want to *pull rank*. He does not
wish to dictate to them in an authoritarian way, as he goes on to express, "we
. . . are workers with you for your joy" (v. 24). In light of the present state of
affairs, this could hardly be enhanced if Paul came immediately.

# A Firm Foundation

"For in your faith you are standing firm" (v. 24). Our strength and stability are
grounded in the One in whom we have placed our faith, not in our acquies-
cence to some human authority. Our comfort and joy should flow from this.
Paul's confidence in verse 24 is rooted in his confidence in the One who
"establishes" them (v. 21). Together with the preceding, Paul's approach
toward "freedom" and "liberty" is clearly seen. Paul was the great preacher of
Christian liberty (cf. Rom. 8:21; 1 Cor. 8:9; 2 Cor. 3:17; Gal. 2:4; 5:1–13). He
does not for a moment presume to interfere with the exercise of one's faith.
He also recognizes (with James and Peter) that genuine faith in Jesus Christ
produces works that are consistent with those who "follow His steps" (cf. 1
Pet. 2:21; James 1:25; 2:14–26). There are those today, just as there were some
in Paul's day, who would use the banner of "Christian liberty," or as some
would have it, "soul freedom" to justify ungodly behavior and even apostasy.
Some, for example, openly reject biblical inerrancy and the deity of Christ as
legitimate expressions of their "soul freedom." Others love to display their
"liberty" with participation in ungodly behavior that offends others—especially other believers who are thus deemed "weaker brothers" (see commentary on 1 Cor. 8:7–13).[3] Those who are true followers of Jesus Christ will
acquire both His mind and His character. Liberty brings "independence, but
it also gives us responsibility. It must not be anarchic."[4]

Just as Paul is confident of the finished work of Jesus Christ on their
behalf, he is also certain that this same Lord Jesus Christ will work in their
hearts. As he said to the Thessalonians, "Faithful is He who calls you, and He
also will bring it to pass" (1 Thess. 5:24). Previously he made the point that
his demeanor in his ministry with the Corinthians was intentionally low-key.
"For I determined to know nothing among you except Jesus Christ, and Him
crucified. And I was with you in weakness and in fear and in much trembling.
And my message and my preaching were not in persuasive words of wisdom,
but in demonstration of the Spirit and of power, that your faith should not
rest on the wisdom of men, but on the power of God" (1 Cor. 2:2–5). This
passage links with the comment above regarding authoritarianism. If Paul
were to make all the decisions, they would never learn how to exercise responsible discernment themselves. Mature Christianity is not like riding on a train

with only one engine pulling everyone behind. It is more like a team of hik-ers who stand on their own feet and, whether blazing a trail or following a guide, pull their own weight. Like a coach, Paul is encouraging these disciples to strap on their hiking boots and get on the trail. Only when they exercise their spiritual muscle will they experience God's enablement and direction.

## Bloody but Unbowed

"But I determined this for my own sake" (2:1). Paul uses the word *krinō* thir-ty-five times in the New Testament; the basic meaning of the word itself is "to judge" or "to make judgment." It is used in several ways to describe:

1. legal judgment—a person judging another person according to human or divine laws.

2. prejudice—a person judging another (correctly or incorrectly). This could include judgment of God by a person.

3. personal choice—made from personal conviction with the authori-tative weight of the individual person.

4. divine judgment—this might be direct, such as the final judgment, or it might be indirect through an agent or circumstances.

5. firm belief—strongly held personal judgment about something, sub-ject to change, though not likely.

6. generic choice—a personal choice as deciding between equally valid options.

Paul's use of the word here should be understood as being within the third category. As their spiritual father (cf. 1 Cor. 4:15), Paul's use of *krinō*, mean-ing "determined" or "resolved," is reminiscent of 1 Corinthians 2:2. In the earlier epistle, he uses the term to denote his resolve to preach only Christ and Him crucified, because he also knew that he would be laying a foundation for the faith of his (as yet future) converts. Against the competing culture and phi-losophy, he had to be sure that the gospel message was clear and distinctive. In this text Paul expresses a similar and equal resolve to build a bridge over the conflicts and misunderstandings created by the immaturity of the fledg-ling congregation and the deceptions of his determined critics.

*Touto*, "this," looks both backward and forward. Having laid the founda-tion for their faith and secured them upon it (1:24), Paul is now "determined" to see this divisive conflict resolved. Over and above his commitment to visit the Corinthian assembly according to his original itinerary was a commitment to himself that "I would not come to you in sorrow again" (v. 1). While there is no mention of it in the book of Acts, it is clear from 12:14, 21 and 13:1 of this epistle that Paul had already visited the Corinthian assembly since writing 1 Corinthians, for the purpose of correcting abuses and dealing directly with those who were challenging his ministry and authority (cf. also the introductions to the commentaries on 1 and 2 Corinthians). Paul had vowed within himself that he would not allow this to happen again. As Paul reflects on these circumstances, he is caused to contemplate the pain he has already experienced in consequence of his ministry with them.

Here and in the ensuing discussion, Paul employs three terms to denote the "pain" through which they have gone. These include *lupeō*, "sorrow;" *thlipsis*, "affliction," and *dakruon*, "anguish." Together these terms express a wide range of emotions experienced as they continue to work through the conflicts that (for Paul) are only obstacles to mutual "joy" (v. 3). Any pastor or decidedly committed parent or leader of any kind knows this pain. It is birthed in "love" (cf. v. 4) and seems always to be necessary to the joy that comes when divisive issues are resolved and the lines of communication are reestablished. "Weeping may last for the night, but a shout of joy comes in the morning" (Ps. 30:5).

---

### *Uses of the Greek Words* **Lupē** *and* **Lupeō**

1. *Extreme grief: almost to the point of depression (2 Cor. 2:7).*

2. *Healthy grief: sadness or grief that promises to produce therapeutic results. Paul often associates grief and pain with salvation and growth (2 Cor. 7:8–11).*

3. *Destructive grief: grief that drowns the person in despair and prevents or perverts growth (2 Cor. 2:7; Phil. 2:27).*

4. *Stinginess (cf. KJV, 2 Cor. 9:7): related specifically to New Testament giving. It is said that the giver should not give with* lupē *or "under compulsion." A person should not give if it induces "pain," or merely because he or she feels compelled to give (legalistically); instead, the giver should have a "cheerful" attitude, recognizing (9:8) that it is God who gives to each in order that each one may abound "for every good deed."*

5. *The grief of regret: whether due to the loss of a personal possession or the death of a friend or relative, there is sadness related to a set of circumstances (cf. Phil. 2:27).*

6. *Spiritual sorrow: an unusual use of the word* lupeō *to denote pain caused by anguish over the spiritual condition of Paul's unsaved Jewish contemporaries (Rom. 9:2).*

---

The fact that an entire vocabulary is needed to unpack the degree of pain experienced by the apostle Paul should set off alarms with anyone who feels called to ministry. The ministry is not a vocation for people who are lazy or of weak character. A young woman recently confessed that when she considered the call of God to ministry, having grown up the daughter of a pastor, her first question was, "Why would I want to bring that kind of pain upon myself?"

If there are those in the assembly who think Paul derived any degree of satisfaction from his previous visit, he assures them that it inflicted no small hurt to his own heart. "If I cause you sorrow, who then makes me glad?" (v. 2). The greatest joy the minister of the gospel can experience is to see that his spiritual children are walking in the truth (cf. 3 John 4). Conversely, nothing is more painful than to have to employ the rod of correction. Unless they have walked where Paul walked, people cannot know the pain that strikes at the heart of those who have to deal harshly with unresolved sin. Such experiences not only test the pastor's love for the "sheep," they also test his character when called upon to defend the "truth" without compromise.

## Joy in Sorrow

"This is the very thing I wrote you" (v. 3). That is, Paul had given instructions regarding disciplinary measures that were necessary in the assembly (1 Cor. 5:1–5; cf. also 7:8). "Lest, when I came, I should have sorrow from those who ought to make me rejoice" (v. 3). His desire is that they would take care of these problems themselves so that when he came he would be able to rejoice in a congregation that acted obediently, and he would see that it had elicited repentant hearts and the restoration of those who had been disciplined. James says that "faith without works is useless" (James 2:20). The real test of obedience is more than lip service. It is measured in changed behavior. Of course, Paul is also interested in the offering for the poor saints in Jerusalem. He does not want to have to pressure the Corinthian believers when he comes to town to receive their contribution. He would rather see that they have voluntarily and cheerfully taken care of that duty on their own. The *Westminster Shorter Catechism* opens with the question: "What is the chief end of man?" The answer: "Man's chief end is to glorify God, and enjoy him forever." For those who imagine that the Christian experience is characterized by sadness, sternness, and the absence of joy, it might be a surprise to learn that this document that gives creedal expression to the denomination that is stereotyped as the religion of Scrooge begins in this way. That which springs forth in joy for the believer is not the same as that which solicits the same emotion in the world. Augustine reflects on his early life of sin: "For I disobeyed, not from a better choice, but from love of play."[5] Later he prays,

Hear, Lord, my prayer; let not my soul faint under Thy discipline, nor let me faint in confessing unto Thee all Thy mercies, whereby Thou hast drawn me out of all my most evil ways, that Thou mightest become a delight to me above all the allurements which I once pursued; that I may most entirely love Thee, and clasp Thy hand with all my affections, and Thou mayest yet rescue me from every temptation, even unto the end.[6]

John Piper loves to repeat, "God is most glorified in us when we are most satisfied in Him." The joy that the believer experiences responds to righteousness and the inner working of God's Spirit in his or her heart. This too is a regular theme of Paul, but especially in this epistle to the Corinthians (Rom. 14:17; 15:13, 32; 2 Cor. 1:24; 2:3; 7:4, 13; 8:2). It is not insignificant that the New Testament term translated "joy" in English translations is *chara*, a variant of the term, *charis*, "grace." Joy in the heart of the saint is a product of grace. And the Source of grace is also the Source of joy.

| Joy in the Heart | |
|---|---|
| *Rom. 14:17* | *Joy is coupled with righteousness and peace by the work of the Spirit.* |
| *Rom. 15:13* | *Joy and peace come in believing.* |
| *Rom. 15:32* | *Joy comes from trusting in God.* |
| *2 Cor. 1:24* | *Joy can be helped along by others.* |
| *2 Cor. 2:3* | *Joy can be found in one's obedience and in the obedience of others.* |
| *2 Cor. 7:4* | *Joy can fill the heart even when one is in affliction.* |
| *2 Cor. 7:13* | *Joy in another believer's heart can bring joy to one's own heart.* |
| *2 Cor. 8:2* | *Joy can produce generosity.* |

"For" (v. 4). This connects with the preceding verse to show why he wrote: "out of much affliction and anguish of heart" (v. 4). Paul's emotional state is graphically revealed. The term, *synochē*, "anguish," occurs only twice in the New Testament (here and in Luke 21:25 in Jesus' description of conditions to prevail during the Great Tribulation). In this context the reference is to how difficult it has been for Paul to deal with the sins and personal criticism that have come from this group. "I wrote to you" (v. 4). Doubtless, Paul's reference here is to a letter now lost.[7] While he is likely referring to some of the issues he dealt with in the first epistle, he does not seem to be referring exclusively to that letter, because, while he did have to deal with some difficulties in that epistle, they do not fit the description that follows (i.e., "affliction," "anguish of heart," "tears"). Furthermore it is difficult to reconcile Paul apologizing for having sent the first epistle to them with the fact of its otherwise very positive tone (contrast the "letter" in question referenced in 7:8). Nevertheless, it likely *does* refer to many of the same issues and voices of opposition to which the first epistle addressed itself. One writer has well noted: "if divisions, carnality, immorality, lawsuits, confusion in worship and excesses at the Lord's table, to say nothing of incest, were not enough to grieve the founder and father of that church to tears, what would it then take?"[8]

"That you might know the love which I have especially for you" (v. 4). Frustration is not what motivates the apostle, rather deep concern and love for his spiritual children. Love is the theme of the gospel. In the words of William Newell, it was "love that drew salvation's plan." Paul never tired of exulting in this truth. "Who shall separate us from the love of Christ?" he asks in Romans 8:35. In 2 Corinthians 5:14 he declares, "For the love of Christ controls us." This love that moved the Father to send His "only begotten Son" (John 3:16), also characterizes those who serve Jesus Christ. "If therefore there is any encouragement in Christ, if there is any consolation of love, if there is any fellowship of the Spirit, if any affection and compassion, make my joy complete by being of the same mind, maintaining the same love, united in spirit, intent on one purpose" (Phil. 2:1–2). His word to the Thessalonians is much the same: "for our gospel did not come to you in word only, but also in power and in the Holy Spirit and with full conviction; just as you know what kind of men we proved to be among you for your sake. You also became imitators of us and of the Lord, having received the word in much tribulation with the joy of the Holy Spirit, so that you became an example to all the believers in Macedonia and in Achaia" (1 Thess. 1:5–7). Paul seems to understand this in two ways. First it is evident that the love of Christ has so marked him that he is literally "constrained" (as in the KJV translation of 2 Cor. 5:14) to proclaim this "good news." In a second sense, this love also "motivates" Paul to serve. That is, Christ's love is such an amazing truth that Paul cannot help but make it known—sometimes even to his own peril (as this epistle demonstrates).

In practical life and ministry, this truth is also important. Sometimes parents struggle with how to discipline their children. Should they use the rod of correction or withhold it? Will discipline drive my child to rebellion? What will happen if we are too liberal? A wise professor once quelled these fears among his young seminary students with sage advice. "Just love your children," he said. "In the end, they will respond well to you if they know you love them."[9] Loving is not a "technique." It is an attitude of the heart that becomes manifestly evident when parents are willing to lay everything on the line to prevent their children from doing anything to bring harm on themselves or their loved ones. Paul loved these people, and they knew it. At the end of the day, this is what made all the difference. "The one characteristic which imparts moral authority to our words and deeds, whether in the pulpit, Sunday school, or the home is love. A loving heart will do more than learning, discipline, and pleading. It is the parent, [or teacher or leader] who loves who is able to exercise an authority over children. This way of love commends itself unto us so that its authority is recognized."[10]

A further reflection on this text is seen in the example of Paul, the pastor, who is not afraid of getting emotionally involved with his people. In this respect he follows the example of our Lord who "wept" over Jerusalem and openly displayed emotion in the face of human suffering and grief (Luke 19:41; cf. John 11:35). Someone has said that a church will often reflect the pastor's family. If the pastor is harsh and detached emotionally from his family, so he will likely be with his church members. If he is warm and embracing with his family, his church will also be a place where people know they are loved and where they "feel" that in tangible ways. Paul demonstrates that emotion is not a bad thing when expressed in the interest of the gospel ministry. "Here we have ample evidence as to why the apostle Paul was so effective in his ministry. He put his whole soul into it. He was indignant, grieved. He wept and he loved alternately, and he was unashamed to manifest it."[11] Effective ministry is like this. It is a mistake to dismiss "emotion" as "emotionalism." If salvation reaches a person at every level—and it does—then our mind, our will, and yes, our *emotions* will be touched. It is certainly true that the manifest expression of that emotion may differ from person to person, but if the transforming power of the Holy Spirit in salvation does not move one's emotion, then they have not been "touched." If we will also be effective in evangelism and nurture, those who are called to church leadership must weep with those who weep, rejoice with those who rejoice, and love with an unfeigned love.

Finally, it should be observed that Paul, the consummate leader, is doing more than merely straightening out a wayward assembly. He is also training leaders. If he comes to town and takes care of all the unpleasant business himself, he will have missed the opportunity to train local leaders in the obligations associated with church discipline. This is another reason he is anxious that *they* do this, not *he*. This will by no means be the last unpleasant issue that will require disciplinary action. Paul never knows when he will be preaching his last sermon to them, so he engages these issues as a laboratory for leadership training.

A vital principle of effective leadership is that the leader must start with the end in mind.[12] The "end" to which Paul is reaching has to do with more than merely resolving conflict. Resolving conflict is, in fact, a means to another end—that of building godly character in the lives of the people. The building of godly character is also a means to the end that they would experience the joy of the Lord when sin is confessed, repented of, and forgiven. This looks toward what follows.

## Study Questions

1. How does this chapter provide an example of problem-solving in the ministry? Suggest five principles you might draw from this section to assist you in your ministry.

2. What is the meaning of the author's reference to a "culture of forgiveness"? How might this be developed in a pastoral ministry?

3. How many times had Paul visited Corinth? Why was his itinerary an issue with them?

4. Truth-telling was vitally important for Paul. Using your imagination, suggest six ways that persons in ministry are tempted to compromise on this principle.

5. Compare 1:24 and 1 Corinthians 2:2–5. How did Paul's message influence his method?

6. How does Paul's discussion of pain and suffering prepare the reader for what follows in chapters 10–13?

7. In what way(s) is Paul's emotional investment in this church demonstrated in this chapter? How should we "imitate" him in this? What are the risks involved?

8. How does Paul use the present conflict issue to train leaders in Corinth?

**CHAPTER 4**

# Restoring a Brother
# 2 Corinthians 2:5-13

### Preview:

*Discipline is one thing; restoration is another. The one is with a view to healing. The other is the process of healing. Sin, of any kind, regardless of its severity, is forgivable at the foot of the cross. Discipline that does not lead to healing is retribution. Restoration that bypasses the process of accountability is a fraud. Those called to leadership in the local church are obligated to apply the benefits of the cross without fail and without partiality. It is to this task that Paul calls the church.*

By this time the apostle has received the report from Titus (cf. vv. 12–14). He now knows that the Corinthian believers have indeed taken responsibility for a very unpleasant matter. They have disciplined the person in the assembly concerning whom Paul had given his advice. In fact, they have taken his counsel to such radical extremes that he now finds it necessary to revisit the matter lest they go overboard in their discipline.

## Who Sinned?

It is difficult if not impossible to know with absolute certainty the identity of this person, let alone his or her sin. The traditional view supported here is that it relates to the person cited in the first letter (1 Cor. 5:1). If correct, the sin is immorality. Others, as noted above, speculate that the sin is something alluded to in 2:5. Tasker follows these in suggesting that the person is not guilty of immoral conduct but of rude and disagreeable conduct. Some speculate that this may have involved an insult directed against Paul[1]—hence his delay in

*43*

coming to them. Others add that it is contrary to the moral position of Paul to suppose that he ever could have tolerated the presence of the incestuous person in the church mentioned in the previous letter.[2]

To this, three things need to be said. First, since the writer is nonspecific, the effort to identify the specific situation beyond mere speculation is futile. Second, it is inappropriate to suggest that there is a sin that is beyond the reach of forgiveness. Paul has already cited the fact that his forgiveness, and certainly that of the Lord, has been extended to persons guilty of gross immoral conduct (cf. 1 Cor. 6:9–11). Consider further the woman at the well (John 4:17, 18) whose "serial adultery" is well documented but whose sins do not present an insurmountable obstacle to the Lord's mercy and forgiveness. The very idea that a particular type of sin—however heinous—would be beyond forgiveness is an affront to the gospel.

Third, regardless of which view one takes on the question, there is no doubt that Paul and his readers knew exactly who it was and what the offense was. This final point is perhaps most important. As noted above, there is no sin that could potentially disqualify the person from the benefits of positive discipline leading to repentance, forgiveness, and reconciliation. It is further evident that this was a situation that required formal church sanction and that their action had yielded the fruit of repentance. The pressing question was: Now what?

Often in our contemporary churches, discipline is a relic of ancient history and avoided at all costs for fear of rocking the boat or worse—legal recrimination by the person who has been called on the carpet. People have the idea that "lifestyle" choices are a matter of one's "right to privacy." The consequence of this is that there are people in many congregations whose lives are characterized by the same carnality and sin common in the surrounding culture. It is, for example, an embarrassing statistic that the divorce rate among evangelical Christians is now equal to or in excess of that in the surrounding unregenerate world. Worse, no one does anything about it. Liberal parents who neglect their children will eventually preside over a household of chaos. Churches who neglect discipline experience the same when it comes to matters of conduct and holiness. But the most tragic consequence of all is that this neglect injures the erring believer most of all. As the child who is never disciplined must learn the harsh lessons of life from the courts, the streets, or prison, believers who are never called to a standard of holiness suffer from spiritual neglect. Never being exercised to godliness, never being required to "walk in a manner worthy" of their calling (Eph. 4:1), they also never enjoy the thrill of growing in grace, the joy of sins forgiven, and what the writer of Hebrews describes as the "peaceful fruit of righteousness." See Heb. 12:11: "All discipline for the moment seems not to be joyful, but sorrowful; yet to those who have been trained by it, afterwards it yields the peaceful fruit of righteousness." The word "trained" in the original text is *gumnazō*, "to exercise, train." It is the word from which the English, "gymnasium" derives. The clear teaching of the New Testament is that discipline is not supposed to be *destructive*, but *constructive*, leading to maturity and holiness.

"If any has caused sorrow" (v. 5). Paul is generalizing in order to state a principal. The Greek verb *lelupēken* is, in the indicative perfect active, suggesting the condition: "if anyone has caused pain or grief that continues to weigh heavy on the hearts of others." It is providential that the writer is intentionally vague. While the text does not disclose the specific sin and/or the sinner in the historical setting, it enables the contemporary reader to, as it were, fill in the blanks. The name could be *ours* and the sin that which besets *us*. What the writer advises in this situation is true in every situation where sin has been properly dealt with and restoration is in order.

There is another subtler lesson to learn here that constitutes the very reason readers are not able to clearly identify the offense or the offender. There is no attempt to dredge up the sins of the past. It has been addressed. Those who needed to know the details have been brought in to deal with it. Now it receives no mention whatever. In the world of the forgiven, there is no need to celebrate the great sins *from which* one has been delivered. Rather, we celebrate the "great salvation" (see Heb. 2:3) *to which* we have been delivered. In fact, "As far as the east is from the west, so far has He removed our transgressions from us" (Ps. 103:12). There are many who would linger at the "waters of Marah" (Exod. 15:23) and complain about how bitter the water tastes instead of drinking from the wellspring of the water of life that never shall run dry (cf. John 4:14; Rev. 22:1). In the world of the forgiven, what belongs to the "old man" is no longer applicable to the "new." As Paul puts it later in this epistle, "the old things [are] passed away; behold, new things have come" (2 Cor. 5:17). It is neither right nor proper to dwell on the character of the old when the new offers so much to celebrate.

Of all the devices used by Satan to destroy or subvert the effectiveness of the gospel, the denial of forgiveness is perhaps the most insidious, for it denies the power of the cross. "But now apart from the Law the righteousness of God has been manifested, being witnessed by the Law and the Prophets, even the righteousness of God through faith in Jesus Christ for all those who believe; for there is no distinction; for all have sinned and fall short of the glory of God, being justified as a gift by His grace through the redemption which is in Christ Jesus; whom God displayed publicly as a propitiation in His blood through faith" (Rom. 3:21–25). Jesus' final words to His small band of disciples were: "Thus it is written, that the Christ should suffer and rise again from the dead the third day; and that repentance for forgiveness of sins should be proclaimed in His name to all the nations, beginning from Jerusalem" (Luke 24:46–47). Peter declared at his own peril, "We must obey God rather than men. The God of our fathers raised up Jesus, whom you had put to death by hanging Him on a cross. He is the one whom God exalted to His right hand as a Prince and Savior, to grant repentance to Israel, and forgiveness of sins" (Acts 5:29–31). Paul and Barnabas repeated the same message to the Gentiles: "Therefore let it be known to you, brethren, that through Him forgiveness of sins is proclaimed to you" (Acts 13:38). When retelling the story of his conversion before King Agrippa, Paul recalled the words of Jesus' commission to him: "But arise, and stand on your feet; for this purpose I have appeared to you, to appoint you a minister and a witness not only to the things which you have seen, but also to the things in which I will appear to you; delivering you from the Jewish people and from the Gentiles, to whom I am sending you, to open their eyes so that they may turn from darkness to light and from the dominion of Satan to God, in order that they may receive forgiveness of sins and an inheritance among those who have been sanctified by faith in Me" (Acts 26:16–18). Not only is forgiveness central to the gospel message, but it is an example that challenges the believer to practice the same. "And be kind to one another, tender-hearted, forgiving each other, just as God in Christ also has forgiven you" (Eph. 4:32). The dark realm of the dominion of Satan is a world where people must bear their own iniquity. In the church where people know not how to forgive, this prince of darkness too often still holds sway. This lesson is vital to the life and health of those whom Paul addresses as the "saints" of Corinth (cf. 1 Cor. 1:2; 2 Cor. 1:1) and equally so in our churches today.

---

### *Thoughts on Forgiving Others*

*1. Be mindful of how Christ forgave you of an insurmountable debt (Col. 3:13).*

*2. Forgiving others is not a sign of weakness, does not affect God's forgiveness of them, and does not, as some who are sorely hurt often fear, justify what they said or did.*

*3. If forgiving someone is difficult, remember that being willing to forgive is the first step.*

*4. Forgiveness is to be done in obedience to God for your own spiritual life (Mark 11:25).*

*5. Reconciliation is the normal goal of forgiveness, but it is not always possible or desirable.*

*6. Forgiving someone does not mean that you have to contact them or that you must now subject yourself to hurtful or dangerous relationships.*

*7. As with God's forgiveness, forgiveness of others does not necessarily remove from them the consequences of their sin.*

# Discipline Is for Healing

"He has caused sorrow not to me, but in some degree—in order not to say too much—to all of you" (v. 5). The sentence structure is awkward here. Paul is saying, to paraphrase, "if someone has caused grief in the assembly, his offense is not so much against me [the apostle] as it is against the local assembly—and that's putting it mildly!" For this reason, the obligation of discipline lies not on the shoulders of the apostle but on the leadership of the local church, and Paul is prepared to go along with their decision (cf. v. 10). It should not be lost to the reader that Paul's approach to this situation is counterintuitive to the magisterial model of church hierarchy. Even though Paul shares their pain, the greatest offense is against the local assembly—which bears the embarrassment and pain and the obligation of dealing with this personal sin. Those who are given the task of adjudicating the sin are those of that same local assembly who have been tasked with the responsibilities of leadership—the deacons and elders. It is a mistake to imagine that the apostles (or any other church leaders, for that matter) ever promoted themselves as peers of the "one mediator . . . between God and man, the man Christ Jesus" (1 Tim. 2:5). There is no *alter Christi* (substitute Christ) to grant indulgence or forgiveness. Only God can forgive sins. Those who imagine that they derive their ecclesiology from the church "fathers" do not go back far enough. If they would go all the way to the apostles, they would see a very different structure taught and practiced.

The Corinthian church's discipline of this individual is enough. "Sufficient for such a one is this punishment" (v. 6). They had gone far enough in bringing the offending person to repentance. Paul's advice now was to "forgive and comfort him, lest somehow such a one be overwhelmed by excessive sorrow" (v. 7). The purpose of discipline is not to destroy but to edify and restore. Therefore, when true repentance is in evidence, the proper response is to "reaffirm your love for him" (v. 8). Contrary to the thinking and practice of many, discipline is not an end but a means. It is not so much like a quid pro quo transaction as it is a "medical" procedure—the means to spiritual health. Those who administer discipline must keep this in mind almost as much as those who receive it. The "end" in view is not punishment, but restoration and healing. Indeed, "looking to yourself, lest you too be tempted" (Gal. 6:1). The work is not finished when the offending person is brought to task. Only when he or she is restored to fellowship is the work considered complete. Only a poorly trained medical doctor would perform surgery only to send the patient out of the hospital to manage his or her healing alone. Neither should the church be content to send ailing believers out from their number without a plan of action to facilitate their healing. They should continue to reaffirm the same love that motivates the disciplinary action in the first place—until the offender has been restored. This, by the way, is what distinguishes grace from law. Its purpose is not simply to exact a pound of flesh for a similar measure of misdeeds. Discipline is not retribution, and repentance is not recompense. Rather, believers appropriate God's grace to love the unlovely, to bind up the wounded, to bring sight to the blind, and to impart joy unspeakable to those who have been alienated from fellowship because of sin.

| Discipline in the New Testament | |
| --- | --- |
| **Example** | **Reference** |
| An accused elder | 1 Timothy 5:19, 20 |
| A sinning brother | Matthew 18:15–20 |
| An overtaken brother | Galatians 6:1 |
| An unruly brother | 2 Thessalonians 3:6 |
| False teachers | Titus 1:10–16 |
| Factious people | Titus 3:8–11 |
| An immoral brother | 1 Corinthians 5 |
| An undisciplined brother | 2 Thessalonians 3:7–11 |

Paul goes on to express why he instructed the church to administer discipline. "That I might put you to the test" (v. 9). He needed to know that the Corinthian assembly possessed the maturity and character to deal with sin in their assembly. It is now clear to him that they did, and in this he rejoices. In 1:3–4 Paul indicated that God's comfort was designed to be shared. Here is his application of this principle in the context of church discipline. As they had received God's forgiveness, they are to forgive. Jesus taught us to pray, "Forgive us our trespasses as we forgive those who trespass against us." Forgiveness is recyclable. When it is given, it comes back again in our own time of need. More than that, Paul was concerned that the church demonstrate the strength of character to do the right thing. He was interested as much in their response as he was in the person being disciplined. Now he knows that his confidence in them was not misplaced. He is convinced that they have the right stuff to confront those in the church who would bring harm through sin, carnality, or a divisive spirit. In time he will come to this. For now he must take care of the matter in hand.

"But whom you forgive anything, I forgive also" (v. 10). Paul awaits the church's decision. He is prepared to stand behind their ruling on the matter. Notice once again that there is no hierarchical structure dictating to the local assembly. The ruling authority was the local church.

There is an important reason Paul is so concerned that they resolve this problem. "So that no advantage be taken of us by Satan" (v. 11). *Satanas* means "adversary" and is the name by which Satan is generally known in the Greek New Testament. Satan is the most commonly used name in our English Bible for Lucifer, the fallen angel (see 1 Chron. 21:1; Job 1, 2; Zech. 3:1, 2; Matt. 4:10; 12:26; 1 Cor. 5:5; 7:5; 2 Cor. 11:14; 12:7; 2 Thess. 2:9). Such an advantage could be gained by Satan either by the despair of an individual Christian or the disunity of the local assembly through the incident in view. "For we are not ignorant of his schemes" (v. 11). The term *noēma*, "schemes," speaks of the working of the mind, of thinking and reasoning. Here it speaks of the machinations and strategies of the archenemy of the gospel. Paul knows that Satan can and will use this incident to distract and diminish the work of God in the Corinthian assembly unless it is properly handled. Satan's first attack is against the gospel (cf. 2 Cor. 4:4). If he can bring disunity to the church, which is the agent of propagating the gospel, then he will also bring dishonor upon the gospel itself. The church that God can best use is the church that exudes God's forgiveness and consolation (on Satan's devices see also 10:3–4; 11:12–14). See also "serpent" (2 Cor. 11:3) and "Belial" (2 Cor. 6:15).

In verses 12–13 Paul shows his confidence in the Corinthian church. "When I came to Troas . . . a door was opened for me in the Lord" (v. 12). The connection of this verse is with verse 4: "that you might know the love which I have especially for you." Further evidence of this love is Paul's behavior while engaged in a very fruitful ministry in Troas: "I had no rest for my spirit" (v. 13). Paul's concern for the evangelization of the lost was overridden by his concern for the Corinthian assembly, and that was saying something (cf. 1 Cor. 9:16)! As important as they are, it is neither love for the lost nor love for the world that distinguishes believers—it is love for one another (John 13:35). "But taking my leave of them, I went on to Macedonia" (v. 13). Paul is eager to meet Titus on the way. See comments on 1:1–2 above. On Titus's report to Paul about the condition of things in Corinth, see 7:5–6.

## Study Questions

1. Suggest an example in your own life or ministry that illustrates the difference between discipline and restoration.

2.  What difference does it make that Paul does not identify the specific sin about which he speaks in this passage? Do you suppose his original readers knew what it was?

3.  Why is spiritual discipline important to those who have sinned? In what specific way(s) does the church leadership fail offenders when they are not properly disciplined?

4.  In what specific way(s) is the work of Satan evident in the situation in Corinth?

5.  Do a brief study of "Satan" using a Bible dictionary and concordance. From this study prepare a brief outline of your findings.

# CHAPTER 5

# The Smell of Victory
# 2 Corinthians 2:14-17

### Preview:

*Followers of Jesus Christ are like the soldiers of a victorious army following their leader in a grand procession. As they march they give off the fragrance of Christ, which in turn divides the race of humanity into two camps—those who are being saved and those who are perishing. Paradoxically, it is the apostles who are the smoke arising from the sacrifice of Christ, not to be identified or confused with those who peddle God's Word for personal gain.*

Beginning with verse 14, Paul offers "the most sustained defense of his apostolic ministry found anywhere in his letters (2:14–7:16; 10:1–13:10)."[1] What follows here also forms the "theological heart of the epistle, providing the framework for understanding the rest of Paul's discussion in chapters 4–9 and perhaps also chapters 10–13."[2] First Corinthians 3:1–18 also contains what Scott Hafemann calls "the most extended interpretation of an Old Testament text found anywhere in his letters."[3]

Much attention has been given to the seemingly harsh transition in the letter from this point. The discussion regarding the mission of Titus and the issues addressed in the previous verses are dropped entirely and not mentioned again until 7:5. This is what has also given rise to numerous theories regarding the possibility of some later editorial remodeling of the epistle. For example, the "severe letter" (see introduction) is sometimes suggested as having been inserted here. However, the tone of this section cannot really be considered all that "severe." There is no reason to say that the sudden transition was not intended by the original author in the first place.[4] On the contrary, having received, as he did, the good report of Titus, there is every reason to consider that he might be led to digress in a benedictory way to place the entire circumstance in the context of the spiritual warfare in which he and his readers are engaged.

## The Means of Victory

The means of victory is God in Christ. Contrary to the sense implied in the King James Version's translation of this verse ("causes us to triumph"), the emphasis is not on *our* victory, but God's victory. The NASB text gives the sense correctly: "But thanks be to God, who always leads us in His triumph in Christ" (v. 14; cf. Col. 2:9–15). The word Paul uses here, *thriambeuō*, is used twice in his letters, here and once in Colossians 2:15. In Colossians 2:15 Christ is the Triumphant One. Here believers are identified as those who follow the Triumphant One. The word *thriambeuō* itself dates back to the worship of Bacchus and was used to show a slave's devotion to his triumphal master.

> In the New Testament it is used [to denote that] the way of Jesus to the cross is paradoxically the triumphal procession of God in which, as *imperator mundi*, He leads the *arcai* as a Roman emperor leads his prisoners, Colossians 2:15. In 2 Corinthians 2:14 Paul describes himself as one of these prisoners. But he regards it as a grace that in his fetters he can accompany God always and everywhere (*pantote . . . en panti topō*, in his missionary work) in the divine triumphant march through the world, even though it be only as the *doulos Christou*.[5]

The imagery pictures the Roman general who marched in victory with his entourage, consisting of two groups: "those who are being saved" and "those who are perishing" (v. 15). The former group referred to those allowed to live as slaves of the empire; they were being led into a new life. The latter group was the condemned; they were being led to their death. Each group carried burning incense. The one was "an aroma from death to death" (v. 16), the other was "an aroma from life to life" (v. 16). Calvary was the mighty display of the infinite power of a sovereign God. There the human race was divided into two categories: those of life unto life and those of death unto death. Barrett's comment is worth noting here: "Paul did not forget (1 Cor. 15:9; Gal. 1:13, 23) that he had fought on the wrong side, and that his position in the triumphal progress was due to a reversal by grace of his just desserts. 'By the grace of God I am what I am, and His grace toward me did not prove vain; but I labored even more than all of them; yet not I, but the grace of God with me' (1 Cor. 15:10)."NEED NOTE

The setting and the imagery in this text were no doubt familiar to both Paul and his readers. They had seen many of these processions and knew all too well the fate of those who followed behind the triumphal military leader as he made his way back to Rome to celebrate his great victory and to lead "captive a host of captives" (Eph. 4:8) and to "make a public display of them, having triumphed over them" (Col. 2:15). Paul makes ample use of the imagery because it forms such an apt metaphor for the victory achieved by God through Christ over the world, the flesh, and Satan (see also Eph. 6:10ff.; 2 Tim. 2:1ff.).

Those who follow behind the Victor sometimes need to be reminded that the One whom they follow is still engaged in a great war. The irony is that, at least in one sense, the war is over and the enemy has already suffered defeat. Calvary and the empty tomb certified this. Christ has died and provided for the remission of sins. Until King Jesus returns and establishes His throne in His earthly kingdom, we are engaged in regular conflict with the subversive opposition forces of the "prince of the power of the air, of the spirit that is now working in the sons of disobedience" (Eph. 2:2). In this situation Paul celebrates the great victory that Titus reported concerning the outcome of their confrontation with those who would harm the church by introducing carnality and division.

## Comfort and Encourage Others

"Do not withhold good from 1those to whom it is due, When it is in your power to do it." (Prov. 3:27)

"The second is this, 'YOU SHALL LOVE YOUR NEIGHBOR AS YOURSELF.' There is no other commandment greater than these." (Mark 12:31)

"In everything I showed you that by working hard in this manner you must help the weak and remember the words of the Lord Jesus, that He Himself said, 'It is more blessed to give than to receive.'" (Acts 20:36)

". . . the Father of mercies and God of all comfort; who comforts us in all our affliction so that we may be able to comfort those who are in any affliction with the comfort with which we ourselves are comforted by God." (2 Cor. 1:3, 4)

"Bear one another's burdens, and thus fulfill the law of Christ." (Gal. 6:2)

"Therefore comfort one another with these words." (1 Thess. 4:18).

"And we urge you, brethren, admonish the unruly, encourage the fainthearted, help the weak, be patient with all men." (1 Thess. 5:14)

When Jesus prayed as He did, "If it is possible, let this cup pass from Me; yet not as I will, but as Thou wilt" (Matt. 26:39), He recognized that there could be no compromise with the enemy. The idea of "peace at any price" or "appeasement" with the enemy was not on His mind. This was a fight to the death against the archenemy of God and of us all. When we pray as He did— and as Paul exemplifies here, we radiate through our lives, attitudes, and actions the reality of His victory. Sometimes believers are given to depression and defeat when they focus on the hardships required of them as soldiers. Paul is not at all blind to these hardships (cf. 2 Tim. 2:3), but he sees the big picture. The hardships are not an indication of defeat, but of the fact that the enemy is still out there. He is very real, and if he sees that we are not on his side, he will do all that he can to discourage us and destroy our effectiveness.

## The Price of Victory

The metaphor of our lives offered up to God as a sweet fragrance conjures up the image of soft lights and sweet music—until we remember that the fragrance of incense is created only when it is *burned*. "For we are a fragrance of Christ to God" (2:15). The words *osmē* and *euōdia* are always used together in Paul's writings. Alone they each mean a type of pleasing fragrance; together they mean an aroma that is exceptionally pleasing. Typically these words are used together with the mention of sacrifice. Here they are used in reference to "those who are being saved," who have a pleasant aroma emanating from the cross, and it this aroma that draws people to Jesus' sacrifice. Barrett translates it, "We are the sweet savour of sacrifice that rises from Christ to God."[6] The thought is of incense rising up to God, used frequently in the Old Testament (Gen. 8:21; Exod. 29:18; Lev. 1:9; Num. 15:3; Ezek. 6:13) as well as in the metaphorical sense in the New Testament (Eph. 5:2; Phil. 4:18). Again Barrett adds, "It seems inevitable that one should fill out the picture by taking Paul's sense to be that the apostles are the smoke that arises from the sacrifice of Christ to God, diffusing as it ascends the knowledge of God that is communicated in the cross."[7] The image is one that Paul also uses elsewhere. "Now I rejoice in my sufferings for your sake, and in my flesh I do my share on behalf of His body (which is the church) in filling up that which is lacking in Christ's afflictions" (Col. 1:24). In his relation to Christ, Paul carries this "aroma" (v. 16) of God's infinite power and unspeakable love wherever he goes. This has the practical effect of dividing humanity. There is in its proclamation the power of death or the power of life. So it was in Paul's original proclamation to the Corinthian believers. This anticipates the next verse. While the immediate reference is to Paul as an apostle, the metaphor is also no doubt given as a word of warning and encouragement to his readers. In their acceptance of the message of Paul, they too join in this train of those who emanate the fragrance of victory in Jesus. But the picture he paints will give pause to any but the absolutely committed. The fragrance of which he speaks contains the consumed remains of the martyrs who witness to these things. These are they as noted above who "fill up that which is lacking" of the sufferings of Jesus.

---

### A Fragrant Aroma

*"And the LORD smelled the soothing aroma; and the LORD said to Himself, 'I will never again curse the ground on account of man, for the intent of man's heart is evil from his youth; and I will never again destroy every living thing, as I have done.'" (Gen. 8:21)*

*"And you shall offer up in smoke the whole ram on the altar; it is a burnt offering to the LORD: ait is a soothing aroma, an offering by fire to the LORD." (Ex. 29:18)*

*"But thanks be to God, who always leads us in His triumph in Christ, and manifests through us the sweet aroma of the knowledge of Him in every place. For we are a fragrance of Christ to God among those who are being saved and among those who are perishing; to the one an aroma from death to death, to the other an aroma from life to life. And who is adequate for these things?" (2 Cor. 2:14–16)*

*"Walk in love, just as Christ also loved you, and gave Himself up for us, an offering and a sacrifice to God as a fragrant aroma." (Eph. 5:2)*

---

The gospel is described as a fragrance manifested in men who are God's representatives, ambassadors on earth. The savor of God, whether good or bad, depends upon those who profess His Name and on their faithfulness in declaring the gospel. When we think of the uncounted flowers which are crushed in order to provide a drop of perfume, we realize that the fragrance of the gospel came from the Cross of Christ, from His suffering and the suffering of His servants like Paul. Wherever a single soul is identified with Christ, a fragrance of the gospel goes forth. By this the knowledge of God is manifested everywhere, in every place. What that fragrance is depends upon the men who manifest it.[8]

"Who is adequate for these things?" (v. 16). Erdman follows the Vulgate translation suggesting that the implied answer to Paul's question is: "I am."[9] See also 3:5–6 below. "One might imagine that Paul would reply in despair, 'No one is sufficient.' Quite the contrary, with startling assurance, he declares himself to be sufficient for such a task. Yet his sufficiency is not of himself. As far as he is concerned, the one condition which he fulfills is that of sincere honesty."[10] Many disagree with this. Tasker observes, "But such a note of self-satisfaction would seem ill-fitted to the context. The logic of the passage seems to demand the answer that no one is sufficient for such a high calling in his own unaided strength."[11] Perhaps the best understanding is to pull both of these ideas together. The seeming paradox is not entirely unique to Paul's letters. While Paul recognizes that perhaps he is not "adequate" (*hikanos*, "to reach," "attain," "worthy"), this obligation is nevertheless that which has been thrust upon him, as he states in Philippians 3:8–14:

> More than that, I count all things to be loss in view of the surpassing value of knowing Christ Jesus my Lord, for whom I have suffered the loss of all things . . . that I may know Him, and the power of His resurrection and the fellowship of His sufferings, being conformed to His death; in order that I may attain to the resurrection from the dead. Not that I have already obtained it, or have already become perfect, but I press on in order that I may lay hold of that for which also I was laid hold of by Christ Jesus. Brethren, I do not regard myself as having laid hold of it yet; but one thing I do: forgetting what lies behind and reaching forward to what lies ahead I press on toward the goal for the prize of the upward call of God in Christ Jesus.

It is evident that this motif was present when Paul considered the work to which he had been called and the price in fulfilling it he expected one day to pay. Yet he also included his readers in the challenge, as he says to the Philippian believers: "Brethren, join in following my example" (Phil. 3:17). Similar language is used in Romans 12:1: "I urge you therefore, brethren, by the mercies of God, to present your bodies a living and holy sacrifice, acceptable to God, which is your spiritual service of worship." This seems to be what is in view in this context. He recognizes that he, indeed, is not "sufficient," yet his sufficiency is in Christ. The language further anticipates 3:4–6, "And such confidence we have through Christ toward God. Not that we are adequate in ourselves to consider anything as coming from ourselves, but our adequacy is from God, who also made us adequate as servants of a new covenant" and 12:9, "And He has said to me, "My grace is sufficient for you, for power is perfected in weakness." Most gladly, therefore, I will rather boast about my weaknesses, that the power of Christ may dwell in me."

Paul then adds: "For we are not like many, peddling the word of God," (v. 17). Some suggest that there were some in the assembly—perhaps traveling preachers, false teachers, who were pretending to be "adequate" but who were instead "peddling" the word. Morgan correctly observes that this "is the [negative] answer to his question, 'Who is sufficient for these things?' Those are sufficient who are not making merchandise of the Word of God, not corrupting it, not distorting it in making merchandise of it; but in sincerity as to God, in the sight of God, speaking in Christ."[12]

In the New Testament, *kapēleuō*, "peddling," occurs only here. In his battles with Judaizers, Gnostics, and wandering philosophers and sophists, Paul uses an expression that the Corinthians would have recognized in their exposure to similar peripatetic preachers in their community. The word itself means to sell something for profit, though it has a wide usage in classical literature, and can mean anything from retail selling to corrupting. Paul's use of the word should be understood as the corruption, or disgracing, of the Word by the selling of it for money. Paul seems to be speaking of people like Simon the sorcerer who pretend to sell spiritual blessings, or the gifts of the Holy Spirit (Acts 8:18–24). Using the editorial "we," Paul makes it clear that he is not in league with such preachers who make merchandise of the Word of God, but "from sincerity" (*eilikrineias:* "clear, open, honest"). The declaration is both an affirmation of Paul's integrity (cf. Acts 20:33) and an insulation from the false, self-seeking propagandists who either make life difficult for him or with whom he is falsely associated (cf. *spermologos* in Acts 17:18; see also 1 Thess. 2:3–5; 2 Cor. 11:4, 12–15).

One further observation on this important text is suggested by Barrett: "The distinction between believers and unbelievers is expressed in their *decision* and not in their *being*, yet rests ultimately upon God's decision (not theirs), and is therefore not absolute in the present but awaits the day of judgment."[13] The suggestion is given here to make clear that Paul is writing with "fundamentally Christian insight and motivation . . . and that his opponents were Jewish rather than Gnostic."[14] Much has been made in recent years concerning the impact of Gnostic ideas on the early church. It is a mistake to read back into the first century what is known of the influence of this later Neo-Platonic movement of the second and third centuries of the Christian era.

Equally important on this account is the evident balance in Pauline thought regarding the sovereignty of God and the free will of man. While salvation is all of God, the obligation to exercise one's will to receive that which is proffered in the gospel is everywhere emphasized in his letters (cf. Rom. 9:15–16; cf. Rom. 10:11–15).

Paul concludes with, "but as from sincerity, but as from God, we speak in Christ in the sight of God." This anticipates, by way of contrast, what follows in the next chapter regarding "letters of commendation" (3:1ff.). Paul's primary commendation is God. His work and ministry are neither for nor with the accolades of others. Certainly he was concerned that his message be heard and well received, but in the final analysis, he considers himself to be answerable to God alone. Not as "those who huckster the Word of God; in other words, we are not of those who are giving out the Word of God for the money we can get out of it."[15]

Some might draw from this a principle not intended. It is true that Paul was a tent-maker. It is also true that, while in Corinth, he supported himself by this means (Acts 18:1–4). In the previous epistle, in order to make a point, Paul reminded his readers that while he was in their city, he and his companions "work[ed] with our own hands" (1 Cor. 4:12). Having said this, Paul never intends to suggest that it would be inappropriate for the minister of the gospel to receive an adequate wage. In his ministry as an apostle and church planter, it was often necessary and prudent to support himself. To this day, bivocational ministers are called "tent-makers" inasmuch as they emulate Paul's example. However, the same writer admonishes elsewhere, "Let the elders who rule well be considered worthy of double honor [literally "double compensation," translated "money" in Matt. 27:6], especially those who work hard at preaching and teaching. For the Scripture says, 'You shall not muzzle the ox while he is threshing,' and 'The laborer is worthy of his wages'" (1 Tim. 5:17–18; cf. also Deut. 25:4; 1 Cor. 9:9, 14). This is now the second time in his letters to Corinth that Paul speaks to this, and it is important that the modern reader not read back into the text a meaning that in fact is the very opposite of what is intended by the writer. Apparently the Corinthians had come to believe that since some were "peddling" their sermons, they must have greater value than Paul who gave out the message for free. Once again he makes it clear that his ministry had nothing to do with money—it was executed in obedience to God's call. As noted elsewhere, the pastor is not a hired hand of the church. He is a minister of God, as Paul charged the Ephesian elders, "Be on guard for yourselves and for all the flock, among which the Holy Spirit has made you overseers, to shepherd the church of God which He purchased with His own blood" (Acts 20:28).

The relative value of the church leader is not measured by the academic degrees that follow his or her name or the salary package commanded. Churches make a grave error in imagining that such worldly standards have anything to do with the measure of a person's character or his or her suitability for being considered for appointment to a ministry. The reverse is also true. Persons with an overly inflated opinion of themselves by virtue of their status, degrees, or salary may very well come up dry when they stand before God. As Jesus charged, "Do not sound a trumpet before you, as the hypocrites do in the synagogues and in the streets, that they may be honored by men. Truly I say to you, they have their reward in full" (Matt. 6:2).

## Study Questions

1. Explain the question raised concerning the internal unity of 2 Corinthians due to the comparison of that which precedes and which follows verse 14 in this chapter. Discuss the issue of the "severe letter" as it pertains to this question.

2. Explain the historical background behind Paul's use of the term *thriambeuō*. How does this passage compare with your understanding of Ephesians 4:8?

3. Who does Paul have in mind with the expression "aroma from death to death?" "Life to life?"

4. Tabulate several areas of your own situation and ministry where "spiritual warfare" is evident.

5. Explain the significance of Paul's use of *osmē* and *euōdia*, especially in relation to Christ and the believer's identification with Him. Can you think of any modern examples of what he is talking about?

6. Explain the purpose of Paul's use of the term "peddling" in this chapter. Relate this to the question of whether preachers/pastors should be compensated for their work.

# CHAPTER 6

# Ministers of the New Covenant
# 2 Corinthians 3:1-18

### Preview:

*Paul concluded the previous chapter by emphasizing his calling as from God and his ministry as an open book before Him. Now he uses the same figure to remind his readers that his ministry was also an open book before them. This gives him an opportunity to address the real issue that gave rise to the opposition to his ministry in the first place. As it turns out, this is not a personal issue, but a doctrinal one. Their attack against the man is nothing more than an attack against his message. The offense is not with Paul, but with the gospel he preaches. If they will examine themselves, they will know this. For it is there that they will see the glory of the new covenant.*

In his letter to Rome, Paul explains, "Israel, pursuing a law of righteousness, did not arrive at that law. Why? Because they did not pursue it by faith, but as though it were by works. They stumbled over the stumbling stone, just as it is written, 'Behold, I lay in Zion a stone of stumbling and a rock of offense. And he who believes in Him will not be disappointed'" (Rom. 9:31–33; see also Gal. 5:11; 1 Pet. 2:8). Robert Grant adds: "Jewish hearers would ask for attestation by miracles, while Gentiles would ask for some kind of philosophical insight. Paul insisted that "to those who are called, both Jews and Greeks, Christ [is] the power of God and the wisdom of God" (1 Cor. 1:22–24)."[1]

In his ministry as the apostle to the Gentiles (cf. Acts 9:15; 13:46–48), Paul's ministry had caused no small stir among those (both Christians and Jews) who were unable to accept this "new work" as from God (cf. Acts

14:1-5, 27; cf. Acts 10:1-11:21). The Jerusalem Council (15:1-29) was eventually called in order to deal with the matter, and it was there that official sanction was given with respect to the matter. All of this, of course, had happened prior to Paul's arrival in Corinth. If Paul had wanted to give them a "letter of recommendation" he could well have pulled out the letter drafted at that time and signed by a veritable "who's who" of the early church. Nevertheless, he recognizes that the real issue is the same one for which he had to contend at Jerusalem (cf. Gal. 1:13-2:21). In the first epistle, Paul underscored that his ministry was from the very start "that your faith should not rest on the wisdom of men, but on the power of God" (1 Cor. 2:5). This was not a political issue, but a battle for the truth of the gospel. If his enemies win, they will have succeeded in undoing everything that had been accomplished to date. He no doubt had this group in mind when he warned that, "savage wolves will come in among you, not sparing the flock . . . speaking perverse things, to draw away the disciples after them" (Acts 20:29-30). In returning to this theme later in this letter, he says:

> I am jealous for you with a godly jealously; for I betrothed you to one husband, that to Christ I might present you as a pure virgin. But I am afraid, lest as the serpent deceived Eve by his craftiness, your minds should be led astray from the simplicity and purity of devotion to Christ. For if one comes and preaches another Jesus whom we have not preached, or you receive a different spirit which you have not received, or a different gospel which you have not accepted, you bear this beautifully [or "rightly"]. (2 Cor. 11:3-4)

Similar conflicts confront churches today from hucksters who seek to draw the people of God "astray from the simplicity and purity of devotion to Christ." Due to the advances in technology, the Internet, and the media, the impact of such enemies is often felt in the most remote settings. No church is exempt from their potential influence. While it is true that many false teachers today are preaching new heresies not current in Paul's day, the answer is still the same—the unvarnished gospel of Jesus Christ. This message is to be set apart from every personality and every program of outreach and evangelism, however famous or "successful" that person or program may appear to be.

General William Booth, the founder of the Salvation Army, was credited with prophetic words concerning the coming twentieth century. "I consider," He said, "that the chief dangers which will confront the twentieth century will be religion without the Holy Spirit, Christianity without Christ, forgiveness without regeneration, morality without God, and heaven without hell." His list could well have provided the outline for a contemporary evangelical bestseller.[2] At the conclusion of his chapter on the "Seven Jesuses I Have Known," McLaren raises the question:

> Why not celebrate them all [Conservative Protestantism, Pentecostalism, Roman Catholicism, Eastern Orthodox, Liberal Protestantism, Anabaptist, and nonviolent Liberation Theology]? Already, many people are using terms like post-Protestant, post-denominational, and post-conservative to express a desire to move beyond the polarization and sectarianism that have too often characterized Christians of the past. . . . What if we enjoy them all, the way we enjoy foods from differing cultures? Aren't we glad we can enjoy Thai food this week, Chinese next, Italian the following week, Mexican next month, and Khmer after that? . . . Isn't there nourishment and joy (and pleasure) to be had from each tradition?[3]

To be sure, Christians should embrace believers across sectarian lines, but one must be careful not to throw out the baby with the bath water. There is an essential core of truth in the gospel that cannot be cast aside however "generous" one may feel. One wonders if these "emerging" theologues were living in Paul's day if the list of "Jesuses" they would include in their theological smorgasbord would include the Jesus of the Judaizers, the Jesus of the Gnostics, and the Jesus of the Ebionites. Consider, for example, the issue for which Paul is ready to take a decisive, not to say "divisive" stand. It was a misunderstanding of how to understand the new covenant in relation to the old. Why, one may ask, is that so important? It is important because it is the theological hinge on which turns the entire edifice of the Christian gospel, conceived from eternity, promised in the Old Testament, executed at Calvary, confirmed by the empty tomb, and consummated in the new covenant. These are not mere preferences to be sacrificed on the altar of acceptance at the temple of tolerance. Such would make good Epicureanism, but it makes for a hopelessly inadequate Christian faith. The central theme of Paul's message was Jesus Christ and Him crucified (1 Cor. 1:23; cf. Rom. 1:16–17). When people turn to Him in saving faith, the results are dramatic and unmistakable. Sins are forgiven, and the power of Christ transforms them with life more abundant than any they have ever known (John 10:10). On this point the writer draws a line in the sand and dares those who cross it to deal with him.

## Living Letters

"Are we beginning to commend ourselves again?" (3:1). Paul almost always uses *sunistēmi*, "commendation," to speak of commending someone in a positive sense. In common usage the term sometimes carries the meaning of an official recognition, such as a police or military commendation, that is, recognizing someone going above or beyond the call of duty. Other times it carries the idea of a recommendation, such as a job recommendation. This is more the feeling here, that of recommending oneself or others for a certain thing. The idea here is to show one's worthiness to teach and lead.

Paul is incredulous that a formal introduction to a church he founded should be necessary; "letters of commendation to you or from you" (v. 1). Such letters of introduction constituted common practice in the early church (cf. Acts 9:1–2; 15:23–29). Due to the prevailing social, political, and religious climate, such letters were both advisable and necessary. Paul here does not disparage their use. He can only be amazed that the Corinthian believers require it of *him*. He lived with them, worked alongside them, taught them, brought them to Christ, and nurtured them in their newfound faith. Now they want to be introduced? This one who was their spiritual "father" (1 Cor. 4:15) is now being called on the carpet to give an account of himself? This could not be coming from the people he knew. It must be coming from his enemies—those who slipped in behind him and who were now calling his integrity into question. In what follows, there is evidence that Paul knew in his heart that this is where the opposition was originating.

So you wish to receive letters of commendation? Do you not realize my letter is "you" (v. 2; the pronoun is plural, literally "my letter is *you all*")? Look at *yourselves*. Consider, in contrast to your former lives that you are no longer "fornicators, nor idolaters, nor adulterers, nor effeminate, nor homosexuals, nor thieves, nor the covetous, nor drunkards, nor revilers, nor swindlers, [as were] some of you; but you were washed, but you were sanctified, but you were justified in the name of the Lord Jesus Christ, and in the Spirit of our God" (1 Cor. 6:9–11). What more evidence do you need? Paul's converts at Corinth were living testimonials to the genuineness of his ministry.

"Written in our hearts" (v. 2). Paul employs the plural together with the editorial "we" throughout this passage. "Known and read by all men" (v. 2). To any who would "take up and read,"[4] Paul's ministry was authenticated (cf. 1 Cor. 9:2). "Being manifested that you are a letter of Christ cared for by us" (v. 3). The apostle is always careful to show that the enabling power of his ministry did not reside in himself but in Christ (cf. 1 Cor. 15:9–10). His use of the term *diakoneō*, "to serve," "minister," "care for," is interesting. It connects with his use of *diakonos*, "servants" (v. 6), and *diakonia*, "ministry" (vv. 7, 8ff.). The reader no doubt recognizes this in relation to the office of deacon (e.g., 1 Tim. 3:8–13). In the sense of "caring for" or "serving," there are also a number of parallels in the New Testament. For example, Jesus is said to have "become a servant (*diakonos*) to the circumcision" (Rom. 15:8). Phoebe is "a servant (*diakonos*) of the church which is at Cenchrea" in Corinth (Rom. 16:1). Epaphras is "a faithful servant (*diakonos*) of Christ on our behalf" (Col. 1:7; cf. also 4:7; 1 Tim. 4:6). Here Paul employs the term to speak of his nurturing care or protection of this assembly.

This "letter of Christ" is distinguished in two ways. First, it is "written not with ink but with the Spirit of the living God" (v. 3). It was supernaturally composed. Second, it was written "not on tablets of stone, but on tablets of human hearts" (v. 3). The reference to "letter" will segue to what follows below where Paul will contrast the "new covenant" as that which is "not of the letter, but of the Spirit" (v. 6). See discussion below. What is important to observe here is that for Paul there is a clear recognition that promises of the new covenant as given to Jeremiah and Ezekiel are being fulfilled in the hearts and lives of those to whom he has ministered the gospel at Corinth (Jer. 31:31ff., esp. vv. 33, 40; Heb. 8–10).

| **The Promises of the New Covenant** |
| --- |
| God promised to put His law in our minds, and to write it on our hearts. (Jer. 31:33; 2 Cor. 3:3) |
| God promised we would be His people, and He our God. (Jer. 31:33; ) |
| God promised that we would know that He is the Lord. (Jer. 31:34; 1 John 2:20) |
| God promised to forgive our sins and not remember them. (Jer. 31:34; Rom. 11:27; Heb. 10:17) |

"Such confidence" (v. 4). This confidence is not only in the genuineness of the Corinthians' conversion experience, but also, in a general sense, "toward God" (v. 4). Paul was not "*self*-confident" but "*God*-confident." Paul understood "how to get along with humble means, and . . . how to live in prosperity." He declares, "In any and every circumstance I have learned the secret of being filled and going hungry, both of having abundance and suffering need. I can do all things through Him who strengthens me" (Phil. 4:12–13). Philippians 4:13 was the life verse of the late Dr. Jerry Falwell. While none will dispute that he was a man of unusual energy, intellect, and strength of character, Dr. Falwell also said many times that most of the work for which he is credited was God's doing—he was only God's instrument in making it happen. In this same vein, Paul's confidence was not in his own dreams and schemes; it was in the certitude that when God had performed a work through him, He would "perfect it until the day of Christ Jesus" (Phil. 1:6). So having laid the foundation for this work, he was still certain that the work will prove not to have been in vain. "Not that we are adequate in ourselves to consider anything as coming from ourselves, but our adequacy is from God" (v. 5; literally "not that we are competent or fit or worthy from ourselves"). The term *hikanos*, "adequate," occurs three times in verses 5 and 6. It has the idea of "enough." As long as Paul had God on his side, it was enough (see also 2:16 above). "To consider" (*logizomai*, think out," "to judge," "to reckon"). Paul's confidence to give account of what God did at Corinth in the hearts of his converts does not reside in himself but "from God."

In keeping with what is said above regarding the powerful influence of the proclamation of the gospel (cf. 2:15, 16), Paul recognizes that when the gospel is preached, God is at work penetrating the hearts of the hearers with His Word. "For the word of God is living and active and sharper than any two-edged sword, and piercing as far as the division of soul and spirit, of both joints and marrow, and able to judge the thoughts and intentions of the heart" (Heb. 4:12). Using the same imagery, Paul says elsewhere, "Take the helmet of salvation, and the sword of the Spirit, which is the word of God" (Eph. 6:17).

## The Letter Kills, the Spirit Gives Life

"Who also" (v. 6). The relative pronoun here does two things. First, it points back to God and, second, it suggests cause or reason (see its use in Luke 8:13). "Made us adequate as servants" (v. 6; literally "made us competent ministers"). The writer answers the question raised in 2:16, "Who is adequate for these things?" This is also the third instance of the term translated "adequate" and "adequacy" in verse 5. Having established his credentials for the ministry, Paul is now elaborating on the distinctive qualities of his ministry. The first is that it was energized by God and not himself or any human agency. The second is that it was in service to a "new covenant" (v. 6). "New" because it was not inaugurated until Christ (cf. Matt. 26:28; 1 Cor. 11:25; Heb. 8:8; 9:15; Luke 22:7–23). "Not of the letter but of the Spirit" (v. 6). *Diathēkē*, "covenant," is always used to refer to a legally binding agreement. In this case the agreement is between man and God, and it replaces an older agreement of the same kind. The import of the word itself is that it refers not just to an agreement but to a legally binding agreement. Paul uses this word specifically because he wishes to emphasize the legal nature of the agreement. Covenant is also a term that defines God's relationship to Israel from Abraham throughout the nation's history. In using the term, there is the sense that God is "personally involved" with his chosen people. Thus this "legal" agreement is more like a "birth certificate" than it is a "court order." It speaks of God's ongoing interest in and relationship with his people.

This expression corresponds with the thought of verse 3, contrasting "ink" with the "Spirit." Here he is more emphatic, "The letter kills, but the Spirit gives life" (v. 6). Paul explains this teaching more fully in Romans 7:6–11. The antithesis between *grammatos*, "letter," and *pneumatos*, "Spirit," has been explained in several ways. Gleason suggests five common views.[5]

First, following Origen, Jerome, and later scholastics of the Middle Ages, this verse has long been used to support a hermeneutic that seeks the deeper, spiritual meaning of the sacred text. The "letter" is understood as "literal sense," while the "spirit" is understood as "spiritual sense." The problem with this understanding is that "spirit" in this context clearly has reference to the "Holy Spirit," not an interpretive method. Beyond this, there is no other example in Scripture where *pneuma* is used to speak of an interpretive approach to the text.

The second approach is to say that *grammatos* refers to the "written text" while *pneumatos* refers to the Holy Spirit as the interpretive guide or "key."[6] The major problem with this view is that Paul is speaking of these as "antitheses," not as two elements working together to effect a proper interpretation.[7] This completely misses the writer's point.

A third view, drawing from Calvin, suggests that the contrast is between external preaching that fails to reach the heart ("legalistic misuse of the Law")[8] and the internal operations of the Holy Spirit through efficacious grace. Barrett supports this idea as follows:

> It was certainly not Paul's intention to suggest that the Old Testament law was merely a human instrument; it was on the contrary, spiritual, inspired by the Spirit of God (Rom. 7:14). But it was easy to misuse it—easy for the Jew to assume that, simply because he possessed it, he was himself superior to the rest of mankind. *Letter* thus points to the way (in Paul's view) many of his Jewish contemporaries understood the law on which their religion was based, and through this to man-made religion in general. . . . *Spirit* points to the new action of God in Christ, where man by faith leaves God to act creatively, no longer expecting to fend for himself.[9]

Again, the point Paul makes both here and in Romans 7 does not have so much to do with the *misunderstanding* of the law, as with "the sin which inevitably results when man in the flesh is confronted by the demands of God. Hence, serving God by the 'letter' should refer, not to the attempt to establish one's own righteousness, but to man's obligation under the old dispensation to carry out the concrete commands of the law of God—a situation which in fact led to obvious sin and death."[10] To this Gleason also notes that the idea that Paul is addressing a "misuse of the Law" cannot be forced into this context where the Law "engraved in stone" could not refer to a misunderstanding, but the Ten Commandments themselves. If Paul had in mind a perversion or misunderstanding of the Law, he would not have later described it as "glorious" (such as he does in v. 9).[11]

A fourth view is that "letter" and "spirit" refer to the outward versus inward obedience to God's law. "One distinguishing characteristic of this view is that Paul's antithesis is not understood as suggesting the end of the Mosaic Law. Thus the change from the Old Covenant to the New Covenant does not entail a change in the Law but rather a change in the believer's ability to obey the Law."[12] Again, there are problems with fitting this idea into this context. Paul notes in verses 9–10, "For if the ministry of condemnation has glory, much more does the ministry of righteousness abound in glory. For indeed what had glory, in this case has no glory on account of the glory that surpasses it." What is stipulated as "new" and "old" in verses 6 and 14 "contrast the new and better from the old and obsolete."[13]

A fifth view, and one that seems most consistent with both this passage and other texts where Paul deals with the same subject (e.g., Rom. 6:6; 7:5ff.; Eph. 4:22; Col. 3:9), is that Paul is simply contrasting the old covenant with the new. Gleason summarizes the evidence for this position.

> On the one side Paul presented the "Old Covenant" (v. 14) as "engraved" (v. 7) on "tablets of stone" (v. 3) and as "the ministry of death" (v. 7), and "condemnation" (v. 9) mediated through "Moses" (v. 7), whose glory "fades away" (v. 11). On the other side he presented the "New Covenant" (v. 6) as "written . . . on tablets of human hearts" (v. 3) and as "the ministry of the Spirit" (v. 8) and "righteousness" (v. 9) mediated "through Christ" (v. 4), whose glory "remains" (v. 11). Therefore to insert a new concept such as "legalism" or "the Spirit as interpreter" into the passage would be foreign to the argument and violate the context.[14]

*Grammatos* clearly has reference to the Mosaic Law as noted above and not to some misunderstanding of it. The "Spirit gives life" is "best understood as referring to the transformation of life by the Holy Spirit according to the New Covenant, as promised in Ezekiel 36:26–27"[15] (cf. Ezek. 37:14; 2 Cor. 1:22; 4:10–12; 5:5, 15). "Paul argues that, as an apostle of the new covenant, he has been called like Moses (2:16b; 3:4–6a), but with a very different ministry (3:6b–18). Moses was called to mediate God's will to a people whose hearts remained hardened, so that without the Spirit, the Law remained merely a "letter" that "kills" as part of a "ministry of death" and "condemnation" (3:6–7, 9)."[16] As Hafemann goes on to note, it would have been fatal for the Israelites to encounter the glory of God—hence the veil on Moses's face.[17]

Since there were certain Judaizers in the assembly at Corinth (see introduction) who were concerned with Paul's defection from Moses's law, Paul uses this occasion to explain his position. The best the Mosaic Law could do was *condemn* the sinner while "the Spirit gives *life*" (v. 6, emphasis mine). It is not implied that the Law of Moses was evil. On the contrary, it is holy, just, and good (cf. Rom. 7:21). The great value of the Law was that it brought sinners to the end of themselves and delivered them to Christ (cf. Gal. 3:24).

## Where the Spirit of the Lord Is, There Is Liberty

Yet this contrast has even further implications. The old covenant "came with glory" (v. 7). Paul alludes to the incident in Exodus 34:29–35. The old covenant, limited as it was, nevertheless, was so glorious that it caused the face of Moses to radiate. Now if this "ministry of death" (v. 7), which was only a transient and temporary measure, so manifested the glory of God "how shall the ministry of the Spirit fail to be even more with glory?" (v. 8). Not only is Paul's message "new," but it is also "better" (cf. Heb. 9:11–28; 10:11–22).

The ministry of the gospel of grace in Christ surpasses the old covenant so much so, that "what had glory, in this case has no glory" (v. 10). The import of this is again reiterated in the words "if that which fades away was with glory, much more that which remains is in glory" (v. 11). The apostle Paul's ministration of the new covenant is justified not only by its surpassing glory (vv. 1–11), but also by its surpassing permanence (vv. 12–18).

"Having therefore such a hope" (v. 12). The "confidence" of verse 4 has now issued in "hope." This hope is sourced in the expectation that if the old covenant was accompanied by the unsurpassed glory of God, how much more can we anticipate the new covenant to be accompanied by glory. "We use great boldness in our speech." Paul now becomes very explicit. *Parrēsia*, "confidence" or "boldness," is often used to show a sense of confidence, sometimes due to a surety that something will happen, sometimes almost as a sense of fearlessness. Here it is neither; rather, it seems to indicate the idea of openness or forwardness in speech despite sufficient reason to fear. In using the expression, Paul seems to be tipping his hand to the fact that he does not expect to be well received.

"And are not as Moses" (v. 13). What follows is an allegorization of the account given in Exodus 34:29–35. "Put a veil over his face" (v. 13). The term *kalumma*, "veil," is used only here together with *anakaluptō* in verses 14, 18 and *kaluptō* (4:3). It is not the term that would be used, for example, of the veil in the temple, which is *katapetasma*. The term *kalumma* could refer to a "covering" or even a "hut." Paul uses this here because it is the term employed in the Septuagint of Exodus 34:29–35 to describe the covering over Moses's face. The veil was not to hide the glory but to obscure it. The people saw his brightness but not directly. It also concealed the "end of what was fading away" (v. 13). The transience of the glory that accompanied the old covenant was not manifestly evident to the children of Israel. For Paul this has typical significance. It seems to suggest the ongoing spiritual condition evident in Israel to this very day.

"Their minds were hardened; for until this very day . . . the same veil remains" (v. 14). For Israel the same obscurity obtains. Their minds are still blinded to the truth as though the veil over Moses's face were thrown over their hearts. "It is removed in Christ" (v. 14). Only the gospel of God's grace exposes the truth to full view. "But to this day whenever Moses is read, a veil lies over their heart" (v. 15). Unfortunately, as far as the Jews are concerned, Christ is still a stumbling block they cannot see (cf. 1 Cor. 1:23). For the apostle, this is no light matter and a concern that caused him great anxiety (cf. Rom. 9:1–4). But now the veil is not so much over the revelation of the glory but over their own hearts (cf. Luke 24:25; Acts 13:27–29).

"But whenever a [person] turns to the Lord, the veil is taken away" (v. 16). The practice of Moses of removing the veil when he turned to the Lord to speak with Him directly is in view here (Exod. 34:29–35). In the same sense, when Israel turns once again to the Lord, they will see and understand—the veil will be removed. "Now" (v. 17; *de*). This connects the reference to "the Lord" in the previous verse with the reference to "the Lord" (v. 17) in the present verse. This Lord is Christ (cf. v. 14).

"The Spirit" (v. 17). While the article does not appear in the original text, the English translation has properly rendered the sense when it includes "that" before Spirit. Paul is not saying "the Lord is Spirit" (in the same sense that is indicated in John 4:24, "God is spirit, and those who worship Him must worship in spirit and truth"). Rather, the sense here is that the Lord is the *Holy Spirit*, the Third Person of the Godhead. It is also important to note here that Paul is not confusing the two persons. Jesus said of His relation to God the Father, "I and my Father are one" (John 10:30). He bears the same relationship to the Holy Spirit. Here is the ineffable mystery of the Trinity—One in essence yet three distinct personalities. "And where the Spirit of the Lord is, there is liberty" (v. 17). Indeed, when Israel turns once again to the Lord and the veil is removed, glorious liberty comes with the confrontation with the Truth (cf. John 8:32; 14:6, 17; 15:26). For further study of the relationship of the Holy Spirit to the ministry of Christ, see John 14:16–17, 26; 15:26–27; and 16:7.

# Beholding and Becoming

"But we all" (v. 18). Reaching a climax, based on the experience of Moses and Israel, Paul now applies the truth to all his readers. "With unveiled face beholding as in a mirror" (v. 18). *Katoptrizomai* is used only here in the New Testament and refers to viewing a reflection of something. It is comparable to James's illustration of viewing oneself in a mirror and seeing what is wrong. However, in Paul's example we do not see what is wrong with ourselves. Rather, we see the glory of God in us. As we gaze upon this image, we are transformed into the same image. One might say that it is like seeing a future version of oneself in the mirror and slowly becoming more like the image.

"The glory of the Lord" (v. 18). As Moses' face reflected God's glory at Sinai, the face of every believer radiates the glory of Christ. That which was reserved for only Moses under the old covenant is made available to all in the new. Some commentaries have attempted to identify the mirror in this text with Christ, the Word, or the believer's heart. This, however, is not clear from the context. What the apostle has in mind, specifically, is difficult to say. The term "beholding" can have the sense of "reflecting." Thus, as Lenski says,[18] the believer himself or herself "reflects" the glory of the Lord just as the face of Moses reflected the glory of the Lord. This view fits most favorably with Paul's imagery. Yet there is more. For Moses the glory eventually faded away, but under the new covenant, the believer is "transformed into the same image" (v. 18). Paul has already established that, as we have borne the image of the earthly, we shall bear the image of the heavenly (1 Cor. 15:49). The apostle John says that ultimately we will be just like Christ "because we shall see Him just as he is" (1 John 3:2). See also John 17:17; Galatians 4:19; and 1 Peter 1:4. "As from the Lord, the Spirit" (v. 18). This transformation takes place by the abiding presence of the Holy Spirit of God. The term *metamorphoō*, "transformed," is used only in Paul (here and Rom. 12:2) and twice in reference to the transfiguration of Christ (Matt. 17:2; Mark 9:2).

## Study Questions

1. Paul addressed his opponents indirectly. How might this be a pattern for handling the perception that "all ministers are suspicious characters"?

2. How might your Bible study group or congregation be "letters of reference" for your discipling efforts? Would it be a "commendation" or a "condemnation"?

3. What are the five different interpretations of "letter" and "spirit" discussed in this chapter? Which view do you support? Why?

4. How do you explain Paul's use of allegory in this chapter? What is his point? Why is this important to his Corinthian audience?

5. In verse 18 Paul indicates that the believer radiates the "glory of the Lord." Thinking in terms of the five senses, what other metaphor(s) do you recall that Paul uses in this letter to show how the believer communicates Christ?

# CHAPTER 7

# Treasure in Earthen Vessels
# 2 Corinthians 4:1-15

### Preview:

*One of the underlying themes of 2 Corinthians is that God's power is demonstrated in weakness. First Paul renounces the hidden things of shame in the proclamation of the truth of the gospel. In doing so the light of this gospel dispels the darkness by which Satan blinds the eyes of those who do not believe. The treasure is then contained in people of clay "that the surpassing greatness of the power may be of God and not from ourselves."*

To the *nuevo rich* of Corinth who prided themselves on their intellectual prowess and who were tempted to view their Christianity as a "superior philosophy," Paul constantly puts himself down. In his first letter, he took most of the first two chapters to remind them that as far as their high-minded neighbors were concerned, this new philosophy (if you please) was "foolishness," and to further show them that God's good hand upon them was hardly due to their superiority, he added, "For consider your calling, brethren, that there were not many wise according to the flesh, not many mighty, not many noble; but God has chosen the foolish things of the world to shame the wise, and God has chosen the weak things of the world to shame the things which are strong." He concludes with, "Let him who boasts, boast in the Lord" (1 Cor. 1:26–27, 31).

The present chapter is a further elaboration on the same theme. Here, however, the underlying theme is power. Power appears to have been an issue in this cosmopolitan city. It was in Corinth that the Isthmian games were regularly held (see introduction to 1 Corinthians). It appears that there were many in their assembly who were also caught up in the "sports culture" where winning the game was the only way to earn respect. These attitudes are still evident today. One of the great challenges to gospel ministries is the task of disabusing people of the idea that God measures success the way the world does. While there is no question that Paul understood the nature of power and, for that matter, how to use it, his approach throughout this epistle and the previous one is to exult in the power of the cross—power through weakness and strength through suffering. What was uppermost in his mind as he wrote was the power of truth.

## Truth and Community

As Paul compares his work and ministry with that of his detractors at Corinth, in what follows, he makes clear that what he had to preach was exactly as God delivered it to him (cf. also 1 Cor. 11:23). He was not trying to manipulate them or deceive them for personal or political advantage. As he begins to enlarge on this point, it becomes clear that what is primarily at stake is not whether he or his enemies win this skirmish; what is on the line is the "truth." Since the truth of which he speaks is the gospel message itself, he is prepared to go to the mat to defend it.

"Therefore, since we have this ministry, as we received mercy, we do not lose heart" (4:1). In light of the superiority and character of the gospel of Jesus Christ under the new covenant, the apostle Paul vigorously and enthusiastically assumes the task of proclaiming its message everywhere. The expression "we do not lose heart" (v. 1) has the sense that Paul was not derelict in discharging his responsibilities to this ministry. The word *egkakeō* is used rarely by Paul to describe discouragement, growing weary, or losing heart and seems to mean the slow fading of purpose, ability, and desire that comes with long-term discouragement or failure. This word does not seem to describe a sudden event but rather a state of being. As the writer uses it here, we see reflected the heart of a marathon runner who goes the distance without losing heart. Paul will explain later why there might be a few reasons for being discouraged. His was an ongoing ministry of adversity. Yet quitting was never on his mind.

"But" (v.2; the strong adversative). What follows stands in sharp contrast to the last statement of verse 1. What Paul denies of himself he impliedly affirms of the false teachers at Corinth.[1] In that regard, Paul demonstrates that he has "renounced the things hidden because of shame." Paul uses *aischunē*, "shame," to describe the shame of hidden sin. Though this word can be applied to many different contexts, the idea is always one of shame or disgrace, whether public or private. This speaks of private disgrace caused by hidden sin. In contrast Philippians 3:9 uses *aischunē* to describe people who publicly acclaim things of which they should be ashamed and who glory in their sin. Here Paul seems to have reference to either disgraceful conduct or secret motives. The latter idea is most likely the meaning. He goes on to speak of the "things hidden" (v. 2).

---

### Do Not Lose Heart

"Now He was telling them a parable to show that at all times they ought to pray and not to lose heart" (Luke 18:1)

"Therefore we do not lose heart, but though our outer man is decaying, yet our inner man is being renewed day by day." (2 Cor. 4:16)

"And let us not lose heart in doing good, for in due time we shall reap if we do not grow weary." (Gal. 6:9)

"But as for you, brethren, do not grow weary of doing good." (2 Thess. 2:13)

"For consider Him who has endured such hostility by sinners against Himself, so that you may not grow weary and lose heart." (Heb. 12:3)

---

His ministry, by contrast, was one of openness and honesty. He was "not walking in craftiness" (v .2). Paul was neither an opportunist nor shrewdly and unscrupulously seeking to achieve his desired aims. He was not "peddling the Word of God" (2:17) or "adulterating the word of God" with false doctrine (v. 2; cf. 2:17). Paul could say, "I have received from the Lord that which I also delivered to you" (1 Cor. 11:23). That which Paul preached was exactly as God revealed it to him. It was "the manifestation of truth" (v. 2). In contrast to those in the Corinthian assembly who were placing undue stress on human credentials, Paul's message commended itself to "every man's conscience in the sight of God" (v. 2). While he never comes right out to accuse his enemies of anything, it is evident that there is an implied object to each of the actions for which he asserts his conscience is clean. Therefore, it is not too much to say that they were guilty of advancing hidden agendas, walking in craftiness, adulterating the word of God, and indeed, peddling their message for personal gain.

The importance of truth in community should not be missed here. "The idea that truth sustains community while deception destroys it is woven into the very notion of truth that we encounter in the biblical [text]."[2] In the Old Testament, truth "was used of things that had proved to be reliable. . . .

'Reliability' would be the best comprehensive word in English to convey the idea. Truth is that on which others can rely."[3] M. Volf cites Paul here together with Jeremiah 9:4–6:

> Let everyone be on guard against his neighbor,
> And do not trust any brother;
> Because every brother deals craftily,
> And every neighbor goes about as a slanderer.
> And everyone deceives his neighbor,
> And does not speak the truth,
> They have taught their tongue to speak lies;
> They weary themselves committing iniquity.
> Your dwelling is in the midst of deceit;
> Through deceit they refuse to know Me, declares the LORD.

"One should put no trust in persons who have taught their tongue to speak lies, insists Jeremiah. The apostle Paul underscores the obverse of the same idea by zeroing in on the relation between trust and truthful speech rather than between distrust and deceit."[4] Volf adds to this several important factors relating to these texts.

> Notice, first, the obvious. In both texts "true" refers to what in some sense *accords with reality*. Jeremiah contrasts "truthful speech" with "speaking lies," and "stating truth" with "falsifying." For both, things ought to be said the way they are, rather than distorted or disguised; words ought to correspond in some unspecified (and maybe unspecifiable) sense to reality.

> Second, neither Jeremiah nor Paul speaks abstractly of the relation between "minds" and "facts," as the Western philosophical tradition liked to state the relation between the knower and the object of knowledge. . . . Instead of forging abstract categories of "facts" and "minds," they narrate the *things people do to each other*. In Jeremiah, neighbors commit iniquity and pile oppression upon oppression. Paul's enemies do shameful things and practice cunning while he does exactly the opposite.[5]

To these Volf adds, "Third, in both texts *truth sustains community and lies destroy it*. By 'the open statement of truth,' Paul is trying to commend himself to the Corinthians, who accuse him of saying, 'Yes, Yes' and 'No, No' at the same time (2 Corinthians 1:17)."[6] Finally, Volf concludes, in "pleading for truth-telling both Paul and Jeremiah appeal to *the character of God*. When Paul speaks the truth, he does so not just before 'everyone' but also 'in the sight of God' (2 Corinthians 4:2)."[7] In much the same way, "for Jeremiah deceit, along with oppression, is a form of refusal to know God (9:6)."[8]

In the contemporary world of pragmatism and worldly ideals of success, we do well to consider the example of both Jeremiah and Paul with respect to Christian integrity in both the leadership and the laity of our churches. Truth may not always be the "easiest" way out of a jam, but the results of failure in this area could ultimately be the destruction of the very community of saints that God has called us to establish.

## Ask the Blind Man; He Saw It All

"And even if our gospel is veiled" (v. 3). Carrying over the analogy of the veil in the preceding chapter, such a veil conceals the truth only from "those who are perishing" (v. 3). "In whose case the god of this world has blinded the minds of the unbelieving" (v. 4). On Satan's control of the world system, see Matthew 4:8–9; John 12:31; 14:30; 1 Corinthians 10:20; Ephesians 2:2; 6:12; and 2 Timothy 2:26. The "lost" of verse 3 are the "unbelievers" of this verse. Such ones are so controlled by Satan that he effectively shields them from the "light of the gospel of the glory of Christ" (v. 4). This is the same "glory" reflected in 3:18.

Two vital inferences should be observed here. The first is contextual. The apostle effectively categorizes those who find his message difficult to accept. In effect, he is saying that the person who is criticizing his ministry at Corinth is not even saved. He is lost, unbelieving, and has been blinded by Satan.

The second inference is theological. While Paul has in mind his own personal defense, he does this on the strength of a larger principle. Whenever the truth of God is presented, it is recognized by "every man's conscience." If it is hidden or "veiled," it is not because God has blinded them, but rather that Satan has prevented them from recognizing it as the truth. The unregenerate person is in bondage—under satanic control—and is incompetent to evaluate the truth of God. Nevertheless, one must be careful here. The problem with the unregenerate is related not so much to the sinner's innate rational faculties (or lack of them). As Paul states so clearly in Romans 1, they know the truth but "suppress" it in their "unrighteousness, because that which is known about God is evident within them." Consequently, their "hearts" are darkened, for "they exchanged the truth of God for a lie" (Rom. 1:18–25).

In God's appeal to sinners, He sent His only Son to earth, to be born of a woman, to live among sinners, to suffer and die, to be buried, and to be raised from the dead to make atonement for the sins of the world. These facts together with the convicting work of the Holy Spirit—of sin, righteousness, and judgment—provide powerful inducements to respond in faith. These are all divine initiatives on behalf of sinners. Add to this the work of the "preachers" of "good tidings" as Paul states in Romans 10:15–21: "How beautiful are the feet of those who bring glad tidings of good things! However, they did not all heed the glad tidings. . . . So faith comes from hearing, and hearing by the word of Christ." He adds in regard to unregenerate Israel from Isaiah 65:2, "All the day long I have stretched out My hands to a disobedient and obstinate people." There is this strange paradox in Scripture where God is seen to offer the wonderful tidings of salvation to the lost through direct and indirect means, yet they *will not* have Him to rule over them (cf. Luke 19:14)!

> The unregenerate are in need of the gospel, but the very thing that provides the only hope of salvation is nonsense to them. The gospel is veiled to those who are perishing. . . . The reply may be that the gospel makes no sense to the perishing because their thought processes are distorted by sin, and they are unwilling. This is correct—that is their problem. But this shows us how human thought processes, clouded as they can be by sin, *cannot* be the court in which we settle what is true and what is false. If our reason has been renewed by the Holy Spirit, it becomes possible for us to see in Scripture, with the eyes of our reason, what God has revealed to us. Prior to this work, the Bible remains spiritual gibberish because the natural man does not understand the things of the Spirit; they are spiritually discerned (1 Cor. 2:14).[9]

At the same time, Satan is also at work to lie, to deceive, and to obscure the truth of this gospel. Make no mistake, each person must choose to receive this work of Christ for their salvation. This is not to say that in so doing they save themselves; rather, by exercising their will to receive the gospel, they meet the conditions so that they can be saved.[10] The work of salvation is all God's work, not ours. "Refusal to believe is the secret and reason of the blindness that happens to men. Oh, it does not matter, people are told, what we believe. Believe me, it does matter. It matters very much what we believe, and whether we believe at all. That is the whole picture here."[11]

"For" (v. 5) connects with the preceding verse. "We do not preach ourselves but Christ Jesus as Lord" (v. 5). Paul's message was clear and simple and could be summed up in a word, or even better, in a name—Christ Jesus. The singular object of Paul's preaching was to confront his listeners with the person of Christ. "And ourselves as your bond-servants for Jesus' sake" (v. 5). As a minister of the gospel, Paul is not his own. He is a voluntary slave of his constituents and compelled by his Master. A further warning here is to the preacher who would follow Paul's example. Preaching is not intended to obscure the truth of the gospel, but to reveal it. We must not, with Moses, throw a veil over the truth to cover it with flowery rhetoric while the people remain in ignorance and darkness. Those who serve Christ to nurture and to guide the flock do well to remember their prime mission. It is not to impress people with erudition, or to score points with professional peers. It was against such pompous piety that John Smyth spoke when he said: "this kind of preaching is rather to put out, than to open the eyes of the blind."[12]

As discussed above, it is important to observe Paul's leadership style. He was not one to "lord it over" his "subjects." Rather, he practiced what might be called "servant leadership." Following the example of Christ who washed the disciples' feet (John 13:5ff.), Paul is a servant to those to whom God has sent him. We do well to exercise the same kind of leadership in the church today. Jesus said, "Whoever wishes to become great among you shall be your servant; and whoever wishes to be first among you shall be slave of all. For even the Son of Man did not come to be served, but to serve, and to give His life a ransom for many" (Mark 10:43–45). J. Oswald Sanders observed, "Those who lead the church are marked by a willingness to give up personal preferences, to surrender legitimate and natural desires for the sake of God."[13]

"For" (v. 6). The particle connects with the preceding verse and forms the basis for it. The expression "God, who said, "Light shall shine out of darkness" (v. 6) refers to the original creation, Genesis 1:3. "Has shone in our hearts" (v. 6). This is the new creation. Some suggest that "our" is used editorially to speak of the apostle himself. The reference would thus connect primarily with Acts 9:3–6; 26:15–16; Galatians 1:15–16 to describe how God revealed this truth to him on the road to Damascus. However, the plural "hearts" seems to lend more support to the idea that Paul has in mind all believers, not just himself. Thus, the miracle of the new birth, while not always accompanied by an outward manifestation of lights, such as the experience of Paul, nevertheless involves a spiritual illumination concomitant with Paul's experience. "To give the light" (v. 6; literally "for illumination"). Just as the comfort of God is to be shared (cf. 1:3–4), the light that penetrates the darkness, illuminates the mind, and regenerates the soul will be reflected to others, and for Paul that was the most exciting aspect of being involved in the gospel ministry. Specifically, for Paul this light was "the light of the knowledge of the glory of God in the face of Christ" (v. 6). This calls to mind Acts 9:3–6. Yet the experience is nonetheless glorious for all who have seen the light (cf. John 1:1–14; 9:24–25, 35–41; 1 Cor. 2:10–14). Jesus said, "I am the light of the world" (John 9:5), and then He proceeded to heal the man born blind! Peter says it this way, "But you are a chosen race, a royal priesthood, a holy nation, a people for God's own possession, that you may proclaim the excellencies of Him who has called you out of darkness into His marvelous light" (1 Pet. 2:9). John adds, "And this is the message we have heard from Him and announce to you, that God is light, and in Him there is no darkness at all. If we say that we have fellowship with Him and yet walk in darkness, we lie and do not practice the truth; but if we walk in the light as He Himself is in the light, we have fellowship with one another, and the blood of Jesus His Son cleanses us from all sin" (1 John 1:5–7).

In the previous chapter (3:1), Paul started this line of thought with a rhetorical question: "Do we need . . . letters of commendation. . . ?" The answer of course was that each of these, his readers, who has experienced Christ and whose heart has been changed by the "Spirit of the living God," is an epistle that is manifestly seen and read by all. In the opening verses of this chapter, Paul seems to come back to the same question but takes the argument a step further. Believers who understand the reality of the gospel—who have seen the "light," with John, these are they who "have an anointing from the Holy One." Not because they are untaught, but because they know the truth and "because no lie is of the truth" (1 John 2:20–21). Here in Paul's words, "For God . . . is the One who has shone in our hearts to give the light of the knowledge of the glory of God in the face of Christ" (v. 6). Someone wants letters of commendation? Who could ask for anything more? As the little chorus says,

> It's hard to believe, but if you don't trust me,
> Ask the blind man, he saw it all.[14]

## Clay Pots

When we think of "clay pots" to describe our bodies, our minds automatically gravitate to that part of our anatomy that tends to obscure our view of the ground! Perhaps this is not what Paul has this in mind, but the metaphor certainly works to the same end. "We have this treasure in earthen vessels" (v. 7). In the wilderness, under the old covenant, God abode in a tent, today He dwells in the hearts of believers. This is the amazing truth, which, for the apostle Paul, forms the principle of empowerment for holy living (cf. 1 Cor. 6:19–20). The stress here is upon "earthen." An earthenware jar is a brittle one. It depicts humanity in its weakness. The wonderful "treasure" is not a product of human genius or clever intellect (humanity in its strength). Yet it resides in people of clay, "that the surpassing greatness of the power will be of God and not from ourselves" (v. 7).

"There is an undercurrent all through this section, revealing Paul's sense of his own physical weakness. He had opened the letter by speaking of great trial coming to him that he had despaired almost of life. There is no doubt that the sense of physical weakness was upon him. He was talking all the time about weakness in the bodily realm and contrasting it with the power in the spiritual realm."[15]

Paul uses the expression *ostrakinois skeuesin*, "earthen vessels," to describe himself (and them) as fragile, worthless, and transitory instruments.[16] Perhaps when he wrote this, he had Isaiah 10:15 in mind, where Assyria is rebuked for taking credit for something God is doing through them. "Is the axe to boast itself over the one who chops with it?" Perhaps it was Jeremiah's prophecy in the Septuagint which uses a similar term, *aggeion*, "vessel," to declare God's word to Israel, "Can I not, O house of Israel, deal with you as this potter does?" declares the LORD" (Jer. 18:1–11). In quoting Jeremiah 18:6, "Behold, like the clay in the potter's hand, so are you in My hand, O house of Israel," Paul uses *skeuos* in Romans 9:21–22. There his point is the same. As instruments of God, we have no reason to boast. He reminds his Gentile readers in Rome, "But if some of the branches were broken off, and you, being a wild olive, were grafted in among them and became partaker with them of the rich root of the olive tree, do not be arrogant toward the branches. . . . Do not be conceited, but fear; for if God did not spare the natural branches, neither will He spare you" (Rom. 11:17–21). There is little doubt that these are the texts in the back of Paul's mind as he writes these words.

One additional thought on "power" is needed. The apostle Paul employs the term *dunamis*, "power" (not to be confused with *exousia*, "authority") many times to describe, for example, the inherent power of God (e.g. Rom. 1:20; Eph. 1:21) and of the gospel (Rom. 1:16; Eph. 3:16, 20). He also uses "power" frequently in the context of God's display of His power through others—whether believers or not (e.g. Rom. 9:17, 22) as discussed above. To the Corinthians, in these two letters, he employs the term almost as many times as he does in all of his other letters combined. "For the word of the cross is to those who are perishing foolishness, but to us who are being saved it is the power of God" (1 Cor. 1:18). "[T]o those who are the called, both Jews and Greeks, Christ the power of God and the wisdom of God" (1 Cor. 1:24). "And my message and my preaching were not in persuasive words of wisdom, but in demonstration of the Spirit and of power, that your faith should not rest on the wisdom of men, but on the power of God" (1 Cor. 2:4). See also 1 Corinthians 4:20; 5:4; 6:14; 15:24, 43, 56. Now he uses the term again in this passage to contrast with the "earthen vessels." "But we have this treasure in earthen vessels, that the surpassing greatness of the power may be of God and not from ourselves." The power of God in the believer is counterintuitive to that which the world emulates. Paul will return to this again in chapter 12 in relation to his "thorn in the flesh." "And He has said to me, 'My grace is sufficient for you, for power is perfected in weakness.' Most gladly, therefore, I will rather boast about my weaknesses, that the power of Christ may dwell in me" (12:9). Again, in the final warning to his readers, "He was crucified because of weakness, yet He lives because of the power of God. For we also are weak in Him, yet we shall live with Him because of the power of God directed toward you. Test yourselves to see if you are in the faith (13:4–5). As he raises the issue here, it is this final warning, "test yourselves," to which Paul is ultimately pointing the reader. The real test of whether one is "in the faith" is whether he or she shares also in the sufferings that precede the glory (2 Thess. 1:5; 2 Tim. 1:8; Heb. 2:9; James 5:10; 1 Pet. 2:19). That this was an issue in this church was already seen in 1 Corinthians 4:8ff.

It is ironic that in much of the discussion today, Paul is entirely misunderstood on this point. It is frequently argued by skeptics (because of passages such as 1 Cor. 7, 11; 1 Tim. 2; et al.) that Paul was a chauvinist at best and a misogynist at worst. Power relations were said to be an important part of his relationship to the churches.[17] This text is certainly reflective of the fact that the issue does come up in Paul's letters. What he says is exactly the opposite of that which many today attribute to him. He celebrates his "power in weakness," not "strength of power." He is not taken with an overly inflated opinion of his importance or with his magisterial authority. His power is not arrogated by virtue of his status in the church or his gender. It resides in Christ who in turn resides in him. And it is therefore shared by all true believers— regardless of status or gender. This is the true message of Paul, not the feminist stereotype often seen in contemporary New Testament studies.

Paul now unpacks what it means to live this way—as a lowly "vessel" to be used (or abused) in whatever circumstances or in whatever task to which this "clay pot" is assigned. It is difficult not to imagine situations where people use things for tasks never intended—using a shoe, for example, to drive a nail, or trying to carry gasoline in a glass jar. Perhaps one should not press the metaphor too far, but it seems to me that this is precisely what Paul does. He is little more than a common "vessel." Yet what he is called upon to do is anything but common! Therein lies the wonder of it all. Against impossible odds, he manifests the provision and power of God "We are afflicted in every way, but not crushed" (v. 8). Paul may be "afflicted in every way," but he will never be "crushed." He may be "perplexed" (v. 8), but he need never "despair" (v. 8). Though he is "persecuted" (v. 9), he will never be "forsaken." He may be "struck down" (v. 9), but he will never be "destroyed."

"Always carrying about in the body the dying of Jesus" (v. 10). The persecutions and sufferings and the trials that confront the believer are the "fellowship of his sufferings" (Phil. 3:10; cf. 1 Cor. 15:31; 4:9; 2 Cor. 11:23; Rom. 8:36; Gal. 6:17). "That the life of Jesus also may be manifested in our body"

(v. 10). This same thought occurs in Romans 8:17. If we share in his suffering, we will also share in his glory (cf. John 14:19; Rom. 6:8–9; 2 Tim. 2:11; 1 Pet. 4:13–14). G. Campbell Morgan told the following story.

> A young fellow entered the ministry, and had remarkable success, and great blessing has attended his life and work. At the time he was a young man fresh from college, a brilliant preacher even then. He preached in my church in Birmingham, and I went home after the sermon and said to Mrs. Morgan, "Was that not wonderful?" She quietly remarked, "Yes, but it will be more wonderful when he has suffered." Well, he suffered, and it was more wonderful.[18]

## The Fellowship of Christ's Sufferings

*I protest, brethren, by the boasting in you, which I have in Christ Jesus our Lord, I die daily. (1 Cor. 15:31)*

*For, I think, God has exhibited us apostles last of all, as men condemned to death; because we have become a spectacle to the world, both to angels and to men. (1 Cor. 4:9)*

*Are they servants of Christ? (I speak as if insane) I more so; in far more labors, in far more imprisonments, beaten times without number, often in danger of death. (2 Cor. 11:23)*

*Just as it is written, "FOR THY SAKE WE ARE BEING PUT TO DEATH ALL DAY LONG; WE WERE CONSIDERED AS SHEEP TO BE SLAUGHTERED." (Rom. 8:36)*

*From now on let no one cause trouble for me, for I bear on my body the brand-marks of Jesus. (Gal. 6:17)*

"We who live" (v. 11; literally "the living"). "That the life of Jesus also may be manifested in our mortal flesh" (v. 11). A diamond is best seen against a black background. The brilliance of the life that is in Christ Jesus is best seen against the background of death. "So death works in us" (v. 12). Paul relates this to his own personal ministry. "Us" is used editorially to refer to the apostle himself. "But life in you" (v. 12). Through a ministry of weakness and suffering, Paul was able to accomplish a very positive ministry in Corinth (cf. 1 Cor. 2:1–4). The tone is not ironic, such as that in 1 Corinthians 4:8–10, although his readers may well have thought so. Nevertheless, Paul is not disingenuous about this. He knows that the power of Christ resides within him, and it has been through him—with all his limitations, faults, and obstacles—that he has seen his Savior do mighty things. To remind us that Paul's experience is not foreign to our own today, Randy Alcorn tells the story of Li Quan, a pastor in the persecuted church of China. Quan, confined to a filthy jail cell, prayed daily for a ministry when suddenly God gave him an idea. He called to the jailer.

"Su Gan, sir, please, I have a request for you."

"Unless you can pay me, I care nothing for your requests."

"Can I do some labor for you?"

Quan saw in the jailer's eyes surprise mixed with contempt.

"This prison is so filthy," Quan said. "There is waste everywhere. The rats and roaches feed on it. You are not a prisoner, but you must feel like you are. Su Gan has to breathe this foul air, to walk carefully because of what oozes out of the cells. Li Quan can help you. Let me go into the cells one by one and clean up this filthy place. Give me water and a brush and soap, and I will show you what I can do! My father, Li Tong was a street sweeper, a great clearer of the ground. The finest in China. And I am my father's son!"[19]

Later when his American friend came to visit, Quan was beaming with joy. They touched hands through the chain-link fence. His friend spoke.

"You smell like . . . soap."

"Yes." Quan beamed, his face and voice surprisingly animated. "This is better than I smelled last time, yes? I have wonderful news! You must tell my family and house church. God has answered prayer. He has given me a ministry!"

"What?"

"I go from cell to cell, bringing Yesu's message."

"But I thought you were in an isolated cell."

"God opened the door. I go to the other men. Most have never had anyone else come into their cell except to beat them. I help and serve them as I clean their cells. I bring them the love of Yesu. Twelve men I have visited. When I left their cells, six I did not leave alone"

"What do you mean?"

"When I left, Yesu was with them"[20]

What is true of the apostle's experience was true for Li Quan, and it is true for the reader. As he instructed the Thessalonian believers, he no doubt wished they would follow his example (2 Thess. 3:7), knowing that they too would see and experience the power of God in and through them (cf 2 Cor. 12:9; Eph. 3:7, 16, 20; Phil. 3:10; Col. 1:11, 29; 2 Tim. 1:7–8). Indeed, it was those who held to a "form of godliness but denied its power" that he exhorted Timothy to "avoid such" (2 Tim. 3:5).

The apostle Paul was able to endure suffering in his ministry not only because he knew that his message was vastly superior to anything offered in the old covenant but also because the gospel of Christ assured him of the glorious prospect of going far beyond the present exigencies of life. This subject he deals with later.

"But having the same spirit of faith" (v. 13). That is, the same Spirit of 3:17, which is the Holy Spirit, often designated by the effects He produces (for example, He is called the Spirit of adoption, Rom. 8:15; the Spirit of wisdom, Eph. 1:17; the Spirit of grace, Heb. 10:29; and the Spirit of glory, 1 Pet. 4:14). Here He is so called because He is the Spirit who produces faith. Thus, in much the same way that David expressed himself in Psalm 116:10, Paul extols the goodness of God. "We also believe, therefore also we speak" (v. 13). The assurance in Paul's heart because of faith caused him to proclaim the gospel with utter confidence in its truth.

"Knowing" (v. 14). This indicates the basis of Paul's confidence expressed in the preceding verse. "He who raised the Lord Jesus" (v. 14) refers to the literal, bodily resurrection of Jesus Christ. "Will raise us also with Jesus" (v. 14). Personal affliction and death become of little consequence when measured against the prospect of resurrection. "And will present us with you" (v. 14). This prospect was expressed by Jude, who said, "Now to Him who is able to keep you from stumbling, and to make you stand in the presence of His glory blameless with great joy" (Jude 24; cf. 2 Cor. 11:2; Col. 1:22). The thought is similar to that of 1 Corinthians 15:19–23 in the idea of "the firstfruits." Throughout Pauline literature the resurrection of Christ is seen as evidence of the resurrection of the believer (Rom. 8:11; 1 Cor. 6:14; Eph. 2:6; Col. 2:12; 1 Thess. 4:14).

"For all things are for your sakes" (v. 15). Everything the apostle endured to carry the gospel to Corinth was for their benefit. "That" (literally "in order that"). The ultimate purpose was "the glory of God" (v. 15), and this Paul envisions as being directly proportional to the sum of gratitude offered in thanksgiving to God for His grace.

## Study Questions

1. Is it ever acceptable to cover up a mistake made in ignorance? How open should the life of the minister be?

2.  How responsible are the lost for their condition?

3.  Have you ever struggled in the midst of being obedient to Christ? How did that struggle impact your walk with Christ?

4.  Contrast how the world defines power and how the gospel defines it. How might we understand the dynamics of power working in our relationships to one another?

5.  Do you know anyone who has suffered persecution for the sake of Christ? Why do you suppose that happened to that person? What would you do in similar circumstances?

**CHAPTER 8**

# We Walk by Faith, Not by Sight
# 2 Corinthians 4:16–5:10

### Preview:

*As the outer person is likened to a clay pot, the inner person is said to be producing an eternal weight of glory. The outer person is decaying while the inner person is developing. We are therefore encouraged to walk by faith, not by sight. In so doing, we will be investing in the eternal rather than the temporal, for we must all stand before the judgment seat of Christ.*

Paul begins by connecting what follows with what has been discussed in the immediate context above with the conjunction "Therefore" (v. 16). It is with reference to the certainty of the glorious resurrection (4:14) that he again declares "we do not lose heart" (v. 16). In 4:1 he used this expression to speak of the superiority of the new covenant. Now he uses it to express certainty in anticipation of the glorious resurrection inherent in the promises of the new covenant. He goes on to explain why this truth is so liberating for him. "Though our outer man is decaying, yet our inner man is being renewed day by day" (v. 16).

## Pots of Glory

The physical body is temporal and passing away. It is subject to decay and through affliction and suffering will eventually be utterly worn out. In the previous letter, Paul reminds us "that flesh and blood cannot inherit the kingdom of God; nor does the perishable inherit the imperishable" (1 Cor. 15:50; cf. Heb. 1:11; Ps. 102:26; Isa. 51:6–8). Yet believers can rejoice that their inner lives are increasing in vitality even as their physical bodies are declining. "The inner man" (v. 16) does not refer exclusively to the soul or immaterial nature, but to a new life imparted to the believer through the work of the Holy Spirit in the new birth (cf. 2 Cor. 5:17–21; Rom. 7:22; Eph. 3:16). Materialism, propagated by godless Marxism in the last century, has generally come to replace the biblical worldview reflected in this chapter. The Bible teaches that human beings have both a material (body) and an immaterial (soul, spirit) nature. That which belongs to the material is subject to death and decay. That which belongs to the immaterial is enduring. When people are born, they are immediately subject to imputed sin and death. This means that the body is subject to demise and decay and the spirit is subject to eternal separation from God. When people are born again, they are given new life "from above" (John 3:3, *anōthen*, from "above"), that is, from the Spirit (John 3:5). In the resurrection we will then be given a new glorified physical body to match the consummation of that work begun in the "inner man" so that we will be finally complete. Paul teaches elsewhere that it is this final glorification for which "the whole creation groans . . . waiting eagerly for our adoption as sons, the redemption of our body" (Rom. 8:22–23; cf. also 1 Cor. 15).

The new life given by the Holy Spirit in the new birth is the particular focus of Paul's attention here. God is working in us that we might become "conformed to the image of His Son" (Rom. 8:29). The so-called youth culture that has overtaken so many today is a sad capitulation to the enemy. In this life, "death" reigns and the "outer man is decaying." But the "inner man" is *developing*. People who have walked with the Lord many years have an inner beauty that transcends the transient beauty of the flesh. Peter speaks of this when he admonishes women. "And let not your adornment be merely external— braiding the hair, and wearing gold jewelry, or putting on dresses; but let it be the hidden person of the heart, with the imperishable quality of a gentle and quiet spirit, which is precious in the sight of God" (1 Pet. 3:3–4). The writer of Hebrews declares, "He Himself likewise also partook of the same [flesh and blood], that through death He might render powerless him who had the power of death, that is, the devil; and might deliver those who through fear of death were subject to slavery all their lives" (Heb. 2:14–15). How pathetic it is for a middle-aged man or woman to struggle to look youthful with plastic surgery, Botox injections, and diet pills. In America this has become a scourge that infects even young people in their teens and twenties who cannot be satisfied with the body God gave them; they feel the need to reinvent themselves through unhealthy dieting, body sculpting, drugs, and excessive exercise. The reality is that none will get out of this world alive—unless we are here for the Rapture. There is a certainty in the life to come that is convincingly demonstrated in the resurrection of Jesus Christ. Peter is probably the best example of this in the New Testament. Before the resurrection he cowered before a little girl who thought she remembered him as a companion of the prisoner Jesus. For "fear of death," he cursed and lied to protect himself from those who might do him harm. But after the resurrection, he was so self-assured in the face of the enemy that he stood on the temple steps in defiance of the angry crowd. Imagine the courage with which he declared: "Therefore let all the house of Israel know for certain that God has made Him both Lord and Christ—this Jesus whom you crucified" (Acts 2:36). What made the difference? It was the knowledge that Jesus Christ had defeated death itself and there was no longer any reason to fear. Believers, of all people, should radiate this assurance. Indeed they do when they take seriously the fact that while this body is failing, our "inner" life is bursting forth with abundant life (cf. John 10:10).

## Be Conformed to the Image of Christ

*For whom He foreknew, He also predestined to become conformed to the image of His Son, that He might be the first-born among many brethren; (Rom. 8:29)*

*And do not be conformed to this world, but be transformed by the renewing of your mind, that you may prove what the will of God is, that which is good and acceptable and perfect. (Rom. 12:2)*

*But we all, with unveiled face beholding as in a mirror the glory of the Lord, are being transformed into the same image from glory to glory, just as from the Lord, the Spirit. (2 Cor. 3:18)*

*Therefore, having these promises, beloved, let us cleanse ourselves from all defilement of flesh and spirit, perfecting holiness in the fear of God. (2 Cor. 7:1)*

*And put on the new self, which in the likeness of God has been created in righteousness and holiness of the truth. (Eph. 4:24)*

*Who will transform the body of our humble state into conformity with the body of His glory, by the exertion of the power that He has even to subject all things to Himself. (Phil. 3:21)*

*And have put on the new self who is being renewed to a true knowledge according to the image of the One who created him. (Col. 3:10)*

*Beloved, now we are children of God, and it has not appeared as yet what we shall be. We know that, when He appears, we shall be like Him, because we shall see Him just as He is. And everyone who has this hope fixed on Him purifies himself, just as He is pure. (1 John 3:2, 3)*

"For momentary, light affliction is producing for us an eternal weight of glory far beyond all comparison" (v. 17). Paul is being modest (contrast 11:16–33). The reader would hardly suspect how intense the affliction was for him. Yet Paul does not patronize his readers, nor is he being cynical. When weighed against eternity and the blessings awaiting our union with Christ, the afflictions of life are light indeed and only for a brief moment (v. 17). The expression "weight of glory" imagines a scale with the sorrows of this life stacked up on the left while on the right is a "pot of glory" outweighing every burden we ever had to bear. Paul had a view of his world and experience that enabled him to see beyond his circumstances, beyond the trials, and even beyond the "the things which are seen." His outlook enabled him to look on "the things which are not seen; for the things which are seen are temporal, but the things which are not seen are eternal" (v. 18). For Paul, the sufferings of life became the platform on which to see the power of God at work. Lest we are tempted to consider this principle to be applicable only to the ancient world, perhaps an example from this writer's own experience will serve to illustrate that God is still in the business of demonstrating "the things which are not seen."

At the end of a particularly grueling week of medical tests, I was standing in the aisle of our new church. The service was over. A woman named Esther made her way to where I stood. Leaning on her cane with one hand, she grabbed my arm with the other.

"God has given me a verse for you," she said confidently.

"You will not die, but live and declare the wonderful works of God." Much as "doubting Thomas" listened skeptically to the women who brought stories of having seen their Lord raised from the dead, I thanked Esther for her "word," but in my heart I wondered. Later I found myself pondering why that happened. *Can it be?* I thought. *Did God direct her to tell me that?* Esther did not know that after the last conversation I had with my doctor, he had scheduled the recent round of tests to discern how far my recently diagnosed cancer had *spread*—a prospect that suggested my condition was much worse than originally thought. I did not know how to receive such a contrary message— even if it did come from God!

It is an amazing thing when God does His work. The text of Psalm 118:17—the verse quoted by Esther—reads in *The Message*: "I didn't die. I *lived!* And now I'm telling the world what GOD did." The psalmist himself was incredulous. He had just come through a battle he did not expect to survive. Pressed to the wall and in desperation, he cried to God for help. At the end of the day, he was still standing—sword in hand. One can imagine him checking his body over to be sure it was true. "I'm alive?" He shouts! "I'm alive!" And for what? He answers his own question. "To tell the world what God just did!"

Eight weeks into my cancer ordeal, I was ready—whether to live or die. We are God's and His to do with as He wills. But it was during this trial that I experienced the "eternal weight of glory" of which Paul speaks here. How exciting it was to think, with Li Quan, *Is this the day I will die?*[1] *Will this be the day I see Jesus? Will I examine the nail prints for myself? Will I see Him "as He is"?* But in reflecting on Psalm 118:17, a quiet confidence began to grow within me that God was going to do something very unusual—perhaps He would deliver me from this "shadow" of death. I began to ask a few trusted friends, my pastor, and my family to pray for a miracle. Asking God for the impossible seemed preposterous. Yet, with Mary, we know that "nothing is impossible" with *Him*.

Later in the week, the doctor called to say that in the last round of tests they found "nothing"! The last ultrasound was completely normal, and he was recommending that we call off the surgery.

He said, "I think we are just chasing a ghost!"

I thought "*Holy* Ghost!" I still do not know how to speak of it. Today my cancer is gone. And so I say with the psalmist, "I'm alive!" And for what? "To tell the world what God just did!" And with Paul to reiterate, "Therefore, we do not lose heart."

As Paul continues, he develops the theme of heaven yet further.

## Our House in Heaven

Paul's confidence in the ministry expressed in the preceding is justified in 5:1–10. In 4:18 he says that his eyes are not on temporal things but heavenly. In this section he explains what he means by this. Since he has already dedicated an entire chapter to the matter of the resurrection, and the "resurrection body" in particular, it would seem that his readers continue to have a problem with this. Among their Greek contemporaries, the reaction to this teaching at Mars Hill was a stumbling block to the intellectuals of the day (Acts 17:32ff.). It is also evident that some in Corinth had similar misgivings.

"For we know" (5:1). This knowledge is based on 4:13–14, "knowing that He who raised the Lord Jesus will raise us also with Jesus and will present us with you." It is this knowledge of faith that has already been ratified in the experience of Jesus Christ. The gospel in Paul's preaching was the message of the finished work of Jesus Christ for the sins of the world—Christ crucified. Faith is the means by which all the benefits of this work are received. This includes that which relates to the past—shedding His blood and offering

Himself as a sacrifice for sins. Theologians speak of this as *propitiation, reconciliation, justification,* and *redemption.*[2] Christ's work, in Paul's preaching, also includes the present—the inner person being renewed each day (4:17). Theologians call this *sanctification.* Finally, Paul anticipates the future when God will pronounce all those who have put their faith in Christ to be righteous. Theologians call this *glorification.* While living on the earth, we stand in the middle between the past and the future, and by faith we rest in confident assurance that our sins have been forgiven. We pin all our hope on this One who said, "I am the way, and the truth, and the life; no one comes to the Father, but through Me" (John 14:6). Salvation is not secured by merely putting our faith in our faith, but trusting without reservation in Jesus Christ Himself. So it is with this sense of utter confidence that Paul proceeds.

| *Bible Passages on Theological Terms* | |
|---|---|
| Propitiation | *Romans 3:25; 1 John 2:2; 4:10; Revelation 5:9* |
| Reconciliation | *Romans 5:10; 2 Corinthians 5:18–20; Ephesians 2:16; Colossians 1:20–22* |
| Justification | *Romans 1:17; 3:24–30; 5:17–19; Galatians 2:16, 20; 3:11; Hebrews 11:4, 7; James 2:21–24* |
| Redemption | *Romans 3:24; Ephesians 1:7; 1 Corinthians 1:30; Titus 2:14; Hebrews 9:12* |
| Sanctification | *Romans 7:7–25; Galatians 5:16–26; Ephesians 4:22–24; Philippians 1:6; Titus 2:14* |
| Glorification | *Romans 8:30; 9:23; Ephesians 2:4–7; Colossians 3:4; 2 Thessalonians 2:13, 14; 1 Peter 5:10* |

"If the earthly tent which is our house is torn down" (v. 1). "Earthly" here has the sense of "terrestrial"—that which is on the earth (cf. 1 Cor. 15:40). The figure has reference to the physical body and the transient character of it. "Torn down" (v. 1; literally "loosened down," "dismantled"). Appropriately used to signify "taking down a tent," here it signifies physical death. "We have a building from God" (v. 1). The tense shows that Paul reckons himself to be already in possession of this new building. This expresses certainty (Rom. 8:30). Paul often speaks of the future as if it were already realized. "But God, being rich in mercy, because of His great love with which He loved us, even when we were dead in our transgressions, made us alive together with Christ (by grace you have been saved), and raised us up with Him, and seated us with Him in the heavenly places, in Christ Jesus, in order that in the ages to come He might show the surpassing riches of His grace in kindness toward us in Christ Jesus" (Eph. 2:4–7). In this text Paul anticipates the time when this present bodily existence will be dismantled. A tent is a place *in which* one dwells when on a sojourn. It is never considered permanent. It is also the place *from which* we interact with those in the present sphere ("that which is seen") who are also on this earthly sojourn.

In contrast to the old body, the new body is pictured as a permanent dwelling: "A building from God, a house not made with hands, eternal in the heavens" (v. 1). There are generally three views taken on this passage: (1) that the "house" (v. 1) is heaven itself, (2) that it has reference to an intermediate body provided for the believer in the interim between the time of his death and the time of the general resurrection, and (3) that it is the resurrection body.

The first view fits well with John 14:2 but does not adequately account for the language in verses 1 and 2 where he says "this house is *in* heaven" and "*from* heaven." It is not given *as* heaven itself. Furthermore, it is discussed here as relating to an endowment given to the believer to enable him or her to participate in the glories of heaven—not as a synonym for that inheritance.

The second view is that this passage teaches an intermediate body. Several suggestions are offered in support of this: (1) Paul believed that he would not die but be changed at once at the rapture of the church (cf. 1 Cor. 15:51–52). However, due to the mounting intensity of the opposition to the gospel and the persecution of those who preached it, the apostle had to face the possibility that such may not be God's plan for him. In the event that he should have to lay aside this body (in death), Paul underscores his certainty that a heavenly home awaits him immediately after death. (2) The inference of verses 3–4 is that the spirit cannot exist without a body. (3) Verses 7–8 imply an immediate change at the time of death. However, it is clear that none of these arguments is compelling.

The third view is that it refers to the resurrection body. In support of this the following arguments are given. First, there is the *negative argument*. There are serious problems with suggesting that this change of body is experienced at the time of death. For example, this would make Paul contradict himself with texts (including the previous letter to this church) in which he not only teaches a corporeal (bodily) resurrection, but specifies that this resurrection is at the future coming of Christ (cf. 1 Cor. 15:15; 1 Thess. 4). Second, there is the *historical argument*. So far as we know, none of the churches established by Paul or his immediate successors held that believers experienced such a change immediately after death. On the contrary, such men as Justin Martyr,

Irenaeus, Polycarp, and Tertullian considered such a doctrine to be heresy. To say that Paul desired to be with Christ in a disembodied state (e.g., as the Swedenborgians teach) violates Paul's expressed desire in verse 3. Then there is the *theological argument*. To say that a temporary body is given until the day of resurrection is opposed to Paul's statement in verse 1 that it is "eternal." A further argument for the view that this is the future resurrection body is that Paul is accustomed, owing to the glory of his future inheritance, to overlooking the intermediate state (cf. Rom. 8:30). Thus Paul seems to pass by the intermediate state as not worthy of comparison with what follows. Furthermore, the "earnest of the Spirit" is given as a pledge to authenticate and to guarantee that about which the apostle is speaking (cf. v. 5). A comparison of Romans 8:23; Ephesians 1:14; and Ephesians 4:30 will show immediately that this ministry of the Spirit has particular reference to the redemption of the body (the future bodily resurrection). It is unlikely that Paul would have consistently made this association in other passages and modified his thinking here without further explanation. At best, the doctrine of an intermediate body is inferential. In fact, the exact nature of the intermediate state is not described in the Scriptures (unless, of course, this text is understood to do so), and therefore specifics regarding it cannot be determined. For a more detailed presentation of this argument, see Peters.[3]

The third view is to be favored primarily for two reasons: first, the sheer weight of the evidence and, second, its faithfulness to all the biblical data. It is incumbent on any student of the Word of God to speak where Scripture speaks and to remain silent where Scripture is silent. While it is acknowledged that it would be a worthy goal to be able to explain the intermediate state, such a noble objective does not justify the fabrication of a doctrine to do so. What is important to note here is that while the saint, at death, ceases to dwell in the body, he or she does not cease to remain in Christ. "While Paul saw death as the end of earthly life, it meant the enrichment, not the negation, of life itself. Death allows *en Christo* corporeality to achieve its goal in consummated *sun Christo* fellowship. Death may terminate the pilgrimage of faith, but it inaugurates the beatific *visio Christi*."[4]

Thus the contrast in verse 1 is between the physical body and the resurrection body. The one is earthly and destined to be dismantled. The other is heavenly, designed and made by God, not human hands, and is eternal. This then understands this text to be in complete harmony with what Paul says elsewhere regarding the eternal state in general and the resurrection body in particular.

"For indeed . . . we groan" (v. 2). In this earthly body. "Longing to be clothed" (v. 2, *ependuomai*, "to have on over"). The term is used by Jesus in

Luke 24:49, "but you are to stay in the city until you are clothed with power from on high." Paul also uses it in Galatians 3:27 to speak of putting on Christ. This term is not characteristically used in a strict sense of a "garment," although that is not entirely absent in the meaning of the term. The idea is more a generic term for "covering." It is found in Revelation 1:13 and 15:6 in relation to clothing. Elsewhere the New Testament biblical writers typically use terms such as *himatizō* (Mark 5:15) and *periballō* (Matt. 25:36; Rev. 11:3). Yet even these are sometimes used in a metaphorical sense (e.g., Rev. 12:1). The writer appears to be playing with several metaphors (clay pots, tent, building, dwelling, etc.) to describe the relation of the "outer man" and the "inner man." When the natural body dies and the believer is given a resurrected body, that is, "our dwelling from heaven" (v. 2), the same duality continues. That is to say that the natural state of the human being is a "duality"—a material/immaterial existence. For this reason it is not incorrect to say that the human (as the "image of God") is *incarnated* in human flesh and that the flesh is not all there is (as materialism would teach), but that together they constitute a unity, to which we generally refer as "person." Some people discount this as "Greek" versus "Hebraic," the latter suggested as the biblical perspective and the former as a view to be discarded as unfaithful to Paul's original thought.[5] It is important to realize that Paul spoke to both the physical *and* the spiritual. His gospel was not just to the saving of the soul; it was that the whole person would be saved. As Garrett notes, when we speak of "soul-winning" we must be careful not to neglect the rest of the human person—the physical.[6] Giving "a cup of cold water" in Jesus' name says it best (Matt. 10:42).

"Inasmuch as we, having put it on, shall not be found naked" (v. 3). After the resurrection we will not be found without a body. Paul argues as he does in 1 Corinthians 15, for a "bodily resurrection," not merely a "spiritual resurrection." He knows well that this will not be received readily by their unsaved neighbors in the community. The truth is the *truth,* and it cannot be changed. There are those today who would compromise on issues viewed as controversial by our politically correct culture. For example, the talk-show hosts hate to hear evangelicals say that there is only one way to heaven. When interviewing people who are deemed to be representative of conservative Christianity, they will always raise the question to which there is no winning response. If the person waffles on the question—trying to placate his audience, he or she is immediately dissociated from those for whom they pretend to speak. If, on the other hand, they speak the truth, the liberal media use such statements as evidence that the spokesperson is an irresponsible bigot. Paul understood this, but he would rather speak the truth than for one second give room for the enemy. The truth of which he speaks is what may be termed the "other half" of the gospel. Salvation involves "reconciliation" with God—the putting away of that which separates us from Him—sin. This might be called the "dark side" of the gospel. The other side of the gospel is the "glorious side." This is spoken of variously as our "inheritance," "blessed hope," "weight of glory," or as Paul has it here, that for which we "groan." The putting away of our sin is a wonderful thing. But it only signifies that *from which* we have been delivered. Here Paul is sharing the incomparable glory *to which* we have been delivered.

"For indeed . . . we groan" (v. 4). Here again, it is due to the burdens of life. Paul also teaches that the entire created universe groans (Rom. 8:23) awaiting the consummation of this promise. We cannot help but imagine what the sun might say, if it could speak, concerning its obligation to "rise on the evil and the good" every day (Matt. 5:45). The entire created order, having committed no evil, groans under the weight of sin until God puts it away forever. A further lesson here is the reminder that the weight of sin, though it be the common lot of all, is but a "light affliction" and does not compare with the "weight of glory" (4:17) yet to be "revealed to us" (Rom. 8:18). We will also do well to hear the admonition that Jesus gives when making reference to the faithfulness of the sun to send its life-giving light to a sin-cursed world. This is "that you may be sons of your Father who is in heaven" (Matt. 5:45). Being a follower of our heavenly Father means that we do not show kindness merely to those who love us in return. Jesus noted that even the "tax-gatherers" and the "Gentiles" do that! Like the sun, the love of God is extended to all—especially those most in need of His mercy.

"That what is mortal will be swallowed up by life" (v. 4). The pressures and trials of life, notwithstanding, Paul is further motivated by a much more positive truth. He anxiously awaits the day when he, together with all the saints, will participate fully in the abundant life promised in heaven.

The assurance of all this is "the Spirit as a pledge" (v. 5; literally "the guarantee or pledge which is the Spirit"). Paul views this in a twofold sense. First, the abiding presence of the Spirit Himself is a continual reminder of the certainty of Jesus' promises. Second, the Spirit Himself generates those inner longings within the heart of the believer that will only be satisfied when he sees Him face-to-face (cf. Rom. 8:23).

"Therefore, being always of good courage" (v. 6). Paul's confidence is not a temporary feeling but a permanent state of mind. "Knowing that while we are at home in the body we are absent from the Lord" (v. 6). So long as this earthly tent is our home, our realization of heaven is detained. "For we walk by faith, not by sight" (v. 7). The KJV correctly renders this as a parenthesis in Paul's thought, for it answers to his confidence in verse 6 and again in verse

8. "We are of good courage, I say, and prefer rather to be absent from the body and to be at home with the Lord." As he noted above, "we look not at the things which are seen, but at the things which are not seen" (4:18).

All things being equal, Paul would just as soon take leave of this "tabernacle" and take up his residence with the Lord in glory. It seems strange to those who do not share this faith or who, perhaps, have never had a "close encounter" that caused them to be brought face-to-face with eternity. For those who have confronted a life-threatening situation, this promise is a "tangible" reality. We *know* that he is right and our hearts resonate with the promise with a longing that will never be satisfied until we see Him. The play on the words *ekdēmeō . . . endēmeō* is lost to the English reader. Paul says that he prefers to be "away from [the bodily] home" and "at home"—that is, present—"with the Lord."

"Therefore also we have as our ambition, whether at home or absent, to be pleasing to Him" (v. 9). Paul lived every day with eternity's values in view. This is similar to what John says: "Beloved, now we are children of God, and it has not appeared as yet what we shall be. We know that, when He appears, we shall be like Him, because we shall see Him just as He is. And everyone who has this hope fixed on Him purifies himself, just as He is pure" (1 John 3:2–3).

Paul adds to this a more sobering thought. "For we must all appear before the judgment seat of Christ" (v. 10). The judgment seat (Gr. *bēma*) was an elevated seat in the square at Corinth where Roman magistrates sat to administer justice and where the athletes who distinguished themselves in the arena received their reward. Not to be confused with the Great White Throne (Rev. 20:11), the judgment in view here is not of the unbeliever but of the believer (cf. 1 Cor. 4:5; Col. 3:4). "That each one may be recompensed for his deeds in the body" (v. 10). That is, be rewarded for the deeds done in this life "whether good or bad" (v. 10). While it is true that for the Christian there is "no condemnation" (Rom. 8:1), it is not correct to assume that God will not hold each responsible for the deeds done in the body. Paul has already unpacked this truth in 1 Corinthians 3:10–15 to which I refer the reader for my comments there.[7]

## Study Questions

1. What is the thematic significance of "therefore" in 4:14? How does it connect the previous context with that which follows? Why is this significant for our understanding of the believer's experience of heaven discussed in chapter 5?

2. How is this text a rebuke to postmodern youth culture and its preoccupation with material things?

3.  Paul had an unusual "worldview" when compared with both the contemporary culture around him and with our own today. Suggest several principles that formed his worldview from this text. What were the practical implications of this? Explain.

4.  The term Paul uses here for our present dwelling, "tent," is distinguished by another term that is used for our future dwelling. Explain this. Why is this a source of encouragement and hope to the writer?

5.  Of the three views concerning the meaning of "a house not made with hands, eternal in the heavens," which is the view chosen by the author of this commentary? Of the arguments discussed, which do you consider the most compelling? Explain.

6.  Explain the significance of the "pledge of the Spirit." You may wish to look at a concordance and a Bible dictionary for help with the question. When is this "pledge" given? How does it relate to our future hope of heaven?

7.  Explain the significance of the "bema seat" judgment. Who will be there? How does this relate to believers? Unbelievers?

# CHAPTER 9

# The New Creation
# 2 Corinthians 5:11–6:10

### Preview:
*Paul is driven by the knowledge that, regardless of the opinions of others, it is God's judgment that matters most. Here he explains first his motive—knowing the fear of the Lord; then his message—a new creation; and finally, his appeal—do not receive the grace of God in vain.*

In that which has preceded and in that which follows, the underlying theme is related primarily to Paul's ministry. It is characterized by trials and opposition (4:7–12). It is driven by the certainty of hope, not in circumstances—"things that are seen"—but in that which is "not seen" (4:13–18). As to that which is not seen, the most exciting thing is the reality that we will one day be with the Lord. Yet this is coupled with a more sobering truth that we must also, in that day, give an account before the "judgment seat of Christ" (5:1–10). With this in mind, Paul continues. He wants us to know that as far as his ministry is concerned, he is driven by the knowledge that, regardless of the opinions of others, he is far more interested in his Lord's opinion (cf. 2:17; 4:2). In what follows he will explain his motive—knowing the fear of the Lord (5:11–15); his message—a new creation (5:16–21); and his appeal—do not receive the grace of God in vain (6:1–10).

## Knowing the Fear of the Lord

What motivates Paul? Why does he put up with such abuse? Why has he "suffered the loss of all things, and count[ed] them but rubbish in order that [he might] gain Christ" (Phil. 3:9)? In a word, it is: "the fear of the Lord" (v. 11). This is best understood in the general sense as it is found through-out the Scriptures as "deep reverence" for almighty God. Perhaps Paul has Proverbs 8:13 in mind here, "The fear of the LORD is to hate evil; pride and arrogance and the evil way, and the perverted mouth, I hate" (cf. 2 Chron. 19:7, 9; Job 28:28; Pss. 19:9; 111:10; Prov. 1:7, 29; 9:10; 14:26–27; 23:17; Isa. 11:2–6; Acts 9:31; Rom. 3:18; Eph. 5:21). The "fear of God" is rooted in recognition of His irrefragable holiness against which the atoning work of Christ is properly understood. For more than two centuries, liberal theolo-gy has attempted to chip away at this in order to make God more tolerant and loving. This trend continues unabated, but regrettably now often from people who otherwise represent themselves as evangelical in their doctrine. John MacArthur Jr. is correct in his response to, for example, "open theists,"[1] who in their misguided desire to emphasize God's love at the expense of His holiness, caricature the traditional orthodoxy as "old model" theology in favor of their "new model" theology.[2] The price paid for such a cosmetic makeover of the God of the Bible is too much. In the end it renders the work of Christ on the cross as excessive overkill—virtually unrelated to the work of the atonement.

> According to the new-model theology, the atoning work of Christ was not truly substitutionary; He made no ransom-payment for sin; no guilt was imputed to Him; nor did God punish Him as a substitute for sinners. None of His sufferings on the cross were administered by God. Instead, according to the new model, atonement means that our sins are simply "forgiven" out of the bounty of God's loving tolerance; our relationship with God is normalized; and Christ "absorbed the consequences" of our forgiveness (which presumably means He suffered the indignity and shame that go with enduring an offense).[3]

Modern Christians need to reflect more seriously on Paul's example here. There is so much emphasis in contemporary evangelical Christianity on the love of God, that His holiness—that is, His *weightiness*—is lost. David Wells has commented on this condition endemic to American Christianity.

> It is one of the defining marks of Our Time that God is now weightless. I do not mean by this that he is ethereal but rather that he has become unimportant. He rests upon the world so inconsequentially as not to be noticeable. He has lost his saliency for human life. Those who assure the pollsters of their belief in God's existence may nonetheless consider him less interesting than television, his commands less authoritative than their appetites for affluence and influence, his judgment no more awe-

inspiring than the evening news, and his truth less compelling than the advertisers' sweet fog of flattery and lies. That is weightlessness.[4]

In this "brave new world," the transcendence of God has been lost to the need to *feel* Him, *touch* Him, and *experience* Him. Wells concludes his analysis of this condition with the following:

> The upshot of all this is that what was once objective in God's being, what once stood over against the sinner, is either being lost or transformed into something we discover first and foremost in ourselves in such a way that God's immanence is typically psychologized. These changes say a lot about our internal landscape and our worldliness, for a God who has thus lost weight is no longer the God of the biblical faith or classical Christianity. A God with whom we are on such easy terms and whose reality is little different from our own—a God who is merely there to satisfy our needs—has no real authority to compel and will soon begin to bore us. This is not the God of Abraham, Isaac, and Jacob. He is scarcely even the God of the philosophers, and certainly not the God of Jesus Christ.[5]

Such thinking has spawned a whole new catalog of designer religions and soft Christianity. Gone is Luther's theology of the cross; enter the pre-Reformation theology of glory—glitzy, twenty-first-century bling-bling Christianity, "God rests . . . inconsequentially upon the church. His truth is too distant, his grace is too ordinary, his judgment is too benign, his gospel is too easy, and his Christ is too common."[6] Such is the style of Christianity that has lost fear of the Lord.

In the immediate context, "terror" has in view the judgment seat of Christ, before which all believers must stand. In light of his accountability before God, Paul goes on, "we persuade men" (v. 11). If "fear" denotes reverence, his response to it is love. It is not his love for Christ that compels him, but the love *of* Christ extended *through* him to persuade others to respond to the good news (see v. 14). Once again he adds in a similar vein, "We are made manifest to God; and I hope that we are made manifest also in your consciences" (v. 11). Inasmuch as Paul's entire life is an open book before God, the Corinthian believers can be assured of his integrity in dealing with them. He continues, "We are made manifest to God; and I hope that we are made manifest also in your consciences" (v. 11). God knows Paul's heart, and he is hopeful that they do too. His object was not to glory in his credentials nor to prove his character to the Corinthians, but simply to authenticate his personal integrity. "We are not again commending ourselves to you" (v. 12). For the most part, the Corinthian assembly by this time was convinced of Paul's genuineness, but Paul was also aware that he still has enemies in the assembly, and the purpose here is to give his followers "an answer" (v. 12).

Paul's ministry was never motivated by or directed to self-interest. "If we are beside ourselves [paraphrase, 'if I appear out of my mind'], it is for God" (v. 13). Paul may be introducing irony here. Some may well have thought he was insane to waste his time with an assembly that demonstrated so little appreciation for his ministry. Nevertheless, if his actions seemed to betray sound logic, he was only acting in obedience to God. "If we are of sound mind, it is for you" (v. 13). The suggestion is that Paul's enthusiasm and spontaneity are held in check in order not to offend the Corinthian believers. "For the love of Christ controls us" (v. 14). Whether Paul appeared to be out of control or under control, Christ's love for him held him in such a grip that it constituted the compelling force in everything he did. Yet even more so, he has come to realize how this love has also extended to his reader: "having concluded this, that one died for all, therefore all died" (v. 14).

Paul has much to say here and elsewhere regarding the relationship of the death of Christ to sinful humanity. He takes up this same theme in Romans 5:18–19. "So then as through one transgression there resulted condemnation to all men, even so through one act of righteousness there resulted justification of life to all men. For as through the one man's disobedience the many were made sinners, even so through the obedience of the One the many will be made righteous." Theologians call this *imputation*. The sin of Adam is imputed to the natural race descended from him. The righteousness of Christ is also imputed to the entire "spiritual" race descended from Him (cf. v. 21). Here Paul is developing the same theme but in a different way. The logic of the text is, as it were, the reverse of Romans 5. In the previous text, Paul argued that through the one act of *righteousness* (Christ's passive obedience to the demands of the Law), justification results "to all men." Here, however, he is saying, inasmuch as "one died for all" we can also say "therefore all died." In other words, Christ died, and since he died for all, it stands to reason that *all* participate in His death. Much has been made over the centuries regarding the so-called extent of the atonement. Paul could not have been more explicit on the question since he looks at it from both sides—that is, from the side of those for whom Christ's *righteousness* is effectual (Rom. 5) and from the side of those regarding whom His *death* was a substitute (here). He is also careful to say that this does not mean that all are saved without exception. Christ's death is for "all" (without exception). However, the expression, "They who live" is nevertheless a specific number. It is they who are "in Christ" (cf. on 5:17, below). Only they share in this "new creation." As Norman Geisler correctly notes, "This did not guarantee the salvation of all, but only their savability."[7]

So, to be faithful to Paul's teaching, it must be noted that there is a *universal aspect* to Christ's saving work and a *particular aspect* to it. While he acclaims Christ's death to be universal in its scope, the new life He brings is not. This must be received by faith. Those who share in this new life are separated from those who "live for themselves" in order that they might live for "Him who died and rose on their behalf" (v. 15; cf. Rom. 5:12–21; 6:1–8; 1 Cor. 15:21–22; Gal. 2:20; Eph. 2:5–6). Note too that the *full gospel* includes the death, burial, and resurrection of Christ Jesus (Rom. 4:24–25). The resurrection also provides incentive to holy living (cf. Rom. 6:4).

Is it any wonder that Paul seemed "beside himself"? The gospel of the saving work of Jesus Christ was limited *by* no one and *to* no one. Yet the task of earnestly persuading men and women to receive this wonderful gift was daunting. D. L. Moody is credited with making the words of fellow evangelist Henry Varley famous. "The world has yet to see what God can do with a man fully consecrated to Him. By God's help, I aim to be that man." There is in Paul's motivation a sense of the adequacy of his message and the sufficiency of his Savior. If, with Moody, one's aim is to be a person "fully consecrated," there is no end to what might be accomplished. In the twentieth century, Dr. Jerry Falwell strove to "be that man." Together, for a century and a half, these two men shook the world with the gospel. Their legacies continue to this day.

## A New Creation

Now Paul turns his attention to his message—the good news of a new creation in Christ (vv. 16–21). "Therefore" (v. 16; Gr. *hōste*, "so that") is inferential. "Therefore from now on we recognize no man according to the flesh" (v. 16). For the apostle the death and resurrection of Jesus Christ has forever destroyed all human distinctions (as he says below, "the old things passed away; behold, new things have come" v. 17). "Even though we have known Christ according to the flesh" (v. 16) "We" is used editorially for Paul himself. There is a man from Galilee "according to the flesh" who has changed the world, but his redemptive work is not to be understood merely in human/fleshly terms. For "now we know Him thus no longer" (v. 16). The historical truth concerning Jesus is important. That "the Word became flesh, and dwelt among us" (John 1:14) is crucial to the historical reality of the Christian faith. Paul is not denying this. However, the most profound accomplishment on behalf of the sins of the world rises far above the human realm to touch the justice of God Himself. This is his point. John reflects the same thought when he declares, "He came to His own, and those who were His own did not receive Him. But as many as received Him, to them He gave the right to become children of God, even to those who believe in His name" (John 1:12–13). His "own" were the Jews. The "as many" were Jews *and* Gentiles, for there is now no difference. What is important regarding Christ's saving work is not that he was a Jew (important as that was to fulfilling the promises to Abraham), but that as the God-man He made propitiation for the sins of the world.

In Christ's coming much is made of the fact that He was the promised son of Abraham, the greater son of David who would inherit the right to his throne. We recognize that these promises remain in force in the present age as promises of the new covenant are granted to the Gentiles. However, it is also important to recognize that it is not merely with respect to the promises to Abraham and David that the apostle to the Gentiles (cf. Acts 15:19ff.) understands his ministry. If there are certain Judaizers in the assembly at Corinth (and there were), Paul wants to make it clear that it is no longer as "Jesus of Nazareth" (*qua* Jew, "according to the flesh") that Jesus is of interest. The ultimate significance is seen in that Jesus is the Christ and that "God was in Christ reconciling the world" (cf. v. 19). Earthly or ethnic connections are of little concern to Paul. We should add too that in saying this, the writer distinguishes the accumulation of information about Jesus from personal faith.

While the error of the Judaizers is not the issue today that it was in Paul's time, we are faced with a related false teaching that is equally damaging to the message Paul preached. This is the "moral influence theory" of Christ's atonement made popular by the liberal preachers and theologians of the late nineteenth century and that generally permeated mainline churches in the last century. The idea is that Christ presents a great example to us of the love of God, and as such, His principle significance in dying was to move us to action with a reciprocating love. Now we certainly do not deny that God loves the sinner. Neither do we say that the redeemed have no good reason to be grateful. However, it is a serious mistake to reduce Jesus' work to little more than a moral example. In such a scenario there would be no reason for Him to have been God. There would have been no vicarious suffering for sin. There would have been no eternal benefits. We would have had only a "man after the flesh" who was of such a moral superiority that he gave to the world the ultimate ideal of how fallen humanity can of their own self-righteousness achieve acceptance before God. Nothing could be further from the truth or from the preaching of Paul (cf. Rom. 1–3).

"Therefore" (v. 17). No longer after the flesh, but in accordance with the creation of a new humanity, "if anyone is in Christ, he is a new creature" (v. 17). What Paul particularizes in verse 16 he generalizes in verse 17. The reason Paul could no longer think of Christ in carnal terms is because of the universal truth that has been applied to him personally. When a person comes into vital union with the risen Lord, that person is now "in Christ" and a participant in a "new creation." (The use of the noun suggests "act of creation" cf. also John 3:3; 15:5; 8:1, 9; Gal. 6:14–15.) "The old things passed away" (v. 17) could be translated "old things are gone." The aorist tense indicates a decisive break with the old life at the moment of salvation. "Behold, new things have come" (v. 17; literally "new things have come into being"). Paul changes to the perfect tense to stress the abiding results of the Christian's union with Christ (cf. Isa. 43:18–19; 65:17; Rev. 21:4–5; Eph. 4:24).

Barrett correctly observes,

> Paul is thinking neither of mysticism . . . nor of ecclesiastical institutions but of a transference by faith in Christ, who experienced the messianic affliction and was raised from the dead as the firstfruits of the resurrection, from the present age into the age to come. Such a transference is properly described as a new act of creation, since the only conceivable analogy to God's act in inaugurating the new age is his creation of the world at the beginning of its story; compare Galatians 6:15.[8]

His point is that the "new creation" is not so much a reference to the establishment of the church or of the "new beginning" the believer enjoys, but rather to the establishment of (as it were) a new race of humanity—Christ the firstfruits. In arguing this way, Barrett is distinguishing the rabbinic usage of the phrase where parallels are drawn between the original creation and God's final redemption and where a person is said to be a "new creature" upon receiving the forgiveness of his sins.[9] "Paul's usage is not as close to the rabbinic as is sometimes suggested, since the rabbis seem to have used *beri'ah hadashah* in the sense of 'new creature', whereas for Paul the sense is rather *creatio nova*, not a new creature but . . . a *new act of creation*."[10]

Paul calls this a "new man" in Ephesians 2:14–22. "For He Himself is our peace, who made both groups into . . . one new man, thus establishing peace, and might reconcile them both in one body to God through the cross." See also Colossians 3:10ff. Again, in a similar context to 2 Corinthians 5, he calls it a "new creation" in Galatians 6:14–15. "But may it never be that I should boast, except in the cross of our Lord Jesus Christ, through which the world has been crucified to me, and I to the world. For neither is circumcision anything, nor uncircumcision, but a new creation." In Romans 6 he declares, "knowing this, that our old self [*anthrōpos*, "man"] was crucified with Him, that our body of sin might be done away with, that we should no longer be slaves to sin. . . . Even so consider yourselves to be dead to sin, but alive to God in Christ Jesus" (vv. 6–11). John comes close to the same idea in Revelation 21:1–2, "And I saw a new heaven and a new earth; for the first heaven and the first earth passed away, and there is no longer any sea. And I saw the holy city, New Jerusalem, coming down out of heaven from God, made ready as a bride adorned for her husband." Whether viewed as a new creation, new man, new body, new temple, New Jerusalem, or bride of Christ, the *en christo* relationship is an entirely new work that brings with it a new relationship with God through the reconciling work of Jesus Christ.

On the importance of this fact in relation to a world that either does not share our faith, or may even be violently opposed to it, Volf correctly comments. "There is a reality that is more important than the culture to which we belong. It is God and the new world that God is creating, a world in which people from every nation and every tribe, with their cultural goods, will gather around the triune God."[11] He adds again in reflecting on this text, "When God comes, God brings a whole new world. The Spirit of God breaks through the self-enclosed worlds we inhabit; the Spirit re-creates us and sets us on a road toward becoming . . . a personal microcosm of the eschatological new creation."[12] Finally, he drives home this point with digital clarity.

> There is a profound wisdom about the nature of our world in the simple credo of the early church "that Christ died for our sins" (1 Corinthians 15:3). At the core of Christian faith lies the claim that God entered history and died on the cross in the person of Jesus Christ for an unjust and deceitful world. In taking upon himself the sin of the world, God told the truth about the deceitful world and enthroned justice in an unjust world. When God was made sin in Christ (2 Corinthians 5:21), the world of deceit and injustice was set aright. Sins were atoned for. The cry of the innocent blood was attended to. Since the new world has become reality in the crucified and resurrected Christ (2 Corinthians 5:17) it is possible to live the new world in the midst of the old in an act of gratuitous forgiveness without giving up the struggle for truth and justice.[13]

"Now all these things are from God" (v. 18). These are all the "new things" (v. 17) introduced to the experience of those who are in Christ Jesus "who reconciled us to Himself through Christ" (v. 18). "To reconcile" is to remove enmity between two enemy parties. In the strictest sense, it involves a "change in relation." Theologically, we typically think of the term in connection with repentance, "a change of mind," and faith, "a turning to," with respect to God in the conversion of the sinner. Since the sinner cannot effect this change for himself, God does it through Jesus Christ in his sacrificial death (cf. Rom. 5:9–10). "And gave us the ministry of reconciliation" (v. 18). This is identical to the "word of reconciliation" in the next verse—announcing the good news "that God was in Christ reconciling the world to Himself" (v. 19). The great message of the apostle was that this was not just another man ("now we know no man after the flesh"). At the "end of the age," that is, in the inauguration of the new eschatological age, Christ put away sin forever on Calvary's tree (cf. Heb. 10:5–12). "Not counting their trespasses against them" (v. 19). This means they are forgiven (cf. Rom. 4:5; Col. 2:13; 2 Tim. 4:16). The present tense here emphasizes a continuous action (cf. 1 John 1:9).

This ministry of reconciliation involves calling upon men and women to demonstrate a changed life, and so Paul considered himself, and all who are in Christ, to be "ambassadors for Christ" (v. 20). With Volf, noted above, they become "personal microcosms" of the "new Creation."[14] Neither Paul nor those who are called together with him usurped authority to this mission. As an ambassador, his ministry at Corinth was *representative*. As an apostle, he came not on his own authority, but at the command of the One who sent him. Thus, his appeal to them is not from himself. Rather, as he says, it is as if "God were entreating through us" (v. 20). Paul's desire is, for the sake of Christ, that they might be "reconciled to God" (v. 20). The verb is not active but passive. The passive voice stresses that he is not calling upon them to change themselves, for he has already established that it is God who does the reconciling (v. 18). Rather, he is asking them to submit to the reconciling work of God.

"He made Him who knew no sin to be sin" (v. 21). Three aspects of Paul's concept of imputation are seen in this passage. In verse 19 God imputes no iniquity (cf. Ps. 32:2). Here he imputes sin to Christ, the spotless Lamb of God (cf. John 1:29; 1 Pet. 1:19). "That we might become the righteousness of God in Him" (v. 21). Then the righteousness of Christ is imputed to the sinner's account. This truth may be viewed from the side of justification, whereby the sinner is declared righteous upon the merits of Jesus Christ (cf. Rom. 3:24–25), or it may be viewed from the side of sanctification, wherein the righteousness of Christ is daily applied. This is the sense developed here and is best understood in conjunction with 3:18. Herein is the essential reason that we "know no man after the flesh." That work concerning which Jesus cried out on the cross, "It is finished!" was to resolve a situation between sinful humanity and a holy God. It was not enough that the Savior be a man; it was required that he also be a suitable "mediator between God and man" (1 Tim. 2:5). Such a one must also be God—not only to bear the full weight of the sins of the world, but also that He might take on himself the wrath of a holy God against that sin. This is what it means that "He became sin for us."

As noted above in the comments on 5:3, those who attempt to redefine God and with it the purpose and meaning of the atonement of Christ create a serious obstacle toward a proper understanding of this text. "Our sins were imputed to Christ, and He bore the awful price as our substitute. Conversely, His righteousness is imputed to all who believe, and they stand before God fully justified, clothed in the pure white garment of His perfect righteousness."[15] MacArthur summarizes:

> Deny the vicarious nature of the atonement—deny that our guilt was transferred to Christ and He bore its penalty—and you in effect have denied the ground of our justification. If our guilt wasn't transferred to Christ and paid for on the cross, how can His righteousness be imputed to us for our justification? Every deficient view of the atonement must deal with this same dilemma. And unfortunately, those who misconstrue the meaning of the atonement invariably end up proclaiming a different gospel, devoid of the principle of justification by faith.[16]

## Doing the Family Business

Having established that the operation of God in reconciling the world to Himself is "in Christ," Paul is eager that his readers understand what this means. Being saved is not to be understood as having been selected out from the mass of humanity and placed on a shelf in a celestial museum. Rather, as Paul understands it, the believer has been chosen to participate in the *work*. God's family business (if you please) is *reconciliation*. The workforce is the *reconciled*.

Those who visit Wal-Mart cannot help but observe that there are no "employees" working there. Rather, they are "associates"! This concept has been revolutionary in the retail business. By the simple act of redefining the workers, they have also redefined everyone's obligation to the bottom line. Likewise, those who are adopted into God's family are expected to contribute to the "family business."

"And" (*de kai*, "and also," v. 1). What follows is based on Paul's teaching in the previous section (5:17–21). "Working together *with Him*" (v. 1). The addition of "with Him" is appropriate since Paul seems to be enlarging on the thought of 5:19—"and has committed to us the word of reconciliation." The masculine, first person plural noun, *sunergountes*, occurs only here in this form. Paul uses the masculine singular *sunergounti* in 1 Corinthians 16:16 with *pas*, "all," to say, "everyone who helps." Here he clearly has in mind the idea that we (that is, Paul and his readers) are linked together with *Christ* (cf. Matt. 11:29) from whom we each receive "grace," that is not to be received "in vain" (literally "to no purpose"). There is no hint here that the salvation of the Corinthian believers is in jeopardy. The grace of which he speaks has reference to 5:21. That they have received this grace denotes clearly that the people to whom he is speaking are genuinely born again. A judicial pardon does not guarantee practical Christian living, and it is the application of the "righteousness of God in him" on a practical level that Paul has in mind (cf. 1 Pet. 1:22; 2:9). Like the associates at Wal-Mart, each one is drawn into the work, and it will be on the basis of their faithfulness to the task that each will stand before the "judgment seat" (5:10ff.). If the thought evoked a sense of "terror" in the apostle, he now lets them know that they too will be there with him.

The thought is similar to what Paul teaches in Ephesians 4:11–12. "And He gave some as apostles, and some as prophets, and some as evangelists, and some as pastors and teachers, for the equipping of the saints for the work of service, to the building up of the body of Christ." The work of the ministry is not restricted to a select magisterium or clergy. It is given to every one of "the saints." Paul seems to view his role as a coach. His task is to teach and motivate, to challenge and equip the saints "for the work of the ministry." Here the work is defined as the work of "reconciliation."

Perhaps it would be useful here to change the metaphor. Suppose for a moment that God is in the oil business. He is building a pipeline across the tundra to supply the lower contiguous states from Alaska. The oil is His grace. We are links in the pipeline. He fills us with His "oil" in order to deliver it on down the line. But suppose we decide to place a valve on the downside of our pipe so the oil that fills us from above can no longer pass through. We would become a *container* instead of a *conduit*. The "oil" is just as rich and useful as ever, but it is "to no purpose." God fills the believer with His grace in order that it might be moved on down the line and fill others also (2 Tim. 2:2). That is the *family business*.

"For He says" (v. 2). Prompted by *dexasthai*, "receive," the apostle recalls to mind *dektō*, "accepted," of the Septuagint translation of Isaiah 49:8. "At the acceptable time I listened to you" (v. 2; literally "in the time of grace I answer thee"). "On the day of salvation I helped you" (v. 2). Consistent with Hebrew parallelism in poetic writing, this line is intended to parallel the previous expression. In Isaiah they constituted a promise to the Servant of Jehovah to sustain him in the time of his ministry. However, the passage not only has messianic implications but is addressed also to Messiah's people, who represent Him. Since his readers have put their faith in the Messiah of whom Isaiah wrote, Paul is justified in making the specific application here. So they do not miss it, he underscores it with the words "Behold, now is the 'acceptable time,' behold, now is 'the day of salvation'" (v. 2). Using an intensified form (*euprosdektos*, "well received"), Paul emphasizes that the time is now. The force of his statement is that God conveys his grace and salvation to people in the day and time suited to Him, and it is incumbent upon all to seize the moment. This is a good example of an analogical use of Scripture not uncommon to Paul (cf. Rom. 10:18).

This passage is most often used by evangelists to encourage people to come to Christ at a time when the Holy Spirit is working upon their hearts. In this sense, the "day of salvation" is always "now"! In keeping with the forgoing context, it seems that Paul is still driving home the point he makes in verse 1. That is, we each are called to the ministry of reconciliation (in God's "day of salvation"). As "Messiah's people" we are called to do His work. Tom Holland considered this text and verses 16–18 the "most significant passage"[17] in this letter concerning "Paul as the *servant* in the Hebraic theological sense."[18] It is evident that Paul saw his own ministry as a servant of the new covenant, as Moses, Isaiah, and Israel were the servants of the old covenant. As the prophets addressed Israel and appealed for fidelity, so Paul appeals to the church at Corinth. The credentials of Paul's ministry are that he is fulfilling all that the suffering servant(s) suffered in their ministry to Israel.

> The question is, does Paul see himself in line as a suffering servant because he is an apostle, or because he is a Christian? The importance of this question is this: if it is because he is an apostle, then it follows that his experience of suffering is part of the apostolic office and need not apply to Christians in general. If it is because he is a Christian, then all Christians are called to this same realm of suffering, and so if *doulos* is applied to Christians, as in Romans 6, it is not to be equated with slavery, but with the covenant figure of the Servant mentioned in the Old Testament. Paul never saw his sufferings as being unique, this is beyond doubt. They were part of the sufferings to which the corporate servant, i.e., the Church was called.[19]

In making this final point, Holland cites 1 Thessalonians 2:14–15. "For you, brethren, became imitators of the churches of God in Christ Jesus that are in Judea, for you also endured the same sufferings at the hands of your own countrymen, even as they did from the Jews, who both killed the Lord Jesus and the prophets, and drove us out."

Concerning "the day of salvation," there is a further application that should not be lost to the contemporary American Christian. God blessed North Africa, and later Europe, with the gospel, and it was in these regions that the first "Christian civilizations" flourished. Over time they fell away, and today North Africa is an Islamic wasteland. The enormous cathedrals of Europe are also empty. Then God blessed America. In our brief history, great churches have been built on the backs of at least three "Great Awakenings." In the twentieth century, America followed Europe in a steady spiritual decline.

Unless God intervenes, there are dark days ahead for this once great Christian republic. Nevertheless, God's work continues as in the book of Acts, "unhindered" (Acts 28:31).[20] Consider, for example, the spread of the gospel in China where there is a vast harvest of souls being brought into the kingdom against enormous obstacles. Christianity is the fastest-growing religion in that country. From fewer than 100,000 Christians in the 1930s, the number of Christian believers has grown by conservative estimates to over 70 million Protestants and 12 million Catholics.[21] When it is God's "day of salvation," the gates of hell shall not prevail against God's church (Matt. 16:18 KJV). The story could be repeated in Korea, sub-Saharan Africa, and across the South American continent. It is happening as God's word to Zerubbabel, "Not by might nor by power, but by My Spirit, says the LORD of hosts" (Zech. 4:6). Paul's challenge to his readers is equally relevant to us today. Seize the moment! "Receive not the grace of God in vain."

## Pressed on All Sides

That which Paul asked of others he demanded of himself. Thus, at this time his thoughts are on his own ministry and the demands made on it based on the principle he has just stated. "Giving no cause for offense in anything" (v. 3). The apostle scrupulously avoided doing anything that would cause someone to reject the gospel on his account. "That the ministry be not discredited" (v. 3).

Ironside observes the practical significance of this text. It is impossible to live our lives in such a way that we will never hurt people's feelings.

> Some people carry their feelings on their sleeves all the time. If you do not shake hands with them, you probably intended to slight them. If you do, you hurt them, forgetting they have rheumatism. If you stop to speak with them, you are interrupting them. If you do not, you are "high-hatting" them. If you write them a letter, they are sure you want to get their money. If you do not, you are neglecting them. If you visit them, you are bothering them. If you do not, it shows you have no interest in the flock. It is impossible to please everyone.[22]

This is not what the writer has in mind. If it were so, I doubt that he would have written either of these letters to the Corinthians. Rather, Paul is saying that he behaves himself in such a way that no one will ever reject the gospel because of its poor showing in his personal life. He also charges all those who follow Christ to do the same—especially those who exercise leadership. See 1 Tim. 3:1–13: "An overseer, then, must be above reproach." He must not be "addicted to wine or pugnacious." He must be "one who manages his own household well. . . . And he must have a good reputation with those outside the church." The reason for maintaining such high standards is that "they obtain for themselves a high standing and great confidence in the faith that is in Christ Jesus."

"But in everything commending ourselves as servants of God, in much endurance" (v. 4; see also my comments on v. 1 above). A careless reading of verses 4–10 might lead one to think that the apostle is spontaneously tabulating disjointed thoughts as they come to his mind. A closer look, however, will reveal a very careful and logical arrangement.

*Agrupnia*, "sleeplessness," is used only here and in 11:27. It likely has in mind the idea that Paul must forgo sleep in order to discharge his obligations as an apostle and to support himself, rather than to indicate that he had a problem with insomnia.

Appropriately placed between a tabulation of the trials encountered by Paul and the various circumstances in which he found himself, he tabulates those spiritual graces with which God enabled him to carry on victoriously. The connection is with "listened to you" and "helped you" of verse 2, and the entire section together demonstrates, from the experience of Paul, that he did not receive "the grace of God in vain" (v. 1). "In purity" (v. 6), may have a moral sense or a constitutional sense. That is, it may refer to freedom from immorality or singleness of motive and purpose. It is not unlikely that Paul has both in view. "In knowledge" (v. 6). The context here implies insight to cope with difficult situations. "In patience, in kindness" (v. 6). The former is a passive idea; the latter is active. In the one there is patient submission to injustice; in the other there is the kind disposition to do good to others, providing enabling gifts, comfort, and assurance (cf. 1:3, 4, 22; John 14:16–17; 1 Cor. 12:7–11). "In genuine love" (v. 6; cf. 1 Cor. 15), "in the word of truth" (v. 7). This refers to the "preaching" of the truth (cf. 4:2). "In the power of God" (v. 7). This is related to Paul's apostolic ministry (cf. Rom. 15:14–21; 1 Cor. 15:10). "By the weapons of righteousness for the right hand and the left" (v. 7). This has in mind, primarily, the righteousness of God in justification (cf. Rom. 5:1–2). Hence the expression is equivalent to "armor of God" (Eph. 6:11) and does not denote one piece of armor, but all of it. By this means Paul was protected on every side.

Prompted by the expression "for the right hand and the left" in the previous verse, the apostle now analyzes the extremes of life and here shows that regardless of the situation, whether riding the wave of popularity or digging in against the onslaughts of opposition, he was always approved a faithful minister of God. As he does in verses 4–5, here too he arranges his thoughts in three groups of triplets. The first triplet includes, "By glory and dishonor, by evil report and good report; regarded as deceivers and yet true" (v. 8). Regardless of the reputation or report that precedes him, Paul never compromised on the integrity of his message. The second triplet: "As unknown yet well-known, as dying yet behold, we live; as punished yet not put to death" (v. 9). In the front lines of the spiritual warfare, Paul can be seen weary but undaunted, beaten but not broken, bruised but unbowed. The final triplet: "As sorrowful yet always rejoicing, as poor yet making many rich, as having nothing yet possessing all things" (v. 10). Paul had learned to abound and be abased; he had learned to have much and nothing. For he had learned, on a practical level, the lesson of our Lord given in Luke 12:15: "For not even when one has an abundance does his life consist of his possessions."

## Study Questions

1. Using the analogy of John MacArthur Jr., how does so-called new model theology undermine the atonement of Christ?

2. In the modern context, the word *terror* has a distinct sociological meaning. How does Paul use this term? How did it motivate him in his ministry?

3. How does 5:14 contribute to the question of the extent of the atonement? Relate this to Romans 5:18–19.

4. Why is the concept of "vicarious suffering" so important to a proper understanding of Christ's atoning work?

5. What exactly is the "new creation" of which the believer is a part? Relate this to other metaphors used by the New Testament writers to describe this truth.

6. Paul describes the ministry of believers as a "ministry of reconciliation." Why do you suppose he uses this term, rather than, for example, a ministry of preaching, witnessing, sanctification, or justification? In this ministry of reconciliation, what part is God's and what part is ours? How does this relate to what the author calls "the family business"?

7. How does the new covenant relate to suffering? Was this just for the apostles, or is it normative for all Christians? How is this reflected in this passage?

# CHAPTER 10

# Perfecting Holiness in the Fear of God
# 2 Corinthians 6:11–7:1

## Preview:

*In seeking to perfect holiness in the fear of God, Paul does two things. First he opens himself up to his readers in order to reestablish a positive relationship with them. Second, he seeks to close the door, once and for all, on idolatry and any uncleanness that would prevent them from reaching the goal of holiness. But here, as we shall see, the uncleanness in mind has to do with the presence and influence of false teachers in their midst.*

For evangelical Christianity in the latter half of the twentieth century, it is difficult to imagine a more divisive issue than that of "perfecting holiness." It was not his message that caused many to forsake the great evangelist Billy Graham after his remarkable sixteen-week New York City Crusade of 1957. It was his perceived compromise with the "ungodly." I am just old enough to remember how divisive this issue was and how acrimonious the debate was between fundamentalists and evangelicals—or "fundies" and "neos" as they were called at the time. This would not be so painful if it were not for the fact that so many in my immediate family came to Christ directly or indirectly through Graham's ministry. I remember arriving at the train station before dawn to take the railroad to New York City. We spent the day sightseeing. Then in the evening we made our way to Madison Square Garden to hear "Billy." My seat was down front toward the stage. I was almost close enough to touch him when he came out.

Sadly, I also remember the deacons of the church gathering later to discuss this "grave error and compromise." People were saying that the fundamentalist "David" had gone to the side of the Philistines. Some of the most critical had been brought to Christ by the very man they now demonized. Even now, forty years later, people still write articles denouncing Graham. So it is a mistake to pass over these verses without considering their relevance to the church today. In the matter of holiness, there is a line to be drawn, but the challenge is where and how to draw that line. My pastor was once called "the most dangerous man in America." This came not from the lips of an abortionist, a liberal, or a pornographer. It came from the president of a Christian college known for its strong stand on holiness. Yet the accusation had nothing whatever to do with holiness or the lack of it. It was more about wire-rimmed glasses, sideburns, music tracks, slacks on women, and blacks traveling with the praise teams.

This section of Paul's letter turns on three imperatives: "open wide to us" (v. 13), "Do not be bound together with unbelievers" (v. 14), and "Make room for us" (7:2). Thus Paul deals successively with (1) sympathy toward himself (6:11–13), (2) separation from the world (6:14–7:1), and (3) surety of reconciliation (7:2–3). The first two of these will be discussed here. The third will be considered in the next chapter.

In seeking to perfect holiness in the fear of God (7:1), Paul does two things. First, he opens himself up to his readers in order to reestablish a positive relationship with them. Second, he seeks to close the door, once and for all, on idolatry and any uncleanness that would prevent them from reaching the goal of holiness. The uncleanness in mind has to do with the presence and influence of false teachers in their midst.

## Be Enlarged

The first step toward reconciliation is enlargement. "O Corinthians" (v. 11). Paul addresses his readers by name in only two other places (Gal. 3:1; Phil. 4:15). In each case it reflects deep emotion. "Our mouth has spoken freely" (v. 11). On the use of this expression, see also Matthew 5:2; Acts 8:32, 35; and Ephesians 6:19. On its significance in this context, compare 3:12. Barrett translates this: "I have let my tongue run away with me"[1] That is, he speaks as one might openly speak to a close friend or family member. It is reasonable to say that Paul takes a *risk* in order that he might heal their relationship. The depth of this risk is indicated by the statement "our heart is *opened wide*" (v. 11; *peplatuntai* from *platunō*, "make broad"). This is a common expression from the Septuagint (Deut. 11:16; 1 Sam. 2:1; Pss. 25:17; 119:32). To enlarge the heart is to increase its capacity for sympathy and understanding (cf. 3:2; 7:3;

Phil. 1:7). He goes further to say that as far as he is concerned, there is absolutely nothing to stop us from engaging in free and open communication. "You are not restrained by us" (v. 12). This is the antithesis of "enlarged." Paul is saying that there is no want of room in his heart for the Corinthians. "But you are restrained in your own affections" (v. 12). That is, if they feel awkward or constrained in relating to him, the problem lies with them, not him. Barrett translates this, "If there is any lack of space it is not on my side, but in your own feelings."[2] When we become parents for the first time, our hearts burst and eyes brim with tears of inexpressible love for the child. When we have a second and then a third child, we struggle initially for fear that we will not have enough love for each. Yet somehow we find it, because our hearts stretch and become enlarged. There is something of that here in Paul. He loves these people without measure and yet, for some reason, they fear to open up to him in the same way.

Perhaps Paul was thinking this way himself, for he goes on as if to chide them mildly, "Now in like exchange—I speak as to children—open wide to us also" (v. 13). The inference is that it would be childish to refuse. If they would but open themselves to the apostle, the problems could be resolved. In this "ministry of reconciliation" there is no room for bickering between the brethren. But in order to bring this about, Paul had to pry these people away from his enemies.

> The perversion of this gospel, whose "ambassador for Christ" he was (2 Cor. 5:20), lay at the heart of Paul's concern for the Corinthian community, at the center of his impassioned polemic against the corrupters of its faith. But the struggle was not a theological debate, not an orderly discussion of the finer points of dogma between mutually respectful partners in an apostolic enterprise. If the methods of Paul's missionary opponents were to succeed, then Paul himself had to be personally discredited, his methods seriously questioned, his motives doubted, and his Christ and his gospel rejected (see 2 Cor. 11:3–6).[3]

Between arrogance and ignorance, there is little room for conversation. During the "neo" wars of the latter half of the twentieth century between fundamentalists and culture-savvy evangelicals, there was plenty of heat but very little light. In place of charity there was invective. The lines drawn in the sand have become retaining walls separating entire quadrants of evangelical believers to this day. One wonders what Paul might have done if he had stepped in to resolve this rift in American Christianity.

Paul calls upon his readers for an open disclosure of their hearts. This requires honesty, courage, and integrity—in a word, *risk*. In my comments on

4:2, I noted that truth and community are linked. "Telling what one believes to be true is a way of being loyal to a relationship; telling what one believes not to be true is a way of defecting from a relationship. . . . We speak truth because community matters to us, and we sustain community that matters to us by speaking the truth."[4] Sadly, the tendency of most is to commit the opposite of what is required to sustain community. It is always easier to lie.

## Be Not Unequally Yoked

After starting with the statement in 6:1, "working together with Him," then adding in 6:13, "open wide to us," which anticipates 7:2, "Make room for us," Paul suddenly stops. "Hold on," he seems to say.[5] If we are "in harness together with Christ," we have no business being involved with these donkeys.[6] We must not "be bound together with unbelievers" (*heterozugountes*, "double yoked," v. 14). The metaphor, as Barrett notes, "was probably strange to his Gentile readers in Corinth."[7] It is related to the Old Testament prohibitions against mixtures (cf. Lev. 19:19, in the Septuagint, *heterozugeō* is used, "coupled with an animal of diverse kind," similarly Deuteronomy 22:10, "You shall not plow with an ox and a donkey together"). In enlarging one's capacity to receive others, the apostle is careful to insist that he has only believers in mind. There is no doubt that it applies to Corinth with all of its vice and pagan associations (cf. 1 Cor. 6:6–20; 8:1–13; 10:14–33). However, in this context the reference is directed against his enemies who have taken hold of the situation in Corinth with such devastating results. What he goes on to describe as from Satan is the work of these who would defile the temple of the living God—the living, breathing church of God at Corinth (cf. v. 16). Thrall argues against the tide of contemporary scholarship that Paul's enemies are not misguided Christians but non-Christian Jews.[8]

"Belial" (v. 15; literally "worthlessness" or "wickedness"). This expression may also be used in the sense of "wicked one" (cf. 2 Sam. 23:6; Job 34:18). Here it is used as a reference to Satan (cf. the parallel use of *ho ponēros*, "the wicked one" in 1 John 5:19). "Unbeliever" is the same term used in the previous verse. If the writer is referring to the false teachers in the assembly, this gives us a sense of how he understands their character as well as their teaching.

"Temple of the living God" (v. 16). In Scripture this expression has a variety of meanings. (1) It may have reference to heaven as God's dwelling place (cf. Ps. 11:4; Hab. 2:20). (2) It may refer to the church as God's temple (Eph. 2:20; 1 Cor. 3:16). (3) It may have reference to the individual believer as a temple of God (1 Cor. 6:19). The plural pronouns in the Old Testament quotation suggest that Paul had the second idea in mind in this passage. That is, collectively, they constitute the temple of God. Accordingly, the promises of God in Exodus 29:45 and Leviticus 26:11–12 apply to their situation as well. "I will dwell in them and walk among them" (v. 16). Paul does not quote directly from the Old Testament here but seems to be employing the language of the Old Testament. "I will be their God and they shall be My people" (v. 16). This great promise to Abraham and to his natural seed is now applicable to all who are sons of Abraham by faith (Gal. 3:6–16). More importantly, it is this temple that is being violated by the enemies of the gospel in Corinth.

"Therefore, come out from their midst and be separate" (v. 17; cf. Isa. 52:11–12). "And I will welcome you" (v. 17; Ezek. 20:34). "And I will be a father to you, and you shall be sons and daughters to Me" (v. 18; cf. Isa. 43:6; Hos. 1:10). In citing these biblical promises, Paul's purpose is twofold. First, it is for edification. Paul looks back to the ministry of reconciliation (5:18), which was motivated by "the fear of the Lord" (5:11), energized by the "love of Christ" (5:14), exemplified by the experience of Paul (6:1–10), and qualified by the promises of God (6:16–18). Yet another purpose is seen in that which follows: it is for exhortation. The apostle Paul always roots practical Christianity in sound Bible doctrine. The exhortation is to holiness before God and ultimately to reconciliation with the apostle.

"Therefore, having these promises, beloved, let us cleanse ourselves from all defilement of flesh and spirit, perfecting holiness in the fear of God" (7:1). The promises of God demand a purity of heart and life on the part of those who receive them.

While many fail to see the connection in these verses with the preceding and following sections, we hope that Paul's readers did not miss the point. In this biting exhortation, Paul insinuates that for his Gentile Christians to allow themselves to be brought under the yoke of bondage (the Law), as these Judaizers are teaching, would be tantamount to plowing with an ox and a donkey. This metaphor is used elsewhere in Paul. In fact, it was the one he used at Jerusalem when he confronted the Twelve with their inconsistency and compromise of the gospel by their treatment of the Gentile Christians. "He made no distinction between us and them, cleansing their hearts by faith. Now therefore why do you put God to the test by placing upon the neck of the disciples a yoke which neither our fathers nor we have been able to bear?" Again he says, "It was for freedom that Christ set us free; therefore keep standing firm and do not be subject again to a yoke of slavery" (Acts 15:9–10; Gal. 5:1).

The practical implications of this principle relate to the need for Paul's readers to make a clean break with these false teachers who are preaching a false gospel with a false Jesus built on faulty foundations. Paul is still endeavoring to break them of these false teachers. In using this metaphor, together with terms like "lawlessness," "darkness," "Belial," "unbeliever," "idols," "unclean," and "defilement," he now associates them with the agents of Satan who are no friends of the gospel of grace.

## Study Questions

1. How would you relate the "ministry of reconciliation" discussed in the previous section with the principle of "perfecting holiness" in this section? Suggest some modern-day examples where this principle was compromised.

2. Why does Paul find it necessary to appeal to the Corinthian believers to "be enlarged" toward him? In this situation, who was it that drew the line of separation from the other?

3. How does Paul employ the Old Testament prohibition against mixtures to direct the church against defiling the church with unbelievers? What does this have to do with his enemies in the Corinthian assembly? What is he *really* saying about them?

4. Suggest several ways these principles should be applied in a contemporary church setting. What other biblical principles should be related to this? Give specific Scriptures where these are supported.

# CHAPTER 11

# Repentance Without Regret
# 2 Corinthians 7:2–16

### Preview:

*In Paul's third imperative, he calls upon his readers to open themselves to him and be reconciled. Three simple steps to reconciliation are given. He then comments on the report of Titus and his encouragement in their response.*

The apostle now continues with what I described in the previous section as his "three imperatives." These included, "open wide to us" (v. 13), "Do not be bound together with unbelievers" (v. 14), and here, "Make room for us" (7:2). This is his third imperative. In the remainder of this chapter, he will begin to prepare the way for the appeal of chapters 8 and 9. This he will do in 7:4–16.[1] This text functions as a hinge to relate his confidence in their response to his earlier challenges to obedience, and also, on the basis of that confidence, to prepare them for his appeal on behalf of the poor saints in Jerusalem. Taking up the offering was not unrelated to the process of reconciliation.

## Three Steps to Reconciliation

Since the church is the temple of God, and since its people ought to be in fellowship with God and His people rather than unbelievers and wickedness, their hearts should be open to Paul. For he has "wronged no one . . . corrupted no one . . . took advantage of no one" (v. 2). The biblical definition of separation has both a negative and a positive side. The negative, expressed in 6:14–17, is that the believer abstains from fellowship with all who are opposed to God. The positive side is that the believer is open to all who are truly the children of God, and such individuals will be evidenced by the quality of their lives. Paul places himself in this category. In the previous letter, the purpose of Paul's exhortation was to encourage them in practical holiness and to wean them from idols. Here his point of departure is the fact that they have taken on the yoke of Christ and they are now "working together with him." The work is "God's business." In doing this work, they must "be separate." They cannot be yoked together with the emissaries of Satan. In the remaining verses associated with this challenge, Paul now returns to his charge to them, "Make room for us in your hearts" (v. 2). He has already indicated that he has made room for them. Now he asks of them the same.

"I do not speak to condemn you" (v. 3). The insinuation is not that the Corinthian church was reprobate or that they were not genuine believers. Paul practiced what he preached. He says, "You are in our hearts" (v. 3). Thus, he conveys his unfeigned love whether "to die together [or] to live together" (v. 3). Neither death nor any other circumstance of life could destroy Paul's deep affection for these people. This affection does not, however, extend in the same way to those who would harm them. It does not extend to those who would, as wolves in sheep's clothing, ravage the flock. This, of course, is the conclusion of the matter with respect to the "three imperatives." In short, Paul says: "I am open to you. Now let go of these who pretend to be your friends—but who are, in fact, the enemies of Christ—and give me your hand."

The practical implications of this lesson are enormous. For marriages in trouble, for families shattered by conflicts, and for that matter, any relationship that may be threatened by external forces, the answer is found in these three steps. There must first be openness on the part of the injured party. Paul was wronged and was profoundly hurt by their behavior and attitude. But he was "enlarged." His love for them was sufficient to transcend the hurt. Then there must be a willingness to let go of the evil. Whether it is a child with bad friends, a teen or adult with an addiction, a spouse with an adulterous relationship, or as in this case, a church involved with false teachers, there must be a willingness to let go. Theologically, we relate this to repentance. Repentance is what happens when we turn "to God from idols" (1 Thess. 1:9). Finally, there must be an embrace. This involves laying hold of righteousness, placing one's faith in the living God, and demonstrating that in obedience to God's ambassadors.

One final thought concerns the enemies about which the apostle speaks. Jesus taught us: "love your enemies, and pray for those who persecute you" (Matt. 5:44). Paul has already urged this church to receive back an offending brother (2:5ff). In some situations the temptation of the "victims" of abuse or wickedness is to demonize their enemies. We even feel entitled to feel hatred toward someone who has committed some wickedness against us. "Deep within the heart of every victim, anger swells up against the perpetrator, rage inflamed by unredeemed suffering. The imprecatory psalms seem to come upon victims' lips much more easily than the prayer of Jesus on the cross. If anything, they would rather pray, "Forgive them not, Father, for they knew what they did."[2]

When former president Ronald Reagan was shot in a treacherous attempt on his life, he later expressed confidence in two things. First, God spared his life for a reason, and he was determined to find out what that was and fulfill it. We all know of his subsequent role in the eventual collapse of the former Soviet Union. The second was that if he would ever get over this, he would have to forgive the man who tried to kill him. Forgiveness is rooted in sacrifice, as the following insight from Volf eloquently explains.

> Christ's crucifixion was more than simply another instance of an innocent person's suffering. The suffering of the innocent as such has no redemptive value, either for the sufferers themselves or for anybody else; it is tragic, rather than redeeming, because it only swells the already overbrimming rivers of blood and tears running through human history. More than just the passive suffering of an innocent person, the passion of Christ is the agony of a tortured soul and wrecked body offered as *a prayer for the forgiveness of the torturers.* No doubt, such prayer adds to the agony of the passion. . . . When I forgive I have not only suffered a violation but also suppressed the rightful claims of strict restitutive justice. Under the foot of the cross we learn, however, that in a world of irreversible deeds and partisan judgments, redemption from the passive suffering of victimization cannot happen without the active suffering of forgiveness.[3]

Is this not what Peter means when he says the following? "For this finds favor ["is grace"], if for the sake of conscience toward God a man bears up under sorrows when suffering unjustly. For what credit is there if, when you sin and are harshly treated, you endure it with patience? But if when you do what is right and suffer for it you patiently endure it, this finds favor with God. For you have been called for this purpose, since Christ also suffered for you, leaving you an example for you to follow in His steps" (1 Pet. 2:19–21).

# Grief and Good Grief

Upon hearing the report of Titus, the sensitive reader once again feels the great emotion of the writer, expressed earlier when he wrote, "Blessed be the God and Father of our Lord Jesus Christ, the Father of mercies and God of all comfort; who comforts us in all our affliction" (1:3–4). In this passage Paul discusses (1) the comfort of his friend Titus (vv. 4–7), (2) the correction in response to his letter (vv. 8–12), and (3) the consolation of his spirit (vv. 13–16).

## Comfort (7:4–7)

"Great is my confidence in you; great is my boasting on your behalf" (v. 4). This expresses joyful confidence. "I am filled with comfort; I am overflowing with joy in all our affliction" (v. 4). Rightly so, for he has just received word from Titus that the Corinthians were actively seeking to rectify the evils and abuses in the assembly.

Upon leaving Troas and coming "into Macedonia" (v. 5), Paul's anxiety[4] over the Corinthian believers was evident (2:12). "We were afflicted on every side: conflicts without, fears within," he declares (v. 5). Those who would follow Paul in leadership must face their fears without fainting. Commenting on this text, J. Oswald Sanders calls to mind the great Reformer Martin Luther.

> Martin Luther was among the most fearless men who ever lived. When he set out on his journey to Worms to face the questions and the controversies his teaching had created, he said, "You can expect from me everything save fear or recantation. I shall not flee, much less recant." His friends warned of the dangers; some begged him not to go. But Luther would not hear of it. "Not go to Worms!" he said. "I shall go to Worms though there were as many devils as tiles on the roofs."[5]

However, not all of us are like Luther. Most—including Paul in this text—must face their fears every day. When called to leadership, we must do so in the power of Christ with confident assurance. In this case Paul's fears were greatly alleviated with the report from Titus. "God, who comforts the depressed, comforted us by the coming of Titus" (v. 6; cf. 11:3–4), that is, by his arrival from Corinth with the news that the church had accepted Paul's letter (the "severe letter," 2:3–4). The report from Titus was a great encouragement to the apostle because of "your longing, your mourning, your zeal for me" (v. 7). The Corinthians had evidenced toward Titus a repentant spirit and a desire to be reconciled to him. We cannot minimize the importance of personal relationships in ministry. When God wanted to communicate with the creature, he did so by personal communication. When it was time to execute His plan to redeem the world, He became incarnate in the person of His only begotten Son. Later John would reflect on the fact that they not only heard from Him, but "we have seen with our eyes," "our hands handled, concerning the Word of Life" (1 John 1:1–3). Here, too, the one thing Paul had that his enemies did not was a genuine relationship with these believers that, in the end, would endure the hardships imposed as he understands them here "from without."

### Correction (7:8–12)

"For though I caused you sorrow by my letter, I do not regret it" (v. 8). Although for a while Paul was sorry that he had written as he did, he is now thankful. "Not that you were made sorrowful, but that you were made sorrowful to the point of repentance" (v. 9; on "repentance" cf. Matt. 3:8; Luke 5:32; Acts 5:31; Heb. 12:17). It is entirely natural to feel sorry that one is caught in a misdeed, but that is not sorrow "according to the will of God" (v. 9). What happened at Corinth agitated the believers to realignment with the will and purpose of God. This made all of Paul's efforts worthwhile. Here Paul expresses temporary regret for having said some things that may have wounded his readers. Regret is here related to Paul's misgivings about his actions toward the Corinthians. Was he too strong? Did he go too far? Until he had heard from Titus, he had second thoughts—regrets that perhaps he handled the situation badly. Who among us has not had similar circumstances where we wondered if perhaps our judgment was wrong, our words too strong, and our attitude has caused offense? Culpability is neither implied nor confessed in this action. Yet the possibility of errors in judgment is the lot of humanity. They come with living as we do in a finite condition, with finite knowledge and finite abilities. They are daily reminders of the folly of hubris to which so many are given. Moral lapses, on the other hand, are not the inevitable lot of humanity. They need not occur, and when they do they require a stronger response than reflected here in the writer. They require "repentance," but repentance of a special kind.

Paul differentiates two kinds of repentance. The first is *hē kata theon lupē*, "godly sorrow." The second is *hē tou kosmou lupē*, "worldly sorrow," as when one feels sorry for causing an unpleasant set of circumstances by his or her behavior. He observes that he is not pleased simply because he made them sorry for what they had done. This would be a mere superficial emotion. When the leader handles a situation badly—or even sinfully—he or she may create circumstances that are subsequently difficult to handle, which makes them sorry. Many a criminal is sorry for the circumstances that caused them to be incarcerated. But the numbers who are sorry simply because they were *caught* far outnumber those who are sorry for *crimes* they committed. In attempting to reconcile parties who are at odds with one another, forgiveness is a seemingly impossible goal because, while sorrow is expressed, there is a failure to come clean—to confess the wrong and to take the further step to see to it that it will not happen again. It is this latter attitude that Paul sees in his readers for which he is overjoyed. "What makes affliction beneficial is not the actual experience of suffering but the reaction to it; a 'godly' or positive reaction brings about spiritual benefit, both now and in the hereafter, whereas a 'worldly' or negative reaction causes irreparable harm."[6]

The second category is sorrow "according to the will of God." This is sorrow that leads to "repentance without regret, leading to salvation" (v. 10). This is contrasted with what Paul calls the "sorrow of the world," which "produces death" (*katergazetai* has the force of "brings about"). It is this response that produces fruit that vindicates the person who experiences it, producing "indignation," "fear," "longing," "zeal," "avenging of wrong," and a demonstration of the person's integrity. Perhaps Paul has in mind Psalm 51:1–11 in contrast with Genesis 27:38–41 (cf. Heb. 12:16–17), where these two kinds of repentance are reflected in David (godly sorrow) and Esau (worldly sorrow). In speaking of the "avenging of wrong" (v. 11), the apostle is not gloating that circumstances have turned out in his favor, but rejoicing that a sense of justice (*ekdikēsin*) had been aroused in them such that they felt a moral obligation to discipline sin in the assembly—even if, perhaps they carried this too far, as is implied in 2:6–7. This is especially hinted in the reference to "fear" (not of the apostle, but the fear of God). "Not for the sake of the offender, nor for the sake of the one offended" (v. 12). Good grief gets right with God.

## Consolation (7:13–16)

Rather it is "for this reason we have been comforted" (v. 13). The consolation Paul could not find (v. 5) is supplied by the report of the spiritual progress at Corinth.

In Paul's discussions with Titus previously, he was convinced that the opposition in Corinth was coming from only a small minority—as he says, "I have boasted" (v. 14). The vast majority of the congregation wanted to do what was right. This conviction is confirmed by Titus's report, so that Paul is able to say, "So also our boasting before Titus proved to be the truth" (v. 14). Their positive attitude was evidenced in that they "received him [Titus] with fear and trembling" (v. 15). Not that they cowered before him, but they treated him with respect and honor (Eph. 6:5).

It is important to recognize in this passage the distinction between the guilt and culpability of the offending party discussed in 2:6–7 and the culpability of the people charged with dealing with it.[7] It is evident in the text that both are guilty—but of different offenses. While we are not entirely certain what the original offense was, we do know that it was originally disregarded— that is, until Paul forced their hand. It is this latter failure to deal with the matter that renders the leadership guilty—not of the original offense, but of ethical and moral failure to step up and address a serious issue that was threatening the very fabric of church life in the assembly. In the end, Paul is overjoyed even in their overaggressive stance in the matter because it shows their heart. This is comparable to Paul's "sorrowful letter" about which he even had second thoughts himself. This is not something for which to feel "guilty." Ethical neglect is another matter. It is here that they were culpable. Nevertheless, they "repented" of their cowardice and faced the matter squarely. For this reason Paul is finally convinced of their heart toward God. This should be a great encouragement to the many in churches to this day that are held accountable before God for the integrity and purity of the congregation. We may not always feel adequate to the situation. We may, with Paul, second-guess the proper action. "No action," however, is not an option. God will not judge us for bad judgment (unless we should have known better), but he will judge us for failure to discharge the obligations of leadership.

A pastor recently confessed that the best thing that ever happened to the churches in the South was the Civil Rights Act of 1964. When that was passed, racism was no longer just a personal prejudice. It was illegal. Until then most pastors hid behind the general ungodly consensus of the members and in so doing shared in the guilt. Today we have similar attitudes reflected in the abortion debate. There are politicians who say that they are personally against the practice but who support the rights of others to perform them. It is not too much of a stretch to associate this with complicit Lutherans in Nazi Germany when they turned a deaf ear to the sound of the cattle cars carrying hapless victims to their death in the extermination ovens. Again, guilt is associated with the ethical and moral crimes. There is also a different kind of guilt associated with those who have been given, in the providence of God, a place of leadership in which they can do something about it and out of neglect or cowardice or both do nothing.

"In everything I have confidence in you" (v. 16). Paul concludes this section fully assured that the Corinthian believers will take whatever steps are necessary to restore unity in the church, to enforce discipline, to be restored to fellowship with himself, and (looking ahead to the next chapter) to be prepared to join with other churches throughout the region in helping out with the collection for Jerusalem. Furnish recognizes this important connection.

> The statement of verse 16 serves as much more than a summary of verses 4–15. It sharpens and focuses the point of those verses in such a way as to form a transition from those fervent expressions of pride and joy to the equally fervent appeal in chapter 8.[8] Titus is returning to Corinth (he is presumably the bearer of this letter) to complete the collection for Jerusalem that he had begun on his first visit (8:6), and Paul has *every confidence* that the same *earnestness* the Corinthians showed before (7:11, 12) will be in evidence again (see 8:7, where the excellence of their "earnestness" is specifically invoked to support the appeal). Here, as elsewhere in his letters, the apostle praises what his readers have already done, only in

order to encourage them to do still more (see, e.g., Phil. 2:12–13; 1 Thess. 4:9–12; Philem. 1:7, 20–21).[9]

## Study Questions

1. Paul discusses "three steps to reconciliation." Can you think of a practical way to implement these concepts into a marriage or group counseling situation?

2. Why is forgiveness so difficult? Do you agree that it requires a sacrifice on the part of the "victim"? How is this illustrated in the text?

3. Paul apparently caused "pain" in the assembly. Why does he now say that he is glad for that? Suggest situations leaders often face in which a willingness to inflict pain is necessary. Why do you suppose leaders would rather avoid such situations? Is that good? Why?

# SECTION II

# Second Trajectory: Practical Needs

## 2 Corinthians 8–9

# CHAPTER 12

# We Are in This Together
# 2 Corinthians 8:1–15

### Preview:

*Paul is commonly credited with being a great theologian and missionary. What is not always known or appreciated of him is that he was also a pretty good fund-raiser. Perhaps this is why pastors tend to gravitate to Paul. He was not only a champion for the truth of the gospel and an effective preacher, but he was also skilled in addressing the practical issues of ministry, including, as illustrated here, how to take up an offering.*

While the writer never mentions money, his readers cannot help but understand his meaning in chapters 8 and 9 with respect to the poor saints at Jerusalem. Concerning this project, we do well to consider what this was for and exactly why the apostle considered it to be a matter of such great importance for *him* to direct.

## Why the Offering?

The idea of taking up the collection for Jerusalem is not a power ploy to exact tribute from the Gentile churches in support of the apostolic church. There is, in fact, no evidence that such a hierarchy existed in the early decades of the church following Pentecost. Thus, the collection is not "to impose an obligation on Gentile churches that would illustrate the supremacy of the mother-church, but in a convergence of Paul's own concerns such as his wish to fulfill a promise of financial aid, to express in a tangible way the interdependence of the members of the body of Christ."[1] This would underscore the principles delineated earlier in 1 Corinthians 12–14. It would enable Paul to keep a promise to the apostles given at the Council of Jerusalem (Acts 15; cf. Gal. 2:10). It would enable the writer to assess the genuineness of the commitment to these principles in the church and, for that matter, all the churches to which he extended this challenge. Additionally (and especially important here), it would bring Jews and Gentiles together in meeting a common need in the church. This latter objective, it is hoped, would also play an important part in reducing hostilities between these two ethic groups. It is apparent that Paul's enemies in Corinth were non-Christian Jews who were poisoning believers with their teachings. But for Paul, the "middle wall of partition" had already been torn down, and as far as he was concerned, it was a nonissue at best and a denial of the gospel of grace at worst. What better way to bring harmony in the ranks than to participate in a common cause such as this. As Naylor has well said:

> In short, Paul envisaged this astonishing, intercontinental money-raising scheme as a means to consolidate the Gentile mission and to make it obvious that the churches proliferating everywhere were one in Christ. . . .

> If we ponder these chapters together with Romans 15 and 1 Corinthians 16, not forgetting Paul's statement in Acts 24:17, we shall probably come to the conclusion that the Gentile collection for the Jerusalem saints was in a way the consummate expression of the apostle's churchmanship, an ultimate and probably unsurpassable demonstration of the oneness of the body of Christ. Think of the wonder of it: before he traveled to Rome and thence (possibly) to Spain, Paul had lived to see erstwhile idolaters sending their monies to Jews brought up to consider Gentiles as unclean, as Simon Peter had been quick to remind the Lord (Acts 10:14), and haughty Jews gladly receiving this benefit as from God. The solvent was the gospel, and there was none other. The scheme was a master-stroke, exhibiting the apostle's genius as a leader.[2]

Paul uses the same logic with Philemon to admonish him against slavery (Philem. 1:4–8). Philemon is commended for his "love, and of the faith which [he has] toward the Lord Jesus, and toward all the saints" (v. 5). Paul then prays that this faith will become more "effective" (*energēs*)—that it will translate into doing the right thing (v. 6). Then he concludes with, "though I have enough confidence in Christ to order you to do that which is proper (*anēkon*, "the appropriate thing"), yet for love's sake I rather appeal to you" (vv. 8–9). The logic is compelling here. Despite the fact that keeping a slave was a legal right under Roman law, the "right thing" for a Christian to do is to free the slave, Onesimus. This is right because it is in keeping with the second great commandment—love your neighbor as yourself, and it is in keeping with the faith shared "toward the Lord Jesus and, toward all the saints (including, of course, Onesimus). To the Galatians he brings this all together to say, "There is neither Jew nor Greek, there is neither slave nor free man, there is neither male nor female; for you are all one in Christ Jesus" (Gal. 3:28).

The collection took eight years to accomplish (from the Council of Jerusalem in AD 50 to Paul's arrest in AD 58). It involved thousands of miles of travel, covering four Roman provinces, and included most of the Gentile churches. At least ten collectors were involved. Since it is here that Titus is first introduced to the New Testament narrative, it is likely that this constituted one of his first responsibilities. The full amount collected was apparently significant since it excited the attention of the Roman governor, Porcius Festus, who hoped to get his hands on some of it (Acts 24:17–26). It nearly cost Paul his life, and it did cost him much of his freedom.

Pentecost and poverty have long distinguished the Christian church (Acts 2:45). "Peter's poignant remark to the lifelong cripple at the gate of the temple, 'Silver and gold I do not have' (Acts 3:6), reveals the financial status of the leader of the church. Were others better off?"[3] Harris outlines several factors leading to "the persistent need for economic relief for impoverished members of the Jerusalem church since its inception."[4] He details as follows.

1.  Due to the impact of the gospel, there was a steady influx of Jewish converts (Acts 2:41, 47; 4:4; 6:7; 9:31; 21:20). These were subject to ostracism and persecution, putting pressure on the resources of the church. Additionally, there were enough needy widows in the church to require attention and administrative oversight (Acts 6:1; cf. Mark 12:42; Luke 21:1–4).

2.  The situation was sufficiently grave to require a voluntary sharing of resources (Acts 2:44–45; 4:34–35).

3.  Throughout the reign of Claudius (AD 41–54) there were repeated famines that caused hardships and starvation, especially among the poor (which consequently included the Christians).

4.  It was expensive to live in Jerusalem. Nearly everything, including water, food, and raw materials, had to be brought in. Everything was subject to taxation, and during times of need, the prices were proportionately inflated.[5]

5.  The Jerusalem church seems to have been a magnet for a disproportionately large number of visitors.

6.  There is documented evidence that Palestinian Jews were subject to excessive taxation from the Jews as well as the Romans. This is reflected in the Gospels giving reference to the tax collectors who

were viewed in a negative light. Zacchaeus is an example of what
people experienced from unscrupulous people taking advantage of
the citizenry (Luke 19:2ff.).[6]

The problems facing the church at this time were especially acute.[7] The
Christians, the poorest of all, had their source of help in the church of
Antioch. Agabus the prophet had announced a famine at hand (Acts 11:28),
and the fellowship determined to send relief. Saul and Barnabas were chosen
to take the contribution to the elders at Jerusalem (Acts 11:30). They, most
likely, were the initiators of its collection. So Paul was quite well trained in
famine relief and in the art of taking collections. God is preparing him for
something greater. A few years later, at the Council of Jerusalem (AD 50),
when Paul and Barnabas, again in Jerusalem, were defending themselves and
the liberty of the Gentile converts, a special plea was added to the decree. The
Diaspora and the Christians were to remember the suffering and the poverty
of the Judean Christians (Acts 15:23–29). This, Paul later says, he was very
eager to do (Gal. 2:10). From that point on, a definite plan of missionary giving became a primary part of every church Paul established (1 Cor. 16:1ff.),
and he urged it upon all those to whom he wrote (Rom. 15:26–27).

The peculiar difficulties at Corinth opened up the whole picture of the
offering. A year earlier, they had demonstrated a special willingness to pledge
(2 Cor. 8:10), and their pledging inspired the Galatians, the Macedonians, and
the Romans. Verbal instructions were followed by questions and written
instructions regarding how they were to give and how the collections were to
be handled (1 Cor. 16:1ff.; 2 Cor. 9:1). There was careful, businesslike handling of all of the finances. Each church was to elect their own financial representative (2 Cor. 8:23). We know who some of these were. From Berea, there
was Sopater; from Thessalonica, Aristarcus and Secundus; from Asia, Tychicus
and Trophimus; from Galatia, Gaius of Derge and possibly Timothy (Acts
20:4). Since no one is specifically mentioned as coming from Achaia, it is likely that Luke or Titus or perhaps even the apostle himself represented them.

The spiritual nature of this offering is evident in the terms Paul uses. He
never calls it "money," because he never seems to think of it as such. Instead,
he calls it "grace" or "generosity" or "blessing" or "partnership."[8] It would
seem that such explicit directions for the offering would be adequate, and
apparently this was the case in Galatia and Macedonia. Corinth had failed,
though they had been first to pledge. Now special action and instruction are
necessary. Hence, there is the special attention devoted to the subject in these
chapters.

The section turns on the concept of "faithfulness." As this is exemplified
in Paul in the previous section, it is now exhorted upon the Corinthian believ-

ers. The writer builds his argument in four ways: first, he illustrates faithfulness by drawing attention to the churches in Macedonia (8:1–6); second, he exhorts the Corinthians to faithfulness as a concrete way of following the example of Christ (8:7–15); third, he demands that the Corinthian believers live up to their commitments lest both he and they be embarrassed (8:16–9:5); and finally, he gives direction to the process by which their faithfulness can be demonstrated (9:6–15).

## Faithfulness Illustrated (8:1–6)

Someone once said, "You must give until you *feel* it in order to get the blessing from the giving." Paul knows some people who have "felt" it. So as he begins his discussion concerning the offering for the poor, the Macedonians immediately come to mind. "Now" (v. 1, *de*, "now then") may indicate a new subject, or it may indicate a transition in a subject already introduced. It would seem that the writer has already prepared the reader for what follows. "We wish to make known to you" (*gnōrizomen*, "we disclose"); the present indicative active verb expresses the writer's *action*, not his *desire*. What he does is to call attention to the performance of others as incentive to awake his readers to the fact that they are falling behind in this important matter. "If *peri de* ('now concerning') in 1 Cor. 16:1 introduces a topic mentioned or discussed in the Corinthians' putative letter to Paul, it is clear that they already knew of Paul's projected collection, and it is probable that they had already indicated their willingness to contribute."[9] They had likely made a "pledge." Now the apostle exhorts them to make good on it. Many people resist making pledges. Usually their reluctance is born of hypocrisy and greed or a misunderstanding of Matthew 5:34. For we all make pledges—unless we pay cash for everything—including our house, utilities, etc. The principle hinted at here is likely drawn from Leviticus 19:11–12. "And you shall not steal, nor deal falsely, nor lie to one another. And you shall not swear falsely by My name, so as to profane the name of your God; I am the LORD." In addition to proportionate giving, Paul also teaches "planned" giving.

"The grace of God which has been given in the churches of Macedonia" (v. 1). The Macedonian churches of Philippi, Thessalonica, and Berea had demonstrated extreme liberality in their giving (cf. 11:9; Phil. 2:25; 4:15, 18). *Charis*, "grace," occurs ten times in these chapters, suggesting a central theme of the writer. Harris observes that it occurs here in six different senses: "God's unconditional kindness" (8:1; 9:8, 14); "privilege" or "favor" (8:4); "act of grace" (8:6); "grace of giving" (8:7); "offering" or "charitable work" (8:19); and "thanks" (8:16; 9:15).[10]

---

### Providing for Those in Need

*"Jesus said to him, 'If you wish to be complete, go and sell your possessions and give to the poor, and you shall have treasure in heaven; and come, follow Me.'" (Matt. 19:21)*

*"But when you give a reception, invite the poor, the crippled, the lame, the blind," (Luke 14:13)*

*"And the congregation of those who believed were of one heart and soul; and not one of them claimed that anything belonging to him was his own; but all things were common property to them." (Acts 4:32)*

*"Yes, they were pleased to do so, and they are indebted to them. For if the Gentiles have shared in their spiritual things, they are indebted to minister to them also in material things." (Rom. 15:27)*

*"Now this I say, he who sows sparingly shall also reap sparingly; and he who sows bountifully shall also reap bountifully. Let each one do just as he has purposed in his heart; not grudgingly or under compulsion; for God loves a cheerful giver. And God is able to make all grace abound to you, that always having all sufficiency in everything, you may have an abundance for every good deed;" (2 Cor. 9:6–8)*

*"This is pure and undefiled religion in the sight of our God and Father, to visit orphans and widows in their distress, and to keep oneself unstained by the world." (James 1:27)*

---

In this regard, the comment by Furnish aptly describes the context into which Paul makes his appeal.

> Here Paul eases himself into the subject of his collection for the poor among the Christians of Jerusalem by describing the enthusiastic participation of the Macedonian churches in the project. But it is significant that he describes their participation first of all as an act of divine grace (v. 1). He attributes it neither to his own successful ministry . . . nor to their own selfless action. It is God's grace working in them, just as it will be when the Corinthians have completed their contribution to the fund (see 9:14).[11]

"That (*hoti*) in a great ordeal of affliction . . . and their deep poverty" (v. 2). "Affliction" and "poverty" stand in sharp relief against "their abundance of joy" and "the wealth of their liberality" (v. 2). Instead of allowing circumstances to inhibit their giving, the churches of Macedonia turned personal and financial distress into a unique opportunity to demonstrate the riches of God's grace. In the original text, verses 3–6 form one continuous sentence. "For I testify that (*hoti*) according to their ability, and beyond their ability" (v. 3). Their giving was not measured inversely according to their own needs, but proportionately to the needs of others. "They gave of their own accord" (v. 3). They did not need to be coerced; their giving was strictly voluntary. As a diamond, created under great pressure, the example of the Macedonians radiates a multifaceted brilliance. First, their generosity was expressed with utter disregard for their own circumstances. On the contrary, as many have observed, it was their own suffering that enabled them to empathize with their brothers in Jerusalem who, as their Lord, were enduring great affliction. Perhaps "in turn, this induced them to part with what money they had. Persecution becomes the furnace in which the grace of giving is refined to a high state of purity."[12] Second, it was with great "joy" that they gave. People who have experienced the forgiveness of sins and reconciliation with God have hearts *seized* (cf. 5:14, *sunechō*) by the love of Christ, which overflows to others. Here Paul recognizes in them the outworking of the grace of God. Third, their giving was *kata bathous ptōcheia*, "out of extreme destitution." Like the widow about whom Jesus remarked, who gave her "two cents," the Macedonians had nothing yet found a way to give as she did—"more than all of them." In such measure their "poverty overflowed in the wealth of their liberality" (*haplotēs*, "singleness," "simplicity."). Without pride or ostentation (as those who give out of their surplus to be seen of others (Luke 21:2–4), their love found a way. The Macedonians offer a wonderful illustration of "grace giving" as preached by Paul. Grace received leads to grace given. *Soli deo Gloria!*

"Begging us with much entreaty for the favor" (v. 4, *meta pollēs paraklēseōs deomenoi hēmon tēn charin*, "with frequent appeals, begging us the grace"). More is to be seen here by what is omitted than what is expressed. That they found it necessary to beg the apostle to participate in the collection for Jerusalem suggests that the apostle may have considered their own needs to be sufficiently extreme to exempt them from participation. But more than that, they appeal for the *grace* ("blessing") of being part of this opportunity to give. "Participation in the support of the saints" (v. 4; literally "the fellowship [*koinōnian*] of the ministry [*diakonias*] to the saints"). Giving is a form of fellowship. In this instance, it is fellowship in the larger ministry of the apostle on behalf of the saints in Jerusalem[13] (note comments on the theme of the previous epistle given in 1 Cor. 1:9).[14] Barrett adds:

> The first step in their ministering to the saints was the offering of themselves to Christ. . . . They also offered themselves to the apostle—and it was God's will that they should. Paul's position as an apostle was a paradoxical one. . . . He would only present himself to his people, not as a lord over their faith (1:24) but rather as their slave (4:5). Yet God had given him authority (for building up, not casting down; 10:8; 13:10), and he

could offer himself as an example (1 Cor. 4:16; 11:1). There could be no question of his right to be taken as an example in the sphere of service to fellow Christians.[15]

"And this, not as we had expected" (v. 5). In light of their own needs, such giving on the part of these believers was totally unexpected. "But they first gave themselves to the Lord and to us by the will of God" (v. 5). The proper order of New Testament giving is expressed here. "First" (v. 5) is understood in order of priority, not chronology. The gift is first to God and then in this instance to Paul. The apostle is rightly astounded by the example of the Macedonian believers. They were dirt poor, yet they begged to be allowed the privilege of parting with what little they had to give to others who had even less.

There is another important principle here concerning which we would be remiss if we neglected to call attention to it. Their giving was "first to God." It was only in a secondary sense that they gave to Paul. In the "will of God," Paul was the immediate recipient of the gift. The ultimate object of the gift was God Himself.

Often when church members find themselves at odds with their pastor, they will vote with their tithe—or in this case, no tithe. In this way they think they are making a statement to the "agent" of God's leadership in their assembly. In reality, their refusal to give is an affront to God. It is against Him that they tighten their fists and close their wallets. We wonder if perhaps some of this was happening at Corinth. We know that many (a minority to be sure) were at odds with him. He knew that too. The example of the Macedonians illustrates the proper perspective on the matter. Of course, Paul also knew that if they would join in this *charis*, they too would receive the blessing that would come their way in their *koinōnia* with this ministry on behalf of the poor in Jerusalem.

Verse 6 completes the sentence begun in verse 3. However, at this point in the sentence, he turns his attention away from the exemplary behavior of the Macedonians and toward his readers to prepare them for another visit from Titus. "Consequently we urged Titus that as he had previously made a beginning" (v. 6). In Titus's previous visit, he had already begun discussing the collection (cf. 1 Cor. 16:1). Paul would be sending him, once again, "so he would also complete in [the Corinthian church] this gracious work as well" (v. 6). At Paul's suggestion Titus is delegated the responsibility of overseeing the offering at Corinth.

We should not miss the historical reference here. The work to which Titus is assigned was begun by him previously. We are not certain when this matter was broached. We have reason to believe that it was already on the table before the writing of 1 Corinthians (cf. 1 Cor. 16:1). It would seem that the key role being played by Titus now is largely due to his previous ministry with them—and the degree of respect and confidence he likely gained with them at that time.[16] Naylor wonders if "Paul has been testing his friend: if Titus can complete this matter he will be better qualified for future ministry."[17] No doubt this was a "test" of Titus's leadership ability, but it is unlikely Paul would have sent a boy on a man's errand. Given the sensitive nature of this project, it is more likely that Titus was chosen because of his diplomatic acumen and not in the interest of developing it. If anyone is being put to the test, it is the people in Corinth for whom, as far as Paul is concerned, the jury is still out (*dokimazōn*, "proving . . . the sincerity of your love also").

## Faithfulness Exhorted (8:7–15)

The theme of this section is "faithfulness exhorted," not "extorted." The commitment to participate in this project was not an endeavor Paul commands, or worse, something into which he *manipulates* them. Rather, he reminds them of their promise; he invokes, once again, the example of the believers to the north in Macedonia; and finally he brings to mind the example of the Savior, "who was rich" yet for our sakes "He became poor" in order that we "through His poverty might become rich" (v. 9). So the three impulses for giving are personal integrity, solidarity with the church, and gratitude to Christ.

"But just as you abound in everything, in faith and utterance and knowledge and in all earnestness and in the love we inspired in you, see that you abound in this gracious work also" (v. 7). As the previous verse explained Titus's commission, here Paul expresses his expectations on their part. "As you abound in everything" (v. 7; cf. 1 Cor. 1:5, 7). With obvious allusions to the richness of their spiritual giftedness referenced in the previous epistle, Paul makes clear that this church, in contrast to the poverty of the Macedonian church, has not only enjoyed great blessing, but has even boasted of it. There is also a touch of irony here. Their boasting was not always a compliment to their spiritual maturity (cf. 1 Cor. 5:6). At the outset, Paul expresses to the Corinthians exactly what he expects of them. "The apostle expresses the conviction that their charity (*charis*) will be on a par with their faith (*pistis*), their eloquence (*logos*), their theological knowledge (*gnōsis*), their religious zeal (*spoudē*), and their Christian love; this last is denoted by the rather curious turn of phrase (*tē ex hēmōn en humin agapē*), which probably signifies: the love which is in you and which I inspired in you."[18] We might say that this is Paul's way of saying, "Faith without works is dead" (James 2:14–22). Of course we are also reminded of 1 Corinthians 13:1–3: "If I speak with the tongues of men and of angels, but do not have love, I have become a noisy gong or a clanging cymbal. And if I have the gift of prophecy, and know all mysteries and all knowledge; and if I have all faith, so as to remove mountains, but do not have love, I am nothing. And if I give all my possessions to feed the poor, and if I deliver my body to be burned, but do not have love, it profits me nothing."

"I am not speaking this as a command" (v. 8). With the exception of verse 9, the first person plural (predominant to this point in the epistle) is replaced with the first person singular. Paul gets up close and personal from here on in this letter. No legal stipulation regulates the believer's giving; it is on account of "the earnestness of others" (v. 8; cf. also Philem. 8, 14). By calling to mind the zeal demonstrated by others, Paul is intent on "proving . . . the sincerity of your love" (v. 8; this is best understood in light of 9:2). Paul has already bragged on them to the Macedonians. Now he is not so sure that his confidence in them was well placed. The only ones who can validate his first impressions are the Corinthians themselves.

> Paul does not command but instead invites, encourages, and lays out divine principles gleaned from Scripture. He hopes that they will respond out of hearts that have been freed by the gospel and fired by God's grace. This does not mean that he sits by passively in wishing anticipation that they will choose the right thing. He is their spiritual director, and he spends two chapters outlining the reasons why they should participate.[19]

"For you know the grace of our Lord Jesus Christ, that though He was rich, yet for your sake He became poor" (v. 9). There is no need to read into this verse any more than is warranted by the context. (On the self-emptying of Christ, see Phil. 2:7 and Heb. 1:2.) The intent of Paul's argument is not unlike that of verse 8; however, he steps it up. "The sacrifice of the Macedonians was one thing, the sacrifice of Christ for others is quite another."[20]

Much has been made of this text in relation to the incarnation of Christ, to which it is an obvious reference. In both instances in which Paul makes reference to this truth, he does so in order to offer an incentive to his readers to follow Christ's example. In Philippians 2 the incentive is to encourage the reader to "have this attitude in yourselves which was also in Christ Jesus, who, although He existed in the form of God, did not regard equality with God a thing to be grasped, but emptied (*kenoō*) Himself, taking the form of a bond-servant, and being made in the likeness of men" (vv. 5–7). Here, too, it is well within the reach of his readers to empty themselves—"to become poor," that through their poverty others might be enriched. While we typically think of the humble human environment into which our Lord came—being born in a lowly stable and identifying with the poor rather than the powerful—this is not likely Paul's intent here. Rather, he has in mind spiritual riches. The

Macedonians were not materially rich, but they were, nevertheless, overflowing with spiritual treasures. The material evidence of their generosity would not have impressed the wealthy elite. Their example of selflessness is exceeded only by our Lord, who emptied himself, became poor—"He made Him who knew no sin to be sin on our behalf, that we might become the righteousness of God in Him" (5:21). "Christ's sacrifice becomes the real motive for giving, not trying to copy or to outdo some sibling community. Paul asks them to respond to what Christ has done for them: 'And he died for all, that those who live should no longer live for themselves but for him who died for them and was raised again' (5:15)."[21] The sense in which Christ becomes an "example" here also needs to be qualified. Paul does not reduce the significance of Calvary to a mere example to be repeated by those who can rise to the same level of spiritual selflessness. He is not "presenting Christ's act of grace as an example for the Corinthians to emulate."[22] Rather, he intends to say, "Do what is appropriate for your status as those who have been enriched by the grace of Christ."[23]

"I give my opinion in this matter, for this is to your advantage, who were the first to begin a year ago" (v. 10; see 9:2). It is only right for Paul to expect the Corinthian church to participate. This was their expressed desire more than a year earlier. "But now finish doing it also" (v. 11). Paul asks only that they follow through with their original commitment. The reference to "a year ago" is likely only a general reference, as one might say, "last year, you expressed your desire, etc." See Barrett for a discussion of how this relates to the various calendars and the date of the epistle presently being penned.[24]

When people fail to live up to their commitments, they hurt themselves as well as those who were counting on them. Paul is concerned here about both. He encourages his readers in terms of their positive performance thus far. "But he clearly, if subtly, communicates that talk is cheap; now is the time to produce. Boswell's old adage that the road to hell is paved with good intentions applies."[25]

"For if the readiness is present" (v. 12). In the ministry of giving, God is concerned first with the attitude of the individual, not the precise amount given. That, of course, varies "according to what [a person] has" (v. 12). Paul does not intend to merely transfer the burden from one group to another. "But by way of equality"—at this present time your abundance being a supply for their need" (v. 13–14). He wants to equalize matters.

Comparing this text with others in Paul's letters dealing with the collection, there are three reasons for participating in this effort. "The first was to show that there is a oneness within the body of Christ: racial differences count for nothing, and between Jew and Gentile there is neither inferiority nor superiority. Secondly, the collection would be a mark of the Gentiles' gratitude to the Jews. Jesus and his apostles were Jewish, and salvation is of the Jews (John 4:22). Romans 15:27 demonstrates Paul's concern that Gentile believers should acknowledge their indebtedness to the Jewish churches (cf. 1 Cor. 9:11). Finally, by way of recapitulation, the contribution for Judea becomes a precedent for future action, when the Jews might be called upon to help poor Gentiles.[26]

As the Scripture says, "He who gathered much did not have too much, and he who gathered little had no lack" (v. 15; cf. Exod. 16:18). Hodge observes, "Property is like manna; it will not bear hoarding."[27] The point here is not to establish some sort of economic parity, as Naylor so aptly puts it, "to create a hands-across-the-ocean commune."[28] Rather, the appeal is to avoid the stingy attitude that leads to hoarding. If there is a need and God's purpose is to supply the need through His agents (in this case, the Corinthian believers), then it is incumbent upon them to be obedient to God's leading. "Applied to the Corinthians, this means that hoarding their abundance will not assure that they will have more for themselves; for if they do not establish a balance among the churches, then God will."[29]

## Study Questions

1. Tabulate and explain the three motives Paul highlights for the church at Corinth to give an offering for the church in Jerusalem.

2. Explain six factors concerning the circumstances being faced by the church in Jerusalem.

3. What is the historical connection between Paul's plan for the offering and the presence of his traveling companions?

4. As Paul searched for an example with which to motivate the Corinthian believers in the matter of giving, what or who does he cite? Why was the failure of the Corinthians on this matter especially problematic to the apostle?

5. While Paul is appealing for an offering, he does not mention money. Tabulate the various terms he uses in this chapter to make reference to the offering.

6. Suggest several reasons why Paul made it a special project to carry offerings from the Gentile believers to their Jewish brethren. What is the lesson for us today?

# CHAPTER 13

# Seek Ye First the Kingdom
# 2 Corinthians 8:16–9:15

## Preview:
*Since there are people who question Paul's motives and perhaps even his methods in this financial initiative on behalf of the saints in Jerusalem, he affirms the personal integrity of all of his delegates. It will be their responsibility to see to the task. And with that he adds the additional challenge, "Now see to it!" He wants this task finished before he arrives.*

## Faithfulness Delegated (8:16–9:5)

The delegation of Titus and the two brothers is just another indication of the care with which Paul undertook this mission. He gives no quarter to those who may be inclined to question his motives or ethics in the matter. Titus illustrates the reciprocity implied in verse 14: "But thanks be to God who puts the same earnestness on your behalf in the heart of Titus" (v. 16). What Paul is asking of the Corinthians in terms of spontaneous loving concern for brethren in need is reflected in the attitude of Titus toward them. Notice here that Paul understands the passion of Titus due to God's leading in his life. This further confirms that this entire effort is a Spirit-directed project. God has lead Paul to initiate the work. He has led the Corinthians to make their pledge. He has placed a burden on Titus and the brothers to assist in executing the plan.

In the comments on 1 Corinthians 5:3ff., Phillip E. Hughes was cited with regard to his observations concerning the protocol expected in dealing with immoral persons in need of discipline.[1] Occasionally, as Hughes notes, we have a window into the life of the early church. In both of these letters to the Corinthians, Paul pulls back the curtain, as it were, to reveal details regarding their church life and worship practices.

---

### Church Life and Worship in Corinth

*Corporate prayer is offered (1 Cor. 14:16).*

*Songs of praise and worship are sung (1 Cor. 14:15, 26).*

*The reception and distribution of gifts are expected and overseen by men appointed to the task, such as deacons (1 Cor. 16:1–4; 2 Cor. 8:19–21; cf. Acts 6:1–6).*

*Giving is also associated with the gathering of believers (1 Cor. 16:2).*

*Giving to the poor is recognized as a Christian form of sacrifice (2 Cor. 9:11–15).*

*The faith is publicly confessed (1 Cor. 15:1–3).*

*The people receive God's blessing (2 Cor. 13:14).*

*They greet one another with a holy kiss (1 Cor. 16:20; 2 Cor. 13:12).*

*People respond to praise and prayer with the affirmative "Amen" (1 Cor. 14:16).*

*Instructions for the Lord's Supper are given, and it is conducted with a prayer of thanksgiving and the breaking of bread (1 Cor. 11:24).[2]*

---

Here too we have further hints of procedures and protocol taken in the early church to ensure full disclosure and integrity in fiscal matters. "We have sent along with him the brother" (v. 18). All that is known of the "brother" is what is indicated here. Since his name is not given, it is useless to conjecture who he was,[3] although Timothy is a likely guess (cf. 1:1). At any rate, he was known "through all the churches" (v. 18). He and Titus will also be joined by a third individual (v. 22), "our brother, whom we have often tested and found diligent in many things." Like Titus, he was "appointed by the churches to travel with us in this gracious work" (v. 19). He was selected by the churches to assist the apostles in overseeing the collection for Jerusalem. Most likely, he was one of the men cited in Acts 20:4. "The point becomes clearer in the two following verses where Paul explains that the presence of this *renowned brother* will certify the integrity of the enterprise. Paul wants to take (or at least is willing to endorse) any step that can be taken to assure that no impropriety occurs or is even suspected."[4]

"For we have regard for what is honorable, not only in the sight of the Lord, but also in the sight of men" (v. 21). Especially in financial matters, the apostle is scrupulously aware of his vulnerability to criticism. These men likely became a pattern for the work of the deacon in the formative years of the church.

> The apostle envisages a cloud larger than a man's hand on the horizon in that some contentious folk will raise awkward questions about the collection, making much of the undoubted fact that the three messengers are not local. Peering into skeptical Corinthian minds, Paul anticipates mutterings to the effect that the delegates who have come are in the process of collecting and now propose to sail away with Corinthian gold. Clutching church money, they will probably never be seen again.[5]

"As for Titus, he is my partner and fellow worker among you; as for our brethren, they are messengers of the churches, a glory to Christ." See similar commendations of Paul concerning Timothy (1 Cor. 16:10; Phil. 2:19–22), Apollos (1 Cor. 16:12), Phoebe (Rom. 16:1–2), and Epaphroditus (Phil. 2:19–22). It is evident that Titus stands out here as the principal agent of the apostle's itinerant ministry, whereas the others appear to be representative of individual churches.[6] Titus is said to be a "partner" (*koinōnos*) and "fellow-worker" (*sunergos*), whereas the other two men are said to be "messengers of the churches" (*apostoloi ekklēsiōn*) and "a glory to Christ" (*doxa Christou*). There is no question in whom Paul has placed his apostolic authority. The others are seen to stand with him to represent the full consent and solidarity of the churches. When Titus and the brothers arrive, Paul admonishes the Corinthians to "show them the proof of [their] love" (v. 24). While there is no doubt that their response to the delegation being sent on Paul's behalf will reflect their affection for Paul, the reference here is clearly a euphemism for the offering, as will be seen in 9:1–5.

While there might be a temptation to do so, the reader should not consider Paul to be disingenuous in the least. Giving them the benefit of the doubt, the mention of the offering—let alone an extended discourse—seemed "superfluous" to him (v. 1). Paul had been "boasting" about this church and their pledge to give generously to the cause that he thought had "been prepared since last year" (v. 2). Indeed, it was their early enthusiasm for the project that Paul had used to encourage the believers in Macedonia in their giving. Now he is not very confident. Their sincerity remains to be seen. He had cited their zeal as an example of sacrificial giving and willingness. Now he is not sure who will be more embarrassed should they not come through—they or him!

"But I have sent the brethren, in order that our boasting about you may not be made empty in this case" (v. 3). Of course, Paul knows that the Corinthian church had been derelict in discharging their original commitment. He is not about to release them from that commitment. He applies pressure and tactfully suggests that he is only concerned that they be on schedule. "As I was saying, you may be prepared" (v. 3). Once again, giving them the benefit of the doubt, Paul says, "I may be wrong about all this. Maybe you have been working on this all year and you are ready even as I write these words." This has to be a stretch since Titus had just arrived from visiting them, and we can be sure Paul knew how much (or how little) progress they had made. So he adds a further contingency that, if it came to pass, failure on their part would be a blow to all of them. In the event they were not ready, consider this as a worst-case scenario: "if any Macedonians come with me and find you unprepared, we (not to speak of you) should be put to shame" (v. 4). Should they fail, Paul's reputation as well as theirs is on the line. Perhaps this is why he sends the "brothers" on ahead to take care of the matter. Considering the gravity of the situation, there is every reason to imagine that his first instinct was to go down there and take matters into his own hands. That he handles it in this way is another compliment to his character.

"So I thought it necessary to urge the brethren that they would go on ahead to you and arrange beforehand your previously promised bountiful gift" (v. 5). That Paul does not come right away with Titus and the brothers is an act of kindness. This will give the Corinthians time to make ready for the offering. No doubt they would have been embarrassed to see their spiritual father with little or nothing to show for all their talk. This will enable them to work with the men to be ready before Paul arrives. In that way neither they nor he will be disappointed.

Paul then adds, "that the same might be ready as a bountiful gift, and not affected by covetousness." Only greed could sabotage this mission. And so the writer warns against the evil of the sin of "covetousness." Harry Ironside tells the story of an effort to take up a missionary offering in a Scottish church.

> One rather close-fisted brother was there, known to be worth something like 50,000 pounds, which in those days was considered a fortune, and as the deacons went around taking up the offering, one of them whispered to him, "Brother, how much are you going to give?"
>
> "Oh, well; I will put in the widow's mite," he said, and prepared to put in a penny.

"Brethren," the deacon called out, "we have all we need; this brother is giving 50,000 pounds!" If he was going to give the widow's mite, he would have to give all he had.[7]

If the truth be known, the stingy Scot lost out in the end. He failed in the *eulogia*—"blessing" or "praise." Consequently, he never knew what price he paid for his failure to open his hands to the needy. The use of the term *pleonexia*, "greed," further intensifies the warning. As Paul uses it here, greed spoils the broth. Just giving is not enough. If the gift is tainted with *pleonexia*, then it can no longer be a *eulogia*. The benefit in return to the giver is lost. When the pastor encourages the people to give, it is not for his personal advantage. It is that they might be blessed by full participation in the building up of the body of Christ. As with the exercise of spiritual gifts, their exercise of the gifts, granted by the Father above, is to distribute blessings and edification to His own. It is not merely for the sake of the poor that Paul exhorts them to give. It is for their sakes as well. If I am correct in my thoughts as to why Paul, in particular, got behind this project, at least one of the positive outcomes of the work would be to put away racism and spiritual elitism in the church once and for all.

# Faithfulness Directed (9:6–15)

"Now this I say" (v. 6; *touto de*, "now this is what I mean").[8] What follows contains the apostle's closing remarks on the matter of the collection for Jerusalem. In so doing, he provides the church with the clearest and most comprehensive treatment of the subject to be found in the New Testament. His approach is to extract principles from both Scripture and experience to demonstrate why and how they are to give. "He makes two fundamental points here, although they may also be understood as two aspects of a single point: God provides the means to be generous (9:6–10) and (therefore) generosity redounds to the glory of God (9:11–15)."[9]

Paul begins with an allusion to their common experience of seedtime and harvest. "He who sows sparingly shall also reap sparingly; and he who sows bountifully shall also reap bountifully" (v. 6; cf. Prov. 11:24–26, Luke 6:38; Gal. 6:7). The metaphor of sowing and reaping is used frequently in Paul's letters to discuss several very different topics. It is used, for example, in 1 Corinthians 15:36–44 to speak of the relationship of the *mortal body* to the resurrection body. The seed goes into the ground and dies. The new body that is resurrected is "from" the dead seed, but like the new life sprouting from the seed, it is a new life altogether. It is a spiritual body. Then again, sowing and reaping are also used in Galatians 6:7–9 to speak of *what one sows* in his life. "Whatever a man sows, this he will also reap. For the one who sows to his own flesh shall from the flesh reap corruption, but the one who sows to the Spirit shall from the Spirit reap eternal life. And let us not lose heart in doing good, for in due time we shall reap if we do not grow weary." We reap what we sow. It may take a lifetime—maybe longer—before we realize the investment, but eventually it will come. This is both a promise and a warning.

In this final word to the Galatians (Gal. 6:9), Paul comes the closest to his subject here. Yet what he instructs here is unique. A person's return is determined by his or her investment. Paul is not so much interested in *what* is invested—we already know, in this instance, it has to do with money. Nor is he interested in the amount that is sown, as such. Rather, he has in mind *how* it is sown. The expression *ep' eulogiais* is ordinarily translated "on the basis of blessings"; or to paraphrase, "with an eye to an abundant harvest," here it has the sense of "freely," or "liberally." While it does not suggest indiscriminate giving, it does denote unrestrained giving. It looks ahead to *hilaros*, "cheerful," in the next verse. The idea Paul captures is that of the farmer who lavishes the ground with seed in anticipation of securing as rich a harvest as possible. Rather than begrudging the land its largess due to the cost of precious seed, the sower scatters it bountifully in anticipation of the day when he will also reap bountifully. It is tempting here to consider that he has in mind an eschatological reference akin to Matthew 13:30: "Allow both [wheat and tares] to grow together until the harvest; and in the time of the harvest I will say to the reapers, 'First gather up the tares and bind them in bundles to burn them up; but gather the wheat into my barn.'"[10]

This does not seem to be what Paul has in mind. There is no exact parallel in biblical or extrabiblical literature. Harris considers it to be a Pauline creation. Although the general thought appears to be contained also in Greek and rabbinic materials, following Gale, Harris considers perhaps it was Proverbs 22:8–9 that gave inspiration to the analogy.[11] Naylor seems to agree.

"Cheerful" means gladness, even merriment. Proverbs 22:9 tells us that "He who has a bountiful eye will be blessed," the background Hebrew being almost literally "The one who is good in eye, he will be blessed." It is likely that Paul alludes to the Septuagint translation of this verse, which states that God "blesses," rather than "loves," the man who is both cheerful and a giver. The overall idea is the same, in that a gleaming eye denotes eagerness, and the person whose eye gleams with joy when he gives (or forgives, Rom. 12:8) will know God's blessing. The Lord has plans for a man of this caliber.[12]

Charles Dickens captures the picture exactly. In his classic *A Christmas Carol*, when the tightfisted Mr. Scrooge is smitten and his stingy heart is set free from its miserly ways, he is absolutely gleeful in his subsequent displays of generosity. Nothing really changed—except his heart—and that made all the difference.

"Let each one do just as he has purposed in his heart" (v. 7). The apostle does not have a minimum quota nor yet a minimum percentage figure in mind. For each individual it is an amount to be determined before the Lord. "Not grudgingly or under compulsion; for God loves ['blesses?'] a cheerful giver" (v. 7). The one giving is to have a willing heart and a sincere desire in order to participate. Paul is not so much interested in their money. Nor is God, for that matter, as the passage from Proverbs 22:9 indicates. The Greek term *hilaron*, from which the English term *hilarious* is derived, is best rendered as the KJV suggests, "cheerful." Giving is not a joke; it is serious business. But it can be a delightful experience.[13]

Paul has struggled with his relationship with these people. He has had to deal with moral issues, theological issues, and attitudinal issues. These, much as the distance separating Lazarus and the rich man, have created a great gulf between them. Repeatedly he has sought for ways to "test" them to discern their hearts. Paul is, of course, interested in their participation in the offering. That is for certain. More than that, he wants to know where their hearts are. If their hearts are right before God—and His apostle—everything else will take care of itself. His appeal throughout this section is to their hearts—not their wallets.

"And God is able to make all grace abound to you" (v. 8). Paul's logic is identical with that of our Lord in Matthew 6:33. When the temporal concerns of life are placed first, God is usually excluded. But when the kingdom of God is placed first, God sees to it that the temporal needs are included. "Paul affirms that God is the source of all human generosity, because it is God who supplies the blessing to make one sufficient in order to perform every good work."[14] "That always having all sufficiency in everything, you may have an abundance for every good deed" (v. 8). Giving is a grace that has reciprocal benefits. This, of course, has been Paul's point all along. The principle of "grace giving" begins and ends with God. Having received from God everything one has, each person is then charged to share those blessings "graciously." In return they will then once again be on the receiving end of God's *amazing* grace. Proverbs 37:25–26 bears out this principle:

> I have been young, and now I am old;
> Yet I have not seen the righteous forsaken,
> Or his descendants begging bread.

> All day long he is gracious and lends;
> And his descendants are a blessing."

"As it is written" (v. 9; cf. Ps. 112:9). "He scattered abroad, He gave to the poor, His righteousness abides forever" (v. 9). Of course, neither Paul nor the psalmist is saying that every believer will always be wealthy or that the believer who gives regularly and faithfully will always be rich. Both experience and the context (cf. 8:2) deny this. They are saying that the abundance of God's riches is available to those who are rightly related to Him. "His righteousness abides forever" (v. 9). The righteous acts of the person who readily gives and supplies the needs of others have eternal value.

Verse 10 should best be rendered "Now he who ministers seed to the sower and bread for your food will supply your seed sown and increase the fruits of your righteousness" (v. 10). The KJV renders it as a prayer to God, when in fact it is an affirmation of the surety of God's supply. "This statement also reflects the basic confession of Judaism that God graciously provides all the bounty of nature. The Hebrew would have understood the opening phrase of Jesus' parable of the rich fool, 'the ground of a certain rich man produced a good crop' (Luke 12:16), to mean that God produced the crop."[15]

In verses 6–10 Paul's emphasis is on the simple truth that God provides the means to be generous. For this reason, he goes on to say in verses 11–15 that generosity redounds to the glory of God. He begins with "You will be enriched in everything for all liberality, which through us is producing thanksgiving to God" (v. 11). This unusual use of the participle, *ploutizomenoi*, "enrich," is not foreign to the New Testament, nor yet to the apostle Paul (cf. Acts 15:21; Eph. 3:17; 4:2; Col. 2:2; 3:16). The purpose for which God blesses some materially is "for all liberality." That is, in the scheme of things, to whom much is given, much is required. The rich fool of Luke 12:19 hoarded his wealth for that serene day when he could relax and enjoy the fruit of his labor—when he could "eat, drink, and be merry." The test of his heart revealed his god. On the throne of his heart was the stuff of today. In the end, only his hollow gods remained. Those who grasp for the things of this world reveal a heart that is far from God.

> The rich fool with his bulging barns and bumper crop wondered where he could store all his good things to preserve them all for himself. It apparently never crossed his mind that he had plenty of storage in the mouths of the needy. Those who are decisive and resourceful in trying to find ways to use God's bounty to help others, as the rich fool was decisive and resourceful in finding ways to feather his own luxuriant nest, are those who are righteous in God's eyes (see 8:2) and who live out God's righteousness.[16]

Giving consummates in a twofold grace. In "supplying the needs of the saints" (v. 12) and "overflowing through many thanksgivings to God" (v. 12). The final result is that God is glorified. As noted above, this process is cyclical. Out of the riches of God's grace He supplies the needs of the believer. The believer, in an expression of gratitude and liberality, shares of his abundance with others. They, in turn, direct their expressions of thanksgiving ("grace") to God from whom the supply originated. Thus, the cycle is complete.

"Because of the proof given by this ministry" (v. 13) connects with 8:24 where Paul uses the noun *endeixin*, "evidence." The "proof" (*dokimēs*) signifies "approval" not "judgment" in a pejorative sense. The evidence of their love is seen in their participation in this *diakonia*, "ministry." Their participation is the measure of their character.[17] So Paul says "they will glorify God for your obedience to your confession of the gospel of Christ and for the liberality of your contribution to them" (v. 13). The act of giving is evidence of obedience to the gospel. As noted above, when people evidence a lack of concern for the needs of the saints, they fail the "test," revealing their true relationship with God. On the contrary, if they are in fellowship with God through a personal relationship, they will evidence the working of His spirit in their lives producing works of righteousness.

"By prayer on your behalf" (v. 14). The connection is with "abundant" (literally "overflowing") in verse 12. Another positive result of faithful giving is that the recipients are induced to bring the giver before the throne of grace. It is in this way that the giver is compensated by the recipient of the gift. This further explains the thought of 8:14.

If Paul were concluding a service here, he might be saying, "Let's all stand for the doxology." In effect, he is gathering together all that has gone before in these two chapters (8, 9) to invite his readers to stand to give "thanks [*charis*, 'grace'] . . . to God for His indescribable gift [*dōrea*, 'free gift,' 'donation']!" (v. 15). The reference is to the gift of God's Son, but the verse is more than a spontaneous outburst of the writer. It is the supreme illustration of the principles Paul has just enumerated. As the example of Christ is applied to the experience of suffering in 1 Peter 2:21, so Paul applies the example of Christ to the grace of giving. We must not lose sight of the reason Paul is caused to ponder the cross as he brings this exhortation to its conclusion. In the words of Andrew Fuller:

> God held the world so dear that He gave His only begotten Son for everyone who will trust in Him. And how did He give Him? He gave Him in His birth as man, in order to be forever one with us. He gave Him in His death on the cross as surety, in order to take away our sin and curse. He gave Him on the throne of heaven, in order to arrange for our welfare, as

our Representative and Intercessor over all the powers of heaven. He gave Him in the outpouring of the Spirit, in order to dwell in us—to be entirely and altogether our own. Yes, that is the love of God. He gave His Son to us, for us, and in us.[18]

With this in mind, the writer challenges the Corinthians and every reader of his letter—including this one—to a more profound demonstration of their love for Him through their manifest love for those who are His.

Finally, it is an expression of great optimism with respect to his anticipation of their response. And as things turned out, there was good reason. As a footnote to these two chapters, Paul reports later to the church at Rome (at his desk in the city of Corinth), "For Macedonia and Achaia have been pleased to make a contribution for the poor among the saints in Jerusalem. Yes, they were pleased to do so, and they are indebted to them. For if the Gentiles have shared in their spiritual things, they are indebted to minister to them also in material things" (Rom. 15:26). This was to be seen in more than material contributions. Paul lived to see many of his spiritual progeny go on to become great leaders in the early church. Titus and Timothy are certainly the most illustrious. Others, such as Onesimus (cited earlier) were less so, however, John McRay reports. "An inscription erected by a freed slave from Laodicea was dedicated to Marcus Sestius Philemon." There is also strong evidence that Onesimus later went on to become a bishop in the region and possibly a significant player in the collection of Paul's writings (see also introduction).[19] If this is so, then we see further evidence of the emerging church of the first century breaking down the walls of separation between Jew and Greek, slave and freeman, male and female; for they are all one in Christ Jesus (Gal. 3:28).

## Study Questions

1. In terms of the way Paul utilizes his companions and demands accountability from those involved in the offering, suggest several principles of leadership gleaned from this text.

2. What do you learn about the policies and procedures of the early church from this text? How much of this do you consider of "descriptive" importance? How much would you consider "prescriptive" for the church today?

3. In what sense is a personal gift to the work of God a measure of the grace and glory of God Himself?

4. What is the significance of Paul's use of "cheerful" in relation to giving? How is this related to his illustration of sowing and reaping?

5. With the success of the offering for the church in Jerusalem, what would you consider to be the most important outcome of this effort besides providing for their material needs?

# SECTION III

# Third Trajectory: Authority Demands Respect

## 2 Corinthians 10–13

# CHAPTER 14

# Weapons of Our Warfare
# 2 Corinthians 10:1–18

## Preview:

*Those who pretend to speak for Christ, but who are in fact the enemies of the gospel must now contend with the true apostle of the Lord. With the suddenness of a summer storm, Paul turns his guns on these servants of Satan. They have raised doubts that he has the strength to stand up to them. He leaves no question of his resolve. He begins by asserting his authority and his credentials, which are not from any human agency, but from God Himself.*

At the dawning of the third millennium, Christians find themselves under siege by an increasingly hostile culture. In reflecting on this "ministry as warfare,"[1] one writer inspired by this text declares: "Countless false teachers and false teachings arise to continually batter the gates of our Christian faith. Long ago, Paul already waged war among the false teachers and false teachings in the Corinthian church."[2]

## A Breathtaking Change

Yet this *ministry as warfare,* appearing as it does at this juncture of the book, introduces another breathtaking change. Chapter 9 closes with such an irenic tone that the reader almost expects a group hug to follow. Paul's attitude changes so drastically from here to the end of the epistle that many speculate these chapters to constitute the text of the "severe letter" mentioned in 7:8 (cf. introduction) or perhaps another document of Pauline or non-Pauline extraction. "Some consider the evidence so convincing that the burden of proof is placed on those who hold to the integrity of the epistle."[3] Nevertheless, since a strong case can be made for the unity and integrity of the text as it stands in the biblical canon, "it is more reasonable to place the burden of proof on those who argue for the partition theories."[4] Barrett, who at the end of the day adopts one such partition theory, rightly observes that in order to properly interpret these letters, it is "of fundamental importance"[5] that three groups be distinguished throughout the epistle. There are, of course, the Corinthian believers concerning whom the writer is deeply distressed because they are being led astray; second, the false teachers who are leading the charge against Paul and his preaching; and third, recognized apostles. His approach toward the believers of the assembly is sometimes harsh but always measured together with his obvious love for them. To these he expresses a full range of emotions one would expect from their spiritual father who is deeply and emotionally involved in their spiritual welfare. With respect to the true apostles, Paul always speaks of them with respect. But when the writer turns his attention (not to say "guns") on the false teachers, his tone, temperature, and manner change dramatically.[6] Well they should. With righteous indignation, David wrote his imprecatory psalms against the enemies of Yahweh (cf. Pss. 7, 35, 55, 58, 69, 79, 109, 137, 139); it should not be surprising, much less considered inappropriate, to see Paul equally upset with the enemies of Christ. In today's multicultural environment, many find this disturbing. If so, perhaps we need to take a closer look at how and where the early church established legitimate lines of separation between truth and error and those who champion them.

Rather than speculating on logical probabilities for why or how the canonical epistle came to be in its present form, it seems better to accept it as it is. It is more reasonable at this point to rely on the work of Paul's trusted followers who were directed by the Spirit of God to save this letter and preserve it in its present form. To try to second-guess how it was composed in the first place on the basis of one's editorial preference two millennia after the fact is presumptuous and, frankly, unnecessary. We have the text, know what it says, and have few doubts about its target audience. What more is needed?

"2 Corinthians is like a river which, as it carries us along, not infrequently breaks into whitewater when tumbling over rocks of controversy."[7] If one keeps in mind the three groups to or about which Paul writes in these letters, it is not very difficult to understand how these last four chapters form the exit landscape of the epistle. The difference in tone is determined by the specific group(s) to which the respective chapters are directed. In the first nine chapters, Paul writes primarily to the majority of the congregation who love and appreciate him—and who value what he has to say. There the tone is fatherly. In the remaining chapters, he turns his attention almost exclusively to that small pocket of resistance that continues to voice opposition to his ministry. Here the tone is polemic. In both cases, his words are an "open letter" to both the saints and the subversives. Everything is on the table. Nothing is hidden from view.

As discussed above and described in the verses to follow, the false teachers appear to be former Jews professing faith in Christ (11:22), but who are actually "false apostles" (11:13). These are the ones from whom the writer has urged the church to separate (6:11–7:1). Since the apostle is now certain that the majority of the believers are with him, he is emboldened to deal more forcefully with those who are not.

The attack against Paul was both personal and ideological, but his first order of business is to defend his integrity as an apostle. This he does in terms of his attitude (vv. 1–6), his authority (vv. 7–11), and his divine commendation (vv. 12–18).

### Paul's Attitude (10:1–6)

Signing his name once again, as noted above, is not evidence that Paul is composing another letter. Rather, it is a way to turn his attention to his enemies. He begins with "I, Paul." (v. 1). In contemporary vernacular it might read something like this. "Okay, let me now speak to those of you who do not believe a word I say. You think I'm a fraud and a coward. I think its time we talked. If need be, we can take this outside!"

A word of practical importance to the reader is in order. Many leaders in our churches today find themselves victimized by unscrupulous wolves among the flock. Too often the real target is the one who stands in the pulpit. Everything is fine until the pastor stands up for a matter of principle or doctrine that is viewed as an attack on the power brokers of the church. This is one of the most difficult obstacles the undershepherd of the church will face. How does the pastor protect the flock when he or she must declare war against the wolves?

We are immediately drawn to the parable of the wheat and the tares (Matt. 13:24–30). Jesus instructed his disciples that the church age would be like the farmer who sowed wheat in his field while an enemy came in the night and scattered tares. The tares (*zizanion*, "darnel") were weeds, but not just any weed. As it grew in the wheat field it looked just like the real thing. It would not be until the time of the harvest that anyone could really tell the difference. The difference of course was that at the end of the season, the fruit-laden wheat would be bent over, while the tares could be seen standing proudly above them. From that vantage they are readily identified. Jesus said to wait until the harvest when God will send his "reapers" who will separate them. Do not try to do this on your own, else you may make a mistake and hurt the innocent. This leaves many with a question. Do we follow Jesus or Paul in this matter? Do we ignore the enemy for now and let God deal with them later as Jesus seems to instruct, or do we call them out, as Paul does, to identify their sinister actions?

The problem arises when we fail to make an important distinction. Jesus is speaking to the character of the entire church age. There will be those who are true to the gospel and those who are not. His counsel is to stay focused on the positive proclamation of the truth. We must resist, but we cannot expect to be able, in this age, to eliminate the archenemy of the church during this age. As Peter notes, "Your adversary, the devil, prowls about like a roaring lion, seeking someone to devour" (1 Pet. 5:8). Only God can—and will—deal with him in His time. Paul on the other hand is addressing a different matter. He is talking about how to address enemy incursions *into* the local body of believers. These can—and must—be addressed. Great harm can be experienced by unsuspecting (and often immature) saints when wolves are allowed to ravage the flock. It is never God's will for the saints to be left unprotected among those who would abuse and devour them.

"Now" (v. 1) indicates the change of subject. "Myself" (v. 1) is emphatic. As a boxer squaring off in the ring, his stance draws a graphic picture. However, do not be deceived by this. His manner is not arrogant. It is characterized "by the meekness and gentleness of Christ" (v. 1; cf. the parallel "mercies of God" in Rom. 12:1). The apostle not only understands that his authority comes from Christ, but even the accompanying grace with which that authority is exercised is from Him. In this case, it has a particularly ironic tone in the words: "who am meek when face to face with you, but bold toward you when absent!" (v. 1). Paul had been charged with demonstrating undue boldness in his letters without the personal strength of character, when confronted directly, to back up what he had to say (10:10).

Holy boldness happens when people, like Paul, are absolutely convinced of the "rightness" of their cause. In today's world, it is on this point that conservatives and liberals divide. Conservatives are convinced that they are right. They draw bold lines between truth and error and between right and wrong. Liberals and postmoderns have abandoned the search for truth. They also have no stomach for conflict. People with no convictions have nothing that commands their loyalty. They have nothing for which they would *die*. Sadly, in their world there is nothing for which to *live* either. The Chinese have an expression, "*Zhen jin bu ba huo lian*": "Real gold fears no fire."[8] Paul fears no fire.

"I ask that when I am present I may not be bold" (v. 2), that is, "Please do not force me to prove this allegation to be false." His accusers have called his bluff. Paul fully intends to pay a visit to Corinth. Though circumstances have made it difficult for the moment, he will, God willing, eventually get there. His warning is that they not push him into coming while he is still angry.

There are, he says, "some, who regard us as if we walked according to the flesh" (v. 2). The charge is not that he is carnal, but that he is lacking divine unction in his ministry and has usurped the apostolic office to himself. This as we have seen was a constant charge thrown by racist and religious enemies against his right to undertake this ministry to the Gentiles.

To this Paul replies: "we walk in the flesh" (v. 3), that is, we are just human, but "we do not war according to the flesh" (v. 3). To paraphrase: "Yes, we are just human, but you have no idea what God is able to do through us!" As the psalmist says, "The LORD is for me; I will not fear; What can man do to me?" (Ps. 118:6).

---

### Be Bold for the Cause of Christ

*"For whoever is ashamed of Me and My words, of him will the Son of Man be ashamed when He comes in His glory, and the glory of the Father and of the holy angels." (Luke 9:26)*

*"For I am not ashamed of the gospel, for it is the power of God for salvation to everyone who believes, to the Jew first and also to the Greek." (Rom. 1:16)*

*"For this reason I also suffer these things, but I am not ashamed; for I know whom I have believed and I am convinced that He is able to guard what I have entrusted to Him until that day." (2 Tim. 1:12)*

*"For which I suffer hardship even to imprisonment as a criminal; but the word of God is not imprisoned." (2 Tim. 2:9)*

*"But if anyone suffers as a Christian, let him not feel ashamed, but in that name let him glorify God." (1 Pet. 4:16)*

---

Although Paul has confessed time and again that his personal attitude was "in fear and in much trembling" (1 Cor. 2:3), nevertheless, his strength is in the Lord. Who among us has not faced similar circumstances? The obstacles are seen as a daunting adversary. We know our weakness and understand all too well that in the flesh the foe is indomitable and the task daunting, "but God." "The name of the LORD is a strong tower; the righteous runs into it and is safe" (Prov. 18:10).

"For the weapons of our warfare are not of the flesh" (v. 4). If Paul did not possess divine authority, he could not possess divine power. His strength was "divinely powerful for the destruction of fortresses" (v. 4). General George Custer was fearless to the point of recklessness. In a letter to his wife, Custer confessed, "I have never prayed as others do, yet on the eve of every battle in which I have been engaged, I have never omitted to pray inwardly, devoutly. Never have I failed to commend myself to God's keeping, asking Him to forgive my past sins, and to watch over me while in danger."[9] He goes on, "After having done so, all anxiety for myself, here or hereafter, is dispelled. I feel that my destiny is in the hands of the Almighty. This belief, more than any other fact or reason, makes me brave and fearless as I am."[10]

Later when Paul's enemies finally got their hands on him in Jerusalem, he was visited by the Lord in the night, who said, "Take courage; for as you have solemnly witnessed to My cause at Jerusalem, so you must witness at Rome also" (Acts 23:11). Paul understood that God was directing his steps, and as long as his work was unfinished, he was indestructible.

"We are destroying speculations and every lofty thing raised up against the knowledge of God" (v. 5). The KJV properly renders the previous verse as a parenthesis. The participle *kathairountes* ("pulling down") connects with "war" at the end of verse 3. Paul continues with the military metaphor in the use of "strongholds." These were high military battlements thrown up in combat. They denote opposition to Paul's work in the gospel. They are "pulled down" together with "every thought" (v. 5) being brought "captive to the obedience of Christ" (v. 5). One cannot help but reflect on 1 Corinthians 1–2. The apostle subsumes all human wisdom, philosophy, and authority under the divine. He acted on the assumption that any of the devices brought against him at the contrivance of men would fall before the power and the wisdom of God (see comments on 4:3; cf. also 1 Corinthians 2:2–8, esp. vv. 7–8: "but we speak God's wisdom in a mystery, the hidden wisdom, which God predestined before the ages to our glory; the wisdom which none of the rulers of this age has understood; for if they had understood it, they would not have crucified the Lord of glory").

An important discussion concerning the import of this text for epistemology (the science that explores how we know what we know) should be noted. Postmoderns tend to be skeptical about our ability to access truth— beyond our personal *experience* of it. Like a bark floating in a vast ocean, we are left to our own devices to define truth for ourselves. "Every thought," says Paul, is subsumed under the authority of Christ. The real war in which we are engaged today is the war of ideas. Many fear terrorists. What is it that motivates them to give their lives? It is the *ideas* that drive them to commit acts of terror. The ideas constitute the "head of the snake." In order to kill the movement, the ideas must be "pulled down." We must take down "every lofty thing raised up against the knowledge of God." Reflecting on this text together with 1 Corinthians 1, Wilson observes:

Human wisdom, on its own, *would not* come up with the folly of the cross. In contrast to human wisdom, Paul speaks the wisdom of God, which is the cross of Christ. The wisdom of the cross was ordained, he says, before the ages. Had the rulers of that age known of the preordained wisdom of God in the cross, they would not have fulfilled it by crucifying Christ. But they did *not* know, and they were God's instruments in securing our salvation. The plain teaching of this text is not just that the cross saves sinners. It is that the cross was ordained before the ages, and that this affirmation causes problems for human wisdom. Paul glories in the fact that it does. The cross saves some sinners and baffles others. The "reason" that both sets of sinners hold in common is not competent to judge these things. All our thoughts must be submissive to Christ (2 Cor. 10:4–5); we must love God with all our minds (Matt. 22:37); and we must never presume that God needs our counsel (Rom. 11:34–35). When the apostle with wonder asks, "Who has been His counselor?" he is not expecting someone in the back row to raise his hand.[11]

God has given us minds to know and reason to understand. With Augustine, we confess, "Thou hast formed us for Thyself, and our hearts are restless till they find rest in thee."[12] When we use human intellectual prowess to elevate strongholds of speculation against the truth and wisdom of God, we not only insult Him, but we also fortify ourselves against the privilege of accessing and knowing *the Truth*. Again, as Augustine observed, whenever we "may find truth, it is the Lord's."[13] It is this truth for which Paul and the early Christians were willing to die. It is sad when the ideas for which people are dying are not *truth*, but satanic *lies*. It is wise to remember that it was through destructive *ideas—lies and half-truths—*that Satan tempted Eve in the garden. And we must be warned that if we fail to engage this war of ideas in our contemporary world, people will continue to be enslaved by "speculations and every lofty thing raised up against the knowledge of God."

"And we are ready to punish all disobedience" (v. 6). Continuing the metaphor, Paul is still at war. He is casting down strongholds. He is leading captivity captive. Now he is prepared to punish all disobedience. "Whenever your obedience is complete" (v. 6). He gives them time to repent. Paul does not intend to deal with them quite so severely until he has given them ample time to prove their change of heart. Sam Johnson was fond of saying, "there's an end on't." The comment echoes Genesis 15:16. God indicates in His covenant to Abraham that his seed would not inherit the land immediately. Rather, they will be enslaved for four centuries. After this, God says, "they shall return here, for the iniquity of the Amorite is not yet complete." We sense that in using this language against his enemies he does two things. He associates them with the ancient enemies of Israel, the Amorites. He lets them know that their day is coming. The irony of such an allusion would likely not be lost on his ethnic Jewish readers who have problems with Paul's gospel because it grants equal access to God's electing grace to Gentiles as well as to them. For this reason this biblical allusion must have had them seething with anger. For Paul this was both racist and a denial of the finished work of Jesus Christ, and it was not going to be tolerated.

### Paul's Authority (10:7–11)

Paul's attitude is fully justified by his delegated authority, as will be shown in what follows. "You are looking at things as they are outwardly" (v. 7). This connects with "those which think of us as if we walked according to the flesh." (v. 2). If such an individual "is confident in himself that he is Christ's" (v. 7), let him know that "so also are we" (v. 7). It is possible, though not entirely certain, that this is the faction within the assembly that identified itself with Christ (1 Cor. 1:12).[14] However, if this is so, the stylistic allusion to Genesis 15:16 above is still interesting in this light. They were more akin to the Amorites, than to Abraham. Their "confidence in Christ" was likewise foreign to that of Paul. Jesus said that in the latter days "false christs and false prophets will arise and will show great signs and wonders, so as to mislead, if possible, even the elect" (Matt. 24:24). Concerning them, Jesus added, "Do not believe them." While the manifestation of Antichrist awaits the final countdown at the end of the church age, John reminds us that "even now many antichrists have arisen" (1 John 2:18) and further adds, with Paul here, "Who is the liar but the one who denies that Jesus is the Christ" (2:22). This is antichrist. At any rate they were giving out that they were from Christ and Paul was not. The apostle was quick to assert that they had no authority or advantage over him. If his enemies pretend to have the true word from God concerning Christ, Paul plays a risky game. What he intends to show is that their message is not the same as his. And for that reason it will not be possible to accept both on equal terms. The church will have to make a choice— whether to follow their spiritual father or these imposters.

"For even if I boast somewhat further about our authority, which the Lord gave for building you up and not for destroying you" (v. 8). The contrast Paul is drawing is between the effects of his ministry and that of his enemies. His work was effective in building them up. So it should be—for that is exactly what Christ authorized him to do. On the other hand, the impact of his enemies who have taken control of the work has been destructive and hurtful. When he adds, "I shall not be put to shame" (v. 8), he is speaking of the lies and misinformation that the false teachers have spread throughout the community.

In adding, "I do not wish to seem as if I would terrify you by my letters" (v. 9), most recognize that this passage could not likely be the "severe letter" mentioned earlier (see also the introduction), because it seems to make mention of it. But he is now adding somewhat of a conciliatory note to say, "I do not wish to *ekphobein*, 'frighten you away'" This also looks ahead to the next verse, where it would seem that the emphasis is on the "letters" rather than the fright caused by them.

We know that Paul intentionally flew under the radar when he first visited the city. He expressly desired to step out of the way and let the gospel do its work, rather than try to overimpress them with his diction or his oratorical skill. Now this comes back to bite him. "In the ancient rhetorical handbooks, *hupokrisis* denoted an orator's "delivery," which included not only his verbal and elocutionary skills but also his bodily "presence," the impression made by his physical appearance, his dress, and his general demeanor."[15] See, "they say, His letters are weighty and strong, but his personal presence is unimpressive, and his speech (*logos*) contemptible" (v. 10). On the contrary, he intends to demonstrate that his actions will correspond to his words. "Such persons we are also in deed when present" (v. 11). He does not give empty threats.

They are pulling the tiger's tail. As strange as it may seem, the modern reader has a better picture of Paul than the Corinthians seem to have had. We have the benefit of all of the New Testament writings, including the accounts of both Luke (Acts 15:4–29) and Paul himself (Gal. 2:1–16), which record other occasions when his strength of character is seen. He calls these enemies "false brethren" (in Gal. 2:4), to whom he gave no quarter—nor yet even to Peter who "stood condemned" for his hypocrisy in the treatment of Gentile believers. On this offense, Paul "opposed him to his face" (Gal. 2:11). Paul's enemies have no idea what they are up against in their opposition of this champion for Christ. Paul is not perfect, and there is no effort here or elsewhere to pretend to be something that he is not. One important fact remains. He was chosen by Christ for a unique ministry to the Gentiles. Those who question his credentials and his character inevitably question the wisdom of His Lord who called him. So it is to that matter he now turns.

The practical significance of this is enormous. All too often churches measure success as the world does by bricks and bodies. Especially in times of trial, when the enemy has sown seeds of discord and the sheep are looking across town for what appears to be a more successful "shepherd," we forget to consult the Great Shepherd of the sheep—who put them (undershepherd and sheep) together in the first place. Success is only measured in relation to the completion of that work for which God brought them together. If this principle is followed, it would be more likely that the pastor will leave on a "high" note rather than a low one. His work will be finished and what he leaves will be a testament to faithfulness in the work. The divine "well done good and faithful servant" will not be determined by how many buildings built, the number of cars in the parking lot, or the amount of money raised in the offerings. It will be based on our faithfulness to the task to which He calls—whether it is to abound or be abased.

### *Paul's Divine Commendation (10:12-18)*

Paul does not measure his credentials as do his enemies who "measure themselves by themselves" (v. 12). Such an approach Paul says is "without understanding" (v. 12). By contrast, he will measure his credentials by an objective standard—"a measure, to reach even as far as you" (v. 13). What he has in mind is his "track record." Where Paul's enemies cited their authority, he cites his accomplishments.

"For, we were the first to come even as far as you in the gospel of Christ" (v. 14). Paul's critics were not responsible for founding the church at Corinth; he was. Paul is not riding on another's coattails. "We are "not boasting beyond our measure" (v. 15), that is, another man's labors. He is an original. The implication is that those who have come in behind him are taking credit for his work. "As we read between the lines we infer that the pseudo-apostles were refusing to share Paul's scruples and (astonishingly) rejoicing in his work at Corinth, substituting their names for his and those of his team as the evangelists who first broke ground in the city."[16] Naylor adds, "This was evil."[17] The power of ego is important in leadership. Obviously, a milquetoast is not likely to do well in a leadership role. It is evident, despite his intentional "laid-back" approach when first coming to Corinth, that Paul had sufficient strength of character to step up to the plate and lead. Often the besetting sin of leaders is pride. Sometimes this causes them to take credit for another person's labor. Preachers with overly inflated opinions of themselves often fall into this trap. In their effort to outdo even themselves, they will steal another preacher's sermons—who's to know? In recent years such behavior has broken into headlines to the shame and embarrassment of all. Whether from pride or sloth, those who are guilty of such pretense bring great harm to the work.

However, since the Corinthians are products of his effort, Paul is not embarrassed to take the credit—not only for their very existence as a Christian community, but even for their ongoing spiritual growth; as he puts it: "as your faith grows, we will be, within our sphere, enlarged even more by you" (v. 15). The principle relates to material possessions but also to the investments of Paul's energies. Asked, "What is the most powerful force in the universe?" Einstein quipped, "Compound interest!" Paul understood the power of the gospel in this way. Do the math; one person, doubled thirty-four times yields a number well in excess of the entire population of the planet. It was certainly with this in mind that Jesus promised His followers they would do "greater works than these" which they have witnessed in His ministry (John 14:12).

The expression *kata ton kanona hēmōn*, "within our sphere," is interesting. The term *kanōn* is used of the canon of Scripture. When so used it designates Scripture as the "standard" or "rule." I say on this account that "Scripture is the rule of faith and practice." The term in its simplest sense has in mind a "measuring rod" such as a yardstick. When Paul uses this term to speak of his ministry, he is indicating that he has been designated a "measure" of the work of the gospel. Recall that Peter was assigned to reach out to the Jews, but Paul was assigned to the Gentiles. None of us can do all the work ourselves. Paul is well aware of that. However, he does not raise the issue to point out the obvious. The Corinthians were part of the work to which he (personally) had been *assigned*—the "sphere measured out to him." He is very sensitive to the fact that his success with this church may well determine his ability to reach out further into the south of Achaia and to other regions. Failure would call in question the entire project.[18] Paul does not intend to allow this situation or any other to inhibit him from going even further to "preach the gospel even to the regions beyond you" (v. 16). Again, it is a simple fact that he can take credit only for what he has accomplished within the sphere of his assigned ministry. To "boast in what has been accomplished in the sphere (*kanōn*) of another" (v. 16), could not be further from his mind.

A historical and theological footnote is in order here. The apostolic office in the early church served as the final court of appeal in matters of doctrinal purity. It is not possible to establish with any degree of certainty that they appointed successors to carry out this function (e.g., the formation of an apostolic succession of bishops). However, it is a mistake to say that they deferred to the local assemblies on doctrinal matters to create, as it were, a patchwork of theological diversity throughout the churches. "Instead, by uniting church leadership and teaching, it must be seen to have established itself as the church's classical solution to the problem of preserving the churches in the faith of the apostolic gospel and hence also in fulfillment of the commission given by the risen Lord."[19] When Paul asserts his authority here and in the succeeding chapters, it is in regard to this function that he does so.

Lest they interpret what he has to say as self-conceit, Paul shows that, in the final analysis, his commendation comes from Christ (vv. 17–18). He was always careful to show that any success he enjoyed in the ministry was due not to his own innate ability but to Christ working in him (cf. Rom. 15:17–18). Thus, his boast is not in himself, but "in the Lord" (v. 17). He reiterates, "For not he who commends himself is approved, but whom the Lord commends" (v. 18). Those who have intruded upon the work Paul established cannot on that account arrogate to themselves legitimate credit for the work. These people simply do not understand how God works. If Paul "boasts it will always be within the limits established by the measure that God has assigned to him, an assignment authenticated by the indisputable fact that he was the first to preach the gospel to the Corinthians. If he boasts, therefore, it is in the Lord; for only the one whom the Lord approves is commended. Paul can claim such approval because he has been granted an assignment from the Lord, who guides his apostolic activity."[20]

## Study Questions

1. Explain why there is such a sudden change in tone at the beginning of this chapter. How does this contribute to developing an interpretive key to this letter?

2. Compare and contrast the parable of the wheat and tares (Matt. 13:24–30) with Paul's instruction in this chapter concerning the enemies of the gospel.

3. How does the pastor protect the flock from bad doctrine and at the same time deal redemptively with those who are spreading it?

4. Explain the relationship between truth and courage. How does Paul's attitude in this chapter illustrate this?

5. Upon what criteria does Paul base his apostolic authority in this text?

6. Why does this writer allege that the modern reader may have a better understanding of Paul as a person than his ancient readers?

# CHAPTER 15

# Fools Talk
# 2 Corinthians 11:1–15

## Preview:

*Boasting was the hallmark of Paul's enemies. He will now boast as they do. But in so doing, he turns the entire process on its head. In what he considers foolishness, he boasts of those things that characterize the true apostle from the false. But before he does so, he expresses his reasons in terms of his fatherly concerns on their behalf and his fear that Satan has led them astray.*

What Paul is about to do is an apparent contradiction to what he has just said in 10:17–18. In order to contextualize this effort, he styles himself as a "fool" and his behavior as "foolishness" (11:1, 16, 17, 21). "Three reasons are given, each introduced by *gar* ("for"), as to why the Corinthians ought to be willing to tolerate his foolish boasting: (1) he is intensely jealous for their highest spiritual good, especially when their corporate purity is endangered (v. 2); (2) they are already tolerant toward theologically deviant visitors to Corinth (v. 4; cf. 11:19–20); (3) he is not inferior to the "superlative apostles" to whom his rivals were apparently appealing (v. 5)."[1]

## Why Play the Fool?

Harris offers an answer to those who wonder if Paul, in this text, does not also violate Proverbs 26:4–5:

> Do not answer a fool according to his folly,
> Lest you also be like him.

> Answer a fool as his folly deserves,
> Lest he be wise in his own eyes.

This is the Old Testament solution to being caught on the horns of a dilemma. Either option is risky. "That is, both ignoring the fool and trying to answer the fool are procedures fraught with danger. If Paul refused to adopt the tactics of his adversaries and refrained from foolish boasting, he would risk losing the Corinthians to a false gospel (11:4), but if he chose to indulge in a temporary foray into foolish boasting, he risked being misunderstood by the Corinthians and playing into the hands of his rivals."[2] At the end of the day, he decides that speaking out (however foolish it seems) is the lesser of two evils.

"I wish that you would bear with me in a little foolishness" (v. 1; *ophelon*, "would that"). He begins with an expression that ordinarily denotes an unattainable wish.[3] Already the apostle is uneasy about what he has to do. For him it is "foolishness" (v. 1). Yet, as repugnant as it is to him, it is necessary.

"But indeed you are bearing with me." Harris has "Yes, do put up with me!"[4] The matter is serious enough for Paul to press home the point. While he considers what he is about to do to be distasteful (at best) and ill-conceived at worst, he braces and continues. He will proceed not as himself, but as a jester. He will gloat, not in his massive accomplishments, but in his *sufferings*. He knows that his adversaries have paid no price and endured no pain in service to Jesus Christ. "The ploy is subtle, a stroke of genius rather than an evidence of despair. In that Paul begs leave for a little folly (11:1), he is aware that the Corinthians will perceive that he has snatched the false apostles' lance from their hands and is tilting it at them with their own weapon. Pierced by their victim's mock boastfulness, the imposters will be seen for what they are—ridiculous"[5]

"For" (v. 2) indicates "reason." What follows answers why they must bear with him. "I betrothed you to one husband, so that to Christ I might present you as a pure virgin" (v. 2). They were in danger of being turned from Christ by being turned off to the ministry of the apostle. As an "ambassador for Christ," he realizes he must win them back to himself in order to win them back to Christ.

In verses 2 and 3, Paul employs another commonplace in the Jewish community—that of the father "responsible for safeguarding his daughter's virginity between the time of her betrothal and the time when he actually leads her into the bridegroom's house (see Gen. 29:23; Deut. 22:13–21)."[6] The metaphor used to speak of the church as a "virgin" betrothed to Christ as a "husband" is used frequently in Paul and elsewhere in the New Testament. This corresponds to a similar analogy in the Old Testament in terms of Yahweh's relationship to Israel (cf. Eph. 5:23–32; Rev. 19:7–9; 21:2, 9; 22:17; see also Isa. 54:5; 62:5; Jer. 31:32; Ezek. 16:32, 45; Hos. 2:2–20).[7] The metaphor is always used in a corporate, not an individualistic, sense. Paul is not saying that each individual believer is related to Christ as a bride. Rather, he is saying that the entire body, as it were, is being prepared as a bride. While used ordinarily of the eschatological union as in Ephesians 5:27, here it is adapted to speak of the local assembly at Corinth. It is never used to speak of the individual's personal or mystical relationship to Christ or to God.

Teresa of Avila, a sixteenth-century Spanish mystic, reintroduced the ancient practice of "bridal mysticism" to the Roman Catholic Church during the Counter-Reformation. This was derived from early heretical Gnostic forms of Christianity where the feminine soul was understood to be united with the masculine divine lover in the "bridal chamber." This union was considered the ultimate sacrament. Teresa described several visions in extremely erotic terms. Such false teachings arise when the metaphor Paul uses for the entire corporate body of the church is adapted to the individual believer. The believer's relationship to Christ is not a "feminine" one. If gender meant anything at all (and it does not) Scripture would emphasize the masculine over the feminine, as seen in the frequent designation of the believer (male and female) as either "children," or more, as "sons" (cf. John 1:12; Rom. 8:29; Gal. 4:7; Heb. 12:7). While Scripture (e.g., Eph. 5:31–32) does employ the bride/bridegroom metaphor to denote the intimate relationship of Christ and the church, it is a serious error to take this to an extreme to define our individual relationship with Him in such terms. In pagan and neo-pagan spiritualities, it was (and still is) commonplace to describe union with the gods and goddesses in erotic terms, as did the Gnostics and fertility cults.[8]

What is implied in the use of the term "virgin" in verse 2 is the idea that they were "pure" and "innocent" when they were first brought to Christ. From a spiritual perspective, their newfound faith in Jesus was unsophisticated, fresh, and new. Phillips translates this, "For in my eyes you are like a fresh, unspoiled girl whom I am presenting as fiancée to your true husband." When the gospel had done its work in their city, Paul had seen the wonder, the joy, and the ecstasy that had come when Jesus entered their lives. When he left them to continue his itinerant ministry, they knew nothing but the pure gospel. They knew only the *truth*. They did not know enough to be cynical or *nuanced*. They were formerly, as Paul said of the Ephesians, "dead in . . . trespasses and sins" (Eph. 2:1–3) until the gospel had transformed them. They were "by nature children of wrath. . . . But God, being rich in mercy, because of His great love with which He loved us, even when we were dead in our transgressions, made us alive together with Christ" (2:3, 5). As little Holly, my granddaughter, explained what happened when she asked Jesus into her heart to save her from her sins, she exclaimed, "My heart hurts!" Their newfound faith and confidence in Jesus Christ had transformed the Corinthians' lives from "nothing" (cf. 1 Cor. 1:27–28, esp. in the use of *exouthenēmena*, "despise," "count as nothing") to a breathtaking display of His grace, such that he had to say of them "that in everything you were enriched in Him, in all speech and all knowledge, even as the testimony concerning Christ was confirmed in you, so that you are not lacking in any gift, awaiting eagerly the revelation of our Lord Jesus Christ, who shall also confirm you to the end, blameless" (1 Cor. 1:5–8). Without a doubt, the writer is recalling these words as he considers the distressing possibility that this is no longer true.

It is not saying too much to suggest that these babes in Christ were babes in the woods—utterly defenseless against the wiles of Belial (6:15), to which they had been subjected after Paul left them. He fears that "as the serpent deceived Eve by his craftiness, [their] minds will be led astray from the simplicity and purity of devotion to Christ" (v. 3). As innocent and unsuspecting as Eve in the Garden of Eden, they have been approached by the serpent and seduced away from their pure, simple faith in the Lord Jesus. The term *panourgia*, "craftiness," "cunning" deserves special note. This was the term apparently used by his adversaries to characterize Paul's dealings with the Corinthians (12:16). It is not surprising then that in 4:2 he asserted he does not act this way. See also 7:2. However, in this instance, he uses a "guilt by association" tactic in observing that this is what Satan did to Eve and, by analogy (through Paul's adversaries), what he appears to have done to them.

## A Different Jesus and a Different Spirit

With the jester's mask still affixed, Paul continues with his second reason for speaking in this way: "For if one comes and preaches another Jesus whom we have not preached, or you receive a different spirit which you have not received, or a different gospel which you have not accepted, you bear this beautifully" (v. 4). The irony of the passage cannot be escaped. That which Paul finds necessary to beg of them in verse 1 (i.e., "bear with him") they had willingly offered to false teachers. To paraphrase: "I speak and you turn a deaf ear to me. Someone else comes along with another message and you hear him gladly. But to make matters worse, the 'Jesus' and the 'spirit' they preach are not the same about which you heard from me." The situation to which the apostle speaks is unique.[9] The reference to a "different spirit" is also curious. We are tempted to connect the dots here[10] with 1 Corinthians 12–14. We wonder if these are the ones who were creating problems with their obsession with the "sign" gifts in their worship of Christ. Perhaps, on the other hand, these are the ones alluded to in 1 Corinthians 4:8 who are said, with tongue in cheek, to be "rich" and ostensibly have already begun to reign as kings, while the apostles are "exhibited as last of all." This has caused some to suggest that the "different spirit" was in contrast to Paul's ministry, which was characterized by hardships and suffering—whence the examples to follow here in this chapter. However, we cannot forget the association of these interlopers with Belial in 6:15. Whatever it is, the writer has justifiable concerns that the inevitable outcome of their work is, and has been, to undermine their spiritual foundation (cf. 1 Cor. 3:10) and to engage in a ministry that was self-seeking and doctrinally problematic.

The relevance for today is huge. If there is uncertainty as to the particular error being propounded by Paul's adversaries, there is little left to the imagination in today's prurient display of aberrant doctrine. False teachers enter our homes through the media—print, television, movies, Internet—and it is pervasive. Name the heresy, check it on the Internet, and one becomes an instant expert on (sometimes *convert to*) an ancient heresy. Many of these are only nettlesome. But most are destructive and dangerous. False religions may speak of Jesus, yet the one they describe (such as in the Koran) is not the same. Cults, such as the Jehovah's Witnesses, speak of Jesus, but he is not the same. Mormons claim to be a sect of authentic Christianity, yet upon examination their god and their Jesus are not the same. There are those who claim to be evangelicals who actually preach a different "god" than "God, the Father of our Lord and Savior Jesus Christ." This in turn changes everything with respect to the person and work of the Savior. "When Paul rebukes the Corinthians because they were being led astray, he recognizes that false teachers still use the *name* Jesus."[11]

"Another" Jesus is identifiable only by the attributes which are predicated of him. If someone were to claim that he knew a Henry Smith, someone else might say, "Oh, I know him too!" But when they get to talking, they discover that one of the Smiths is over six feet tall, and the other is barely over five. One is three hundred pounds, and the other is one-hundred fifty pounds. It would not be long before they decided they were talking about different people with the same name. They decided this on the basis of the differences between their *attributes*.[12]

There are many who use the same *names* for God but who change his attributes and are preaching a very different "god."

## Not the Best Preacher in the World

Although Paul was "not in the least inferior to the most eminent apostles" (v. 5), it was not immediately evident in his personal ministry. He was "unskilled in speech," and this was apparently offensive to some. Perhaps Paul reflects something of his rabbinic training here. He is "firmly denying that rhetorical skill can be used as an index of a preacher's true knowledge, something the Corinthians were apparently being encouraged to believe."[13] He could not have been criticized "in knowledge." As for the message that he preached, "in every way we have made this evident to you in all things" (v. 6). The tone is possibly ironic in contrast with verse 4. They may have criticized his style, but they could add nothing to his sermon. He may simply be reminding them once again, as he did in 3:2, that they are his "letter, written in our hearts, known and read by all men . . . a letter of Christ, cared for by us."

The reference to the *huperlian apostolōn*, "eminent apostles," is problematic. Older commentaries and patristic writers generally favor the idea that it refers (as Gal. 2:9) to the original Twelve. As such it is taken to mean that Paul defends his status with the most "eminent" of the apostles. This interpretation can be readily adapted to the context.[14] Recent expositors, however, tend to view the reference in light of Paul's continuing "fool's speech." Using hyperbole, Paul dubs them "super-apostles." The adverb *huperlian* is a pejorative that one would not have expected to be used in relation to those who hold legitimate status in the early church as did the original apostles. It is used here to "describe the consummate conceit characteristic of the [pseudo-]apostles in question."[15] Tasker, who supports this view, adds, "This verse cannot then be used, as it has so often been used in the past, either in the debate about the primacy of Peter, or as evidence for an alleged conflict between Paul and the older apostles."[16]

"Did I commit a sin in humbling myself. . . ?" (v. 7; cf. 1 Cor. 9:1–18). Irony fairly drips from his pen. Their only legitimate criticism was his self-effacing manner. ". . . because I preached the gospel of God to you without charge?" (v. 7). In eighteen months of ministry, Paul never once extracted from them a living wage. "I robbed other churches" (v. 8) is hyperbolic and intended to shame them. "Taking wages from them to serve you" (v. 8). Paul, no doubt, has the impoverished Philippian church primarily in mind (Phil. 4:15–16). He could have mentioned the fact that he worked with his own hands to sustain a living on his first arrival in Corinth. It is suggestive of his restraint that he does not. "In everything I kept myself" (v. 9). Paul's behavior at Corinth was unimpeachable. He was not going to start now in allowing his readers to force him to compromise his principles (cf. Acts 18:3; 20:34–35; 1 Thess. 2:9; 2 Thess. 3:8; 1 Cor. 9:15–18). It is not certain what prompted their criticism. "Perhaps they felt that his manual labor (Acts 18:3; 1 Cor. 4:12) was inconsistent with his apostolic status. Or they may have thought that he had breached the conventions of patronage according to which a visiting teacher would be fully supported by wealthy patrons."[17] If that is so, Paul will rub it in rather than appeal to their sense of political correctness. "This boasting of mine will not be stopped in the regions of Achaia" (v. 10). It is significant that Paul readily receives aid from the Macedonian churches and refuses it from those at Corinth. For a reconstruction of the stages of Paul's support during the time of his first visit to Corinth, see Harris.[18] The contribution from the Macedonians (cf. v. 9) "may, with confidence, be identified with the return of Timothy and Silas to Corinth mentioned in Acts 18:5. The former had come from a mission to Thessalonica and the latter, most probably from a mission to Philippi."[19]

Then to those who question his motives, Paul answers his own question: "Why? Because I do not love you? God knows I *do*!" (v. 11). This is an oath. The writer swears, as it were, upon the knowledge of his heart known only to God. Paul defends his integrity with an appeal to the secrets of his heart that only God has seen. Commonplace in courtrooms from Paul's day to this, such an oath presumes that even when no one else sees the truth, God does. It is sad that in contemporary culture most people conduct their lives as though their innermost secrets are not known even to God. Such radical thinking has even permeated the ranks of so-called evangelicals whose god is too small to embrace everything. Open theists express doubts about what God knows and when He knows it. It is helpful to be reminded what Scripture teaches on this subject and why it is that Paul is able to appeal to His comprehensive knowledge as he does.

> Scripture is not unclear as to how God gets this extraordinary knowledge. God knows . . . because He controls all the events of nature and history by His own wise plan. God has made everything in conformity with the purpose of His will (Eph. 1:11). Therefore, God knows all about the starry heavens (Gen. 1:15, Ps. 147:4, Isa. 40:26, Jer. 33:22) and about the tiniest details of the natural world (Ps. 50:10–11, 56:8, Matt. 10:30). "God knows" is an oath-like utterance (2 Cor. 11:11, 12:2–3) that certifies the truth of human words on the presupposition that God's knowledge is exhaustive, universal, and infallible. God's knowledge is absolute knowledge, a perfection; so it elicits religious praise (Ps. 139:17–18, Isa. 40:28, Rom. 11:33–36). So God "knows everything" (1 John. 3:20).[20]

Why indeed does Paul refuse their help? Is it because he has no interest in them and no desire for their help? Hardly, but as he says, "that I may cut off opportunity" (v. 12) for my enemies to level any criticism. "Those who are looking for things to criticize will find no help from me." What is especially interesting about this statement is that Paul knew early on in his ministry in Corinth that there were people who were looking for things to find fault with him. His refusal to receive anything from them was calculated from the beginning. Those who are in ministry and who "rule well" in their oversight of the church have every right to receive wages (1 Tim. 5:17–18). However, it is in this matter that they are also vulnerable. Giving is to God, as was so eloquently developed in chapters 8 and 9. It is not given to the preacher. In the giving it is directed to God, and in the receiving it is received from God—not the human agent. When this principle is not understood, or if it is being perverted, great harm can come. Paul made sure that his integrity was, as he instructed Timothy later to require of all leadership, "above reproach" (1 Tim. 3:2). Again and again we hear reports that yet another great ministry has been brought under attack because the leadership of the church has not been "above reproach" in the matter of finances. Satan is shrewd enough to injure the cause of Christ, on his own—without the willing help of the saints.

The statement: "Those who desire an opportunity to be regarded just as we are in the matter about which they are boasting" (v. 12) is intended, once again, to call out his enemies. If they wish to take credit for Paul's ministry, they must do so by showing that they measure up to his character. There is method in Paul's madness. He knows that if they are to bring accusation against his integrity, theirs will have to match his own—that is, they will be forced to stop merchandising the gospel. Of course, he is equally certain that this is not going to happen. Either way, Paul wins the argument.

"For such men are false apostles (*pseudapostoloi*), deceitful workers, disguising (*metaschēmatizō*) themselves as apostles of Christ" (v. 13; cf. Phil. 3:2). Despite their claim to be *apostoloi*, Paul rejects this and employs a term seen only here in the New Testament—perhaps coined—to describe them. They are mere *pseudo-apostles*. This again confirms our understanding of the reference to the "most eminent apostles" in verse 5. As a "fool," the writer styles them as such, but in fact they are false and deceitful. Their apostolic role is a fraud. From all outward appearances, "these are not unbelievers who maliciously plot to infiltrate the church as undercover agents. They 'are professing Christians whom he roundly accuses of doing the Devil's work.'"[21] "The three-fold use of the verb *metaschēmatizō* (vv. 13, 14, 15), which has been translated "disguise" is significant for Paul's argument, because it allows him to explain how the super-apostles have been able to deceive the Corinthians: Satan is working through them."[22] Matera continues:

> Paul explains how the intruding apostles have been able to deceive the Corinthians. They have come to Corinth appearing to be "apostles of Christ" and "ministers of righteousness," but in fact their appearance is merely a disguise; for unlike Christ, who has the power to change and conform themselves to be Christ's apostles and ministers of righteousness, their appearance is merely a disguise, a masquerade, a sham.[23]

The warning here is appropriate for any church, whether ancient or contemporary. The "ministry" can become a "business." When this happens integrity is often the first casualty. Lacking divine appointment and unction, these imposters use the tactics of the world, the flesh, and the Devil to achieve success in their own eyes. This is not to say that the "business" of the church should be haphazard. Rather, it is to say that the leadership of the church or parachurch ministry must be God-called and Spirit-led. Paul consistently quantifies his success in terms of the impact of the gospel on the lives of those to whom he was called to preach. It is evident throughout this text that his detractors—these false apostles—were measuring success by other self-serving means.

"No wonder" (v. 14, *kai ou thauma*). Harris notes that "*ta thaumata* is used of jugglers' tricks."[24] With their amazing tricks and smooth rhetoric, it is no surprise that they have been able to deceive the Corinthian believers, "for even Satan disguises himself as an angel of light" (v. 14; on *metaschēmatizō*, "disguise," see comment above on v. 13). The passage calls to mind the culmination of our Lord's discussion with the Pharisees in John 8. The specific allusion Paul makes is not altogether clear. Perhaps it is to Job 1:6. While the specific description "angel of light" does not occur in Jewish literature, there are many references to his making appearances, singing hymns like the angels, transforming himself into the "brightness of angels," or descriptions of him as the "Prince of light" wearing the "form and brightness of an angel," etc.[25] It is mere speculation to suggest with Garland that this is a Hebraic idiom.[26] "What is important for Paul is that the shining stars dazzle and make the ones working in the trenches, like Paul, look frumpish and unspiritual by comparison. But Satan is more likely to take the guise of a shining star with glamorous appeal than a foot soldier. Satan is seductive, insidious."[27]

"Therefore it is not surprising if his servants also disguise themselves as servants of righteousness" (v. 15; on *metaschēmatizō*, "disguise," see comment above on v. 13). What is not surprising is their behavior. While the writer certainly has in mind the perversity of their theology, his point here is that they are acting in character with the one whom they follow—Satan. "They may deceive themselves and others that they are doing God's work, but their narcissism and superior air reveals that they serve someone other than God. They only masquerade as apostles in the same way that Satan masquerades as an angel of light."[28] What gives them away is their boastfulness. On that account one would expect them also to act deceitfully—to "disguise themselves." Nowhere in this text does Paul give them the benefit of the doubt with respect to their faith in Christ. On this I make two comments. In the first place, arrogance is a dead giveaway. For those who are called, as Paul, to protect the flock of God, it is important to evaluate what one sees before trying to assess what one cannot see. If what is seen is arrogance, it is likely that what cannot be seen—behind the mask—is a savage wolf (Acts 20:28–30). The second comment is this. Do not be surprised when they show up at your door. They will come. Just be prepared when they do. They will also be known by their fruit (Matt. 7:20).

Since their works show them to be the emissaries of Satan, their "end shall be according to their deeds" (v. 15). They are not only the enemies of Paul's ministry, but they are enemies of God. We are reminded of Paul's confrontation with the magician in Acts 13:7–11. When Paul (as Saul) was attempting to share the gospel with Sergius Paulus, the proconsul, Elymas the magician repeatedly interfered. Paul, "filled with the Holy Spirit, fixed his gaze upon him, and said, 'You who are full of all deceit and fraud, you son of the devil, you enemy of all righteousness, will you not cease to make crooked the straight ways of the Lord?'" With that he cursed him with blindness. Paul was hardly given to cowardice. Here, too, he makes clear that these imposters who have attempted to interfere with the work of God are likewise subject to the severest judgment. "Any minister who passes darkness off as light, lies as truth, or sin as an alternative lifestyle must reckon with God's judgment. He argues that these nameless rivals are aligned with the forces of evil, are thoroughly evil themselves, and therefore should be expelled from the community. Their end will be destruction (see Rom. 3:8; Phil. 3:19), and the same will hold true for any who fall sway to them."[29]

## Study Questions

1. Compare and contrast Paul's behavior in "playing the fool" with Proverbs 26:4–5. Does he violate or follow the advice of the ancient sage? Why does he do this in the first place?

2. Discuss the "betrothal" idea in verses 2–3. How is this concept misunderstood and misused in the church today?

3. Were Paul's enemies unbelievers or just misguided believers? What evidence is found in this chapter to help answer this question?

4. What is the identifying characteristic of false teachers highlighted in this chapter?

5. Who are the "eminent apostles" referenced in verse 5? Do you agree with the assessment of Tasker? Explain.

# CHAPTER 16

# Playing the Fool for Jesus' Sake
# 2 Corinthians 11:16-12:21

### Preview:

*As a jester, Paul continues now with his foolish speech. In what can only be understood as a parody of himself as an apostle of Christ, he spoofs his enemies in their conceits and brags on that which marks him out as a true apostle. The one who would follow a man who died on a cross is going to be characterized by affliction, pain, persecution, weakness, and an entire catalog of sorrows. Paul can "boast" of these. But his enemies have none to declare in their boasting. Paul exposes them to be the impostors they really are. The true signs of an apostle are not signs, but suffering. Paul concludes with the explanation that he made himself a fool, not to make fools of them, but because he loves them and takes responsibility for their spiritual welfare.*

Paul continues now with his fool's speech. Verse 16 begins the speech proper. The length of attention given to getting ready for this is another indication of how distasteful the enterprise is to him. His enemies have apparently made such outrageous claims about themselves—contra Paul—that he is forced to speak. "From Paul's response to those claims, one may infer that the rival apostles (1) took special pride in their Jewish heritage, (2) pointed to various specific accomplishments as evidence that they were Christ's true ministers, and (3) boasted of being the recipients of extraordinary visions and revelations."[1] Paul will respond in turn to each of these claims with examples of his own.

# The Proof of His Boast (11:16–33)

"Again . . . receive me even as foolish" (v. 16). Hering suggests, "accept me as though I am mad" is the better sense.[2] Although it runs cross-grain to every fiber of Paul's being, the spiritual welfare of this congregation requires drastic measures. Thus, it has become necessary to "boast a little" (v. 16). In doing this, he again is quick to qualify himself. "I am not speaking as the Lord would" (v. 17). Paul has reached the limits of his patience. What Paul is about to do is out of character—with his mission from the Lord, with the example of Christ, and with his apostolic and prophetic office. So why does he do it? He answers, "but as in foolishness, in this confidence of boasting." You have driven me to it! See what you have done to me! Growing up in a household with six siblings (five boys) gave new meaning to the term *chaos*. We often heard Mom, well beyond the end of her rope, declare, "You are going to drive me insane if you do not stop your bickering!" Unless we worked things out, ordinarily that meant we would likely be subjected to an event measurable on the Richter scale!

The use of *hupostasei* is unusual. As in our text, it is ordinarily translated "confidence," giving the idea that his attitude of confidence is proof of his madness. However, "there is good reason to take the basic sense as imposed by etymology: *'upostasis'* is a 'sup-position' or 'hypo-thesis', the *supposition* is that Paul is really boasting, thanks to a fit of madness (cf. 9:5 for this sense of *'hupostasis'*)."[3] Again, he still has on his fool's mask. In this character, with tongue firmly fixed in cheek, he continues.

"Since many boast according to the flesh" (v. 18; literally "since many glory after fleshly standards"), "I will boast also" (v. 18). If the Corinthians wish to qualify Paul on strictly human standards, he will give them a *curriculum vitae*. It will be unlike any they have seen. Paul has a hard time assuming the character of a fool. He presses on, but the irony fairly drips from his pen. You "bear with the foolish gladly" (v. 19). "Since you so readily receive fools, I shall attempt to qualify myself as one." "Being so wise" (v. 19; cf. 1 Cor. 4:8). This trait seems to be characteristic of their brand of wisdom. Their faulty sense of values has created a warped sense of discrimination. "You bear with" (v. 19), he says, strange and abusive people. "You bear with anyone if he enslaves you, if he devours you, if he takes advantage of you, if he exalts himself, if he hits you in the face" (v. 20; cf. Gal. 1:7; 1 Pet. 5:3). In this strange turn of events, these believers had forsaken their own loving father in the faith and had subjected themselves to spiritual tyrants who were self-seeking and destructive of true spirituality.

Sadly, even after Paul had resolved this problem at Corinth, throughout its history the church has again and again had to rescue saints who have fallen prey to such people. A few years ago, Stephen Arterburn and Jack Felton, in their book *Toxic Faith* documented this phenomenon in contemporary Christianity. Charlatan preachers feed off the flotsam and jetsam of performance-based religion to appeal to the craving for pain-free living, or naiveté and brokenness, to support "ministries" characterized by power, abuse, and what can only be termed, religious addiction.[4]

"To my shame I must say" (v. 21; literally "by way of disparagement") "we have been weak by comparison" (v. 21). Strangely, their tolerance had not been extended to the apostle. "But in whatever respect anyone else is bold (I speak in foolishness), I am just as bold myself" (v. 21). While in reality it amounts to nothing if one wishes to discuss personal qualifications, Paul will advance his own. Here Paul boasts about his nationality. In referencing his ethnic credentials, the language again supports our understanding that Paul's enemies were primarily Jewish. "Are they Hebrews? So am I. Are they Israelites? So am I. Are they descendants of Abraham? So am I" (v. 22). The adjective *Hebraios* in the sense of "full-blooded" is used in the New Testament only here and in Philippians 3:5; cf. Acts 6:1.

Then Paul boasts of the cost of his commitment to Christ. "Are they servants of Christ? (I speak as if insane)" (v. 23). Furnish translates the participle *paraphronōn*, "I must be out of my mind to talk this way."[5] The expression is hypothetical. If they are ministers of Christ as they claim to be, then "I more so" (v. 23). Discipleship cannot be purchased at bargain prices (Luke 9:23). The cost exacted of the apostle Paul is measured by the tabulation that follows. "labors," "imprisonments," "beatings," and "deaths" are all given in the plural in the original text. They bespeak a lifestyle more than occasional events.

"Often in danger of death" (v. 23; literally "in many deaths"). This is tantamount to saying, "I die daily" (1 Cor. 15:31). Hering suggests "mortal dangers."[6] Paul's point is transparent. He never knew if today would be his last on earth. "Thirty-nine lashes" (v. 24). Deuteronomy 25:3 forbids the Jews to inflict more than forty stripes on an offender. Scrupulous in their observance of the Law of Moses, they were in the habit of giving no more than thirty-nine (so as not to go over the limit of the law). He goes on to elaborate further. "Once I was stoned" (v. 25; cf. Acts 14:19). "Three times I was shipwrecked, a night and a day I have spent in the deep" (v. 25). Since Paul penned this letter long before the shipwreck recorded in Acts 27, it must be reckoned that the incidents of which he speaks find their mention in Scripture only here. There are numerous occasions recorded in Acts 13:1–20:5 when Paul likely traveled by sea. Since Luke, the author of the book of Acts, did not accompany him much of that time (apparently only in Acts 16:10–17), it is not surprising that some of the details have been omitted from his account. Furnish offers the following helpful summary of possibilities.

> Acts reports no experiences of shipwreck endured by Paul up to this point in his ministry (that of Acts 27 is later), but the apostle was frequently on the sea: Acts 13:4 (from Seleucia to Cyprus), 13 (Paphos to Perga); 14:25–26 (Attalia to Antioch); 16:11 (Troas to Neapolis via Samothrace); 17:14–15 (Macedonia to Athens); 18:18–22 (Corinth to Caesarea via Ephesus), 27 (Ephesus to Achaia [probably Corinth]). To these one may add the emergency visit Paul had made to Corinth from Ephesus (2 Cor. 2:1) . . . and probably his journey from Troas to Macedonia in order to meet Titus (2 Cor. 2:13; 7:5).[7]

Travel by sea was at best perilous, and most people took their lives in their hands when they set sail. There were no lifeboats, and the small barks on which they sailed were ill-equipped for dangerous storms that frequented the high seas.

"Dangers from rivers" (v. 26; literally "perils of rivers"). Along the roads traversed by Paul there were numerous rivers that seasonally swell with floodwaters, and which to this day are legendary for the perils they pose for the traveler. This is especially so along the Alpine district and the road extending through Lebanon from Jerusalem to Antioch. "Dangers from robbers" (v. 26). The area from Perga to Antioch in Pisidia was especially known for this (Acts 13:14). "Dangers from the Gentiles" (v. 26). Halfway through the list of Paul's perils from "outside," he includes his enemies at Corinth. What is implied by this is explicitly stated in 11:13. "Often without food" (v. 27). The context does not view this as a ritualistic observance practiced by the Pharisees. Rather, it is an "involuntary abstinence." While it is admitted that *nesteia* is ordinarily used of ritualistic fastings (cf. Luke 2:37; Acts 14:23), it is unlikely that such is the sense here. From its connection with "hunger and thirst" (v. 27), a touch of irony is suspected. No doubt Paul's Jewish adversaries at Corinth made a practice of ritualistic fasting and took pride in it. On the other hand, Paul fasted because the pressures of a faithful ministry required it of him.

"Apart from such external things" (v. 28; literally "not to mention those things which are besides"). Paul could go on to enumerate the things that came upon him "daily" (v. 28) in the "concern for all the churches" (v. 28), but he declines. Instead, he chooses to boast, not in his ability to endure hardness, but in his weakness. "Who is weak without my being weak?" (v. 29; cf. 1 Cor. 9:22). "Who is led into sin without my intense concern?" (v. 29; literally "who is caused to stumble, and I am not indignant?"). The apostle was deeply concerned about the weaker believers, and he "burned" with indignation when he thought of those who would lead them astray. On the relation of his weakness to the evidences of God's strength, see also 12:10; 13:9; 1 Corinthians 4:10.

"The God and Father of the Lord Jesus, He who is blessed forever, knows that I am not lying" (v. 31; for similar language see 11:10; Rom. 11:1; Gal. 1:20; 1 Tim. 2:7). It is not certain whether this is intended to underscore what he has reported above or to introduce what follows—or both. Perhaps he is pausing to review in his mind where he is going with all this. Perhaps he wants the reader to know that despite the "fools mask" he wears, at this point he is speaking the truth. At any rate, in pausing to catch his breath, he thinks of how this all began. From his calling on the road to Damascus to the present he has lived the life of a fugitive.

"In Damascus the ethnarch under Aretas the king was guarding the city of the Damascenes in order to seize me, and I was let down in a basket through a window in the wall, and so escaped his hands" (vv. 32–33). What he says is in essential agreement with Acts 9:22–25. The difference is relating to who, in fact, instigated the attempt on his life. Luke reports that it was the Jews who sought to "do away with him." Here he says that it was the Nabatean king who tried to "seize" him. I see no reason why the two accounts cannot be reconciled. In the case of the Jews, their intent was to *analein* "destroy," "put him to death." Here Paul indicates that Eretas the king was intent on "arresting me" (*piasai me*). Some imagine that it was his Jewish enemies who put the king up to making the arrest so that they, in turn, could get their hands on him, although, as noted below, this is not the only possible way to reconcile the two accounts. The identity of the king in question is likely the Arabian Eretas IV, who reigned in the area east of Palestine from the Euphrates to the Red Sea, throughout most of the period from 9 BC—AD 39, a span of nearly a half century.

It is worth noting that Eretas IV lived throughout the period of the life and times of Jesus Christ. And he was only a short distance away from the momentous events that occurred during this historic time. Naylor summarizes from Josephus the following account.

> Aretas was father-in-law to Herod Antipas, called by Jesus "that fox" (Luke 13:31–32), and the ablest son of his father Herod the Great. In AD 23 Antipas became infatuated with Herodias, wife of his half-brother Herod Philip, and to marry her he divorced his own wife, the daughter of Aretas, the incestuous union leading to the death of John the Baptist. Angered by his daughter's humiliation, Aretas went to war against Antipas and inflicted a severe defeat on him in AD 32. Herod then appealed to Caesar

Tiberius, who commanded Vitellius, governor of Syria, to march against Aretas and bring him to Rome dead or alive. Tiberius died before this could be accomplished (AD 37), and the campaign was called off.[8]

Because no Roman coins from this time period have been found, it "is thought that in AD 34 Aretas recaptured Damascus, a town which had already been taken by one of his predecessors, but which had fallen into Roman hands in 63 BC. So Paul's flight could be placed between AD 34 and 39. If the visit to Damascus in question is the one following his conversion, a date as close as possible to AD 34 must obviously be chosen."[9] Hering also calls attention to Galatians 1:17 where Paul mentions a second visit to Damascus followed by a period of unspecified length in Arabia.[10] This latter point would at least open the unlikely possibility of two separate events—one recorded by Luke and another by Paul. Nevertheless, if Paul entered the city during this tumultuous time, one can imagine more than one scenario in which he might have been wanted by either his former Jewish allies or the king. He originally set out on his way to the city as their Jewish *Goliath*, but he left as a Christian *David*. We can be sure that the Jews were painfully aware of Paul's conversion. We cannot know with any certainty how much the king knew or even if his desire to bring in this "person of interest" was due to his former association with the Jewish community or that of the new breakaway movement—about which the king likely knew very little.

"Through a window in the wall" translates *dia tou teichous*, "through the wall." Our translation probably has the sense correctly, as it cannot mean "over" the wall.[11] The incident recalls Joshua 2:15 in the daring effort of Rahab on behalf of Joshua's spies. First Samuel 19:12 records another similar escape by David from Saul. In walled cities where, for security reasons, there were limited ingress and egress options, such an exit, ignominious as it was, reflects the outlaw status to which the writer had been reduced almost from the very inception of his confession of Christ.[12] Why Paul does not continue at this point to pursue this discussion we do not know. Perhaps he was interrupted or distracted. At any rate, this is all he says of this, and when he begins chapter 12, his mind is clearly elsewhere.

## The Consequences of His Boast (12:1–10)

This passage turns on the concept of "glory" (*kauchaomai*, "boast"). Paul's adversaries were boasting after the flesh (11:18). His boasting is of another sort. One almost senses an attitude of frustration here. He has entered into something especially obnoxious to him—boasting of himself. In the previous chapter, his focus was on earthly, physical experiences. Yet there is something even more important—something he had hoped he could avoid. Nevertheless, two factors converge to force him to speak. The first is the contempt of Paul's adversaries for his personal appearance and delivery (10:10; 1 Cor. 2:1–4). The second is that the nature of Paul's boasting in chapter 11 requires explanation. Left as it is, one might suspect that he derived a perverted pleasure from physical suffering.

As to the first criticism, Paul will stop their mouths forever. As to the second, he will demonstrate that his attitude was fully justified in consequence of his unparalleled spiritual privilege. Some suspect that Paul is still engaged in fool's speech. The text is understood as a parody of sorts. He has a vision he cannot talk about and an illness God cannot or will not heal.[13] Harris suggests rightly that Paul can argue as he does on the basis of fact, just as well as fiction. The change in style further supports this.[14] Beyond this he explicitly asserts, "For if I do wish to boast *I shall not be foolish*, for I shall be speaking the truth" (v. 6, emphasis mine). There is a "raw force"[15] to the passage that is lost when interpreted as an extended parody. We take these events then to refer to real events that have occurred in Paul's experience of God and which he had hoped he would never be required to discuss.

The experience of God in private devotion is often characterized by personal intimacy. Much as the private times shared with a spouse, it is the sort of thing we, like Mary, ponder in our hearts rather than put on open display. Often one's prayer time can be more a time of silent adoration than spiritual chatter. Peter comes to mind on this latter point (Matt. 17:4–6). Does not the Lord's rebuke of him sound familiar to all of us? Sometimes the Scriptures can be a catalyst to contemplate the Lord, or to boldly "state our case" if we are especially anxious about something. But there are many times when we, with Brother Lawrence, "practice the presence of God" either in the quietness of the hour or the busyness of the day. We come to "know" God in His dynamic presence. These private moments are always special but in most cases "unspeakable." We see the reality of God's presence in the eyes of the aged saint who because of physical infirmity is called to be a "prayer warrior." When the pastor visits to bring comfort, he comes away renewed and fortified by the power of God's presence radiating from this dear saint who has been blessed to be in God's presence for extended periods of time. While she cannot begin to voice what she has come to know in the school of prayer, like Moses (2 Cor. 3:7–11), her countenance radiates that she has "been with Jesus" (Acts 4:13).

We would be shocked if such a one began to "boast" of her heightened spirituality. Yet in Paul's case this is precisely what he has been driven to. "Boasting is necessary, though it is not profitable" (12:1). What Paul does he is forced to do, but from his perspective, it is embarrassing and distasteful. "I will go on to visions and revelations" (v. 1). The connection is with "infirmities" of 11:30. How is it that Paul takes pleasure in his infirmities? The answer is that they constitute a reminder of something that, no doubt, stands out as the most extraordinary experience of his life. "Of the Lord" (v. 1). Paul is speaking of visions of which the Lord is the Author, not the object. He may very well have seen the Lord at this time, although if he did, he does not say. However, what follows is not intended to give attention to the one who received the vision, but God who gave it.

"I know" (v. 2; *oida*, "know") "a man in Christ" (v. 2; i.e., "a Christian"; cf. Rom. 16:7). "Fourteen years ago" (v. 2) connects with "know" not "in Christ" (v. 2). The time reference does not inform us about how long he has been "in Christ," that is, how long he has been saved. Rather, it points to the time of this unique experience. The date is not precise enough to pinpoint the exact time or event to which he alludes. Some suggest that this occurred when he was stoned in Acts 14:19. Others date it to the time when he was at Tarsus, waiting for the Lord to point out his work, somewhere between Acts 9:30 and 11:25.[16] "Whether in the body I do not know, or out of the body I do not know, God knows" (v. 3). This does not connect with "vision" but "man." It is not that he is unsure as to whether it was a dream or a vision (internal or external) but uncertainty as to whether he was in a bodily or disembodied state. This is especially interesting given the next comment: "such a man was caught up" (v. 2; *harpazō*, "to snatch away"). Luke uses this term in regard to Philip in Acts 8:39, and Paul has already used it to speak of the Rapture in 1 Thessalonians 4:17. John uses it to speak of the ascension of Christ (Rev. 12:5). Inasmuch as he has already used this term to speak of the common experience of believers occurring at the coming of Christ for the saints, it is not inappropriate to speculate if Paul came at this time to understand this "mystery," as he calls it in 1 Corinthians 15:51. He frequently mentions things that were *revealed* to him or that are *mysteries*— often in connection with the ultimate transformation and translation of the saints into the presence of Christ. Just as frequently he also relates these truths to the uniqueness of the body of Christ as composed of both Jews and Gentiles. Perhaps the experience about which he speaks includes more than a revelation of God's glorious presence, but also a time when God revealed truth to him regarding the uniqueness of the church and the church age (cf. Rom. 11:25; 16:25; 1 Cor. 2:10–11; 4:1; Eph. 3:3–10; Col. 1:24–27; see also Rev. 3:20).

He was taken, he reports, "to the third heaven" (v. 2). The exact sense of this expression is not clear. Later rabbis were accustomed to dividing the heavens into seven strata. However, it is not certain if this notion dates back to the apostolic age. In any case, if this were the sense, it would indicate an assumption only to the area of the clouds. Some who take this view see the reference to "paradise" in the next verse to be yet a further assumption. Other commentaries suggest that a threefold division was often employed among the Jews: the air (Lat., *nubiferum*), the sky (Lat., *astriferum*), and heaven (Lat., *angeliferum*). However, there is no evidence that ancient sources reflect a consensus on the point. Some held to four heavens. Many Jewish and Christians writers spoke of seven heavens. The Gnostics spoke of ten heavens.[17] Thus, the best that can be offered is that Paul's precise meaning cannot be established with absolute certainty. At any rate what follows makes the question merely academic.

He "was caught up into paradise" (v. 4). This term is used in the Septuagint in Genesis 2:8 in describing the Garden of Eden. In Paul's day "Paradise" was used commonly by Jewish writers to speak of heaven (Luke 23:43; Rev. 2:7). Thus, whether the "third heaven" (v. 2) is viewed on the way to heaven or synonymous with it, Paul's celestial journey eventually took him to heaven. "And heard inexpressible words" (v. 4). Not words that "could" not be uttered, but which "may" not be uttered. As Paul renders it "a man is not permitted to speak" (v. 4). Paul was forbidden to communicate what he saw and heard to anyone. See comment above on verse 2. If this is taken to mean that he was forbidden to speak of *everything* that happened, he would be violating that injunction by writing this chapter. We take this to mean, that among the things he saw and heard, there were things that were both inexpressible and forbidden to be communicated upon his return.[18]

"On behalf of such a man" (v. 5; *huper tou toioutou*, "regarding such a one"). Again, the direction of Paul's boast is not toward himself but in regard to the experience the Lord afforded him. "I will boast" (v. 5). Such divine favor and privilege justifies his response. "On my own behalf I will not boast, except in regard to my weaknesses" (v. 5). Paul is careful to keep the attention of his readers on the true object of his boast.

"For if I do wish to boast" (v. 6). The connection is more with what is implied in the preceding verse than in what is stated. The inference is that, in the flesh, Paul had a natural inclination to want to exalt himself because of this privilege—as though he warranted God's favor in some way. Paul will boast, but not in an empty claim. "For I shall be speaking the truth; but I refrain from this" (v. 6). What Paul says is absolutely true, yet even now he is reluctant to share it with his readers, "that no one may credit me with more than he sees in me" (v. 6). Paul does not even wish to share this glory vicariously. His only interest is to exalt the Lord.

What follows explains Paul's attitude, "because of the surpassing greatness of the revelations, for this reason, to keep me from exalting myself" (v. 7; literally "in order that I might not, by the abundant excess of the revelation, be uplifted"). "There was given me a thorn in the flesh" (v. 7; *skolops*, "a stake or pole with a sharp pointed end, "thorn," "splinter"; cf. Gal. 4:13–14; cf. also Num. 33:55 where the Septuagint uses this term to describe the inhabitants of Canaan who would become "pricks in your eyes and . . . thorns in your sides"; cf. Ezek. 28:24). The use of the dative here should be understood in the locative sense as this translation has it. This then would support the meaning that the pain experienced by Paul is more akin to a splinter in the foot than the torture of impalement on a stake.[19] If the Septuagint readings have inspired this metaphor, it is also interesting that Paul modifies it. A thorn in the eye would cause blindness. An arrow in the side would bring death. A thorn in the side, however, would only bring a nagging debilitating irritation and pain. This painful experience is also "a messenger of Satan" (v. 7). As such Paul does not identify its source as much as its agent. It is a persistent problem allowed by God and used by Satan, as he did Job, to discourage Paul and to break him down.

Just what Paul means by this "thorn" has provoked no small debate. Harris observes wryly, "Although Paul has not identified the 'thorn,' commentators have not been slow to attempt the impossible. Paucity of data and the ambiguity of Paul's language have frustrated—and will always frustrate—all efforts to reach finality."[20] Perhaps Naylor is right that "ignorance is bliss because, as with the undefined afflictions of many psalm-writers, Christians who suffer can identify with the apostle in his over-arching personal weakness."[21] The views suggested are so varied that it is easier to classify them than to list them. These include (1) temptations from the Devil, (2) Paul's opposition from his adversaries, (3) an intense bodily pain or recurring physical affliction, such as eye trouble, migraines, malaria, or (4) some form of spiritual or psychological distress.[22]

What is known of it is that it was given in consequence of the magnitude of his revelations from God (v. 7), it was painful enough for him to seek its removal (vv. 7–8), it was given by God (v. 7), it was a tool of Satan (v. 7), it was permanent (vv. 7–9), it was intended to keep him humble (v. 7), it was a source of shame and/or embarrassment to the apostle (v. 7), and it was at once a source of great weakness and strength (vv. 9–10).[23] A fairly strong circumstantial argument can be sustained in favor of the view that it was eye trouble (see Acts 13:9; 23:1; Gal. 4:13–15; 6:11). However, as Alford has observed, "it may also have been something else besides this, and to such an inference, probability would lead us; disorders in the eyes, however sad in their consequences, not being usually of a very painful or distressing nature in themselves"[24] Tasker agrees and argues that it "must be acknowledged that the general impression of Paul that the reader obtains from his Epistles, not least from 2 Corinthians, and from Acts, is of a man with an exceptionally strong constitution and remarkable powers of physical endurance. This is not really compatible with the view that he was the constant victim of a physical ailment."[25] On this basis he argues for the view more common in the Reformers and older patristic interpretations that the "thorn" was of a spiritual nature. He follows Chrysostom and others that perhaps it had more to do with people such as Alexander the coppersmith (2 Tim. 4:14), Hymenaeus and Philetus (2 Tim. 2:17),[26] and all others—including the pseudo-apostles who are engaged in yet another piece of the Devil's business in Corinth to humiliate Paul and to cause him pain—to which he gives ample testimony throughout this letter. Nonetheless, we agree with those who caution the reader to unwarranted dogmatism on this question.

So troublesome was this affliction that Paul "entreated the Lord three times that it might depart" (v. 8). Subsequent to Paul's third request, God gives him an answer: "No." "My grace is sufficient for you, for power is perfected in weakness" (v. 9). The trial must remain but would be accompanied always by the enduring grace of God. The principle is a timeless one. It marks God's relationship to humankind from the beginning. He creates *ex nihilo*, "from nothing." He waits until Abraham and Sarah are not only old, but *too old* to bear children, and then *ex nihilo* gives them Isaac. From servitude and ignominy He creates *ex nihilo* a nation to be His elect. "The Almighty will brook no rival, and if and when he deigns to employ men as his instruments it is because they accept that they are weak, possessing all the durability and strength of a fading flower."[27]

Thus, for Paul this and every affliction reminded him "that the power of Christ may dwell in [him]" (v. 9). Paul concludes that this is the reason I have such an attitude—i.e., "I am well content with weaknesses, with insults, with distresses, with persecutions, with difficulties" (v. 10). Not that I should suffer, but "for Christ's sake" (v. 10). What Paul had discovered was that when he suffered for the sake of Christ there was a kind of divine alchemy. As he says, "for when I am weak, then I am strong" (v. 10). Paul concludes that he has "become foolish" (v. 11), stopping the mouths of his adversaries and establishing once and for all his right to speak as he does.

The lesson of Paul's life experience falls today on deaf ears. In a materialistic age, the idea that there are things of value beyond our "stuff," seems incomprehensible to most. Consequently, we *devalue* that which costs us little and *value* that which exacts the greatest price. But in spiritual matters this means we lose the best to gain the least. Perhaps this is why we think of heaven as having been paved with gold. The metal we prize the most here will be little more than paving bricks there. This is especially true when testing the *metal* of a person's character. Not all that glitters is gold. Not all who present themselves as "eminent apostles" will prove in the end to be the real thing.

## The Credentials of the Apostle (12:11–18)

Paul has at length concluded a task that has been manifestly repugnant to him. He now goes on to review his credentials as an apostle and to demonstrate why this "fool's speech" need never to have been given—especially to his own children in the faith. This he discusses in terms of his position as their spiritual father (v. 11), his performance against great adversity (vv. 12–14), and his integrity as seen in his actions (vv. 15–18).

"I have become foolish" (v. 11, "I have played the fool"). We can almost see his flush of embarrassment. "You yourselves compelled me" (v. 11; "you" is emphatic). The sincerity of Paul's affection for these people is measured by the pain he is willing to endure to secure theirs. "Actually I" (v. 11; also emphatic) "should have been commended by you" (v. 11). That these people whom Paul loved so much failed to take the initiative in defending him against his critics was painful to acknowledge. Barrett considers this a key verse in the letter for understanding the situation at Corinth and identifying specifically who his enemies were.[28] The Corinthian believers themselves are cited here for their silence—not their opposition to him. They said nothing when they should have spoken up for him.

With his fool's mask still affixed, he declares, "Actually I should have been commended by you, for in no respect was I inferior to the most eminent apostles, even though I am a nobody" (v. 11). Once again the comparison is with those who claim to be "superapostles" (not the Twelve). Paul has made such a spectacle of himself that, given their criteria of greatness, he should have been readily acknowledged by them. It is with irony that he declares, "I can't believe you would not have acknowledged my credentials!" But having said that, he then adds, "but I am a nobody." If Paul is a "nobody" and he comes behind none of these "eminent apostles," where then does that leave them? The obvious conclusion is something less than "nobody"! Those who received this letter must have been chagrined to receive such a rebuke. What insult, what disappointment, what grief they have brought upon him and themselves in their failure to acknowledge and respect their spiritual father. The price he paid to make his way to their city, together with the glorious outcomes experienced by them in their newfound faith, should have been sufficient. If it was a matter of "heart," there was only one who really passed the test—and he was not among the interlopers who came later.

"The signs of a true apostle were performed among you" (v. 12). The expression here is elliptical, suppressing a negative reaction; that is, signs, indeed, were truly demonstrated but apparently never recognized. First among the signs of a true apostle has already been noted, which is the manner in which they were exercised, "with all perseverance," Furnish translates, *en pasē hupomonē*, "with utmost endurance."[29] It was not out of self-interest that he performed these signs. Rather, it was against great odds, fierce persecution, and great personal limitations. In the expression "by signs and wonders and miracles," the translation in our text is supported by Furnish, who argues, "Here all three words stand in the dative case, expressing the means by which the apostolic signs had been exhibited in Corinth."[30] It is further noted that these same terms are listed together in Acts 2:22; 2 Thessalonians 2:9; and Hebrews 2:4. Romans 15:19 is given as an additional instance where *en* with the dative (*en dunamei pneumatos hagiō*) also seems to have this meaning.[31]

However, contra Furnish, the force of the argument is lost when one takes this as a dative of means. This sense is supported by Barrett, who explains:

> Miracles were no contradiction of the *theologia cruces* he proclaimed and practiced, since they were performed not in a context of triumphant success and prosperity, but in the midst of the distress and vilification he was obliged to endure. The miracle the Lord did not perform was that of removing the angel of Satan sent to buffet Paul. . . . But both sides of the picture are important and valid, and if the signs were performed in a context of endurance **my endurance was accompanied by** (these five words are not in the Greek but seem to be implied by the dative case in which the three nouns following stand) **signs and portents and mighty works**.[32]

The point of emphasis is Paul's "endurance," not the signs *per se*. As in the classic Dickens novel *Great Expectations*, the main character, Pip, despises the one person who loved him as a son, admired him the most, and was responsible for giving him a vast fortune. Only after great adversity does Pip later discover who his true benefactor was. Sadly, by that time it was too late to show his gratitude as he should. Here Paul appears as a vagabond in the eyes of the very ones upon whom—against great adversity—he has showered the signs and ministrations of his apostolic mission. Rather than give him the credit, by their silence they have become complicit in support of a cadre of false teachers whose intent is to undermine and destroy the effectiveness of their true benefactor—Paul.

Finally, Calvin reminds us that when we speak of "signs, wonders, and miracles," we are not talking about three different kinds of miraculous happenings. Rather, we are considering the supernatural work of God from three different angles. "Paul calls them *signs*, because they are not empty shows but are appointed for the instruction of mankind; *wonders*, because they ought, by their novelty, to arouse men and strike them with astonishment; and *mighty deeds*, because they are more signal tokens of divine power than what we behold in the ordinary course of nature."[33]

So the writer is still driving home the point made in the first eleven verses of this chapter. The credentials of those who follow the One who died on a cross are best noted in the sacrifices they continue to make—not necessarily the miracles. If and when they are blessed, as was Paul, to enjoy a special relationship with God through revelations or signs, God sees to it that there is a balance so they will not become proud. For Paul this was the "thorn" in his flesh. "Not withstanding the honour accorded to him by God, his affliction has abased him and possibly makes him look ridiculous. Obviously, as the patent object of divine chastisement, Paul cannot lord it over his fellows. Pinned to the ground, so to speak, he is in no position to lift himself up."[34] In fact, it is his being in this condition that marks him most indelibly as God's instrument. However, for the Corinthians, the true evidence of Paul's calling was lost to them. They were looking for the dramatic—a display of supernatural powers. Instead, he just insinuated himself into their city as a vagabond, and in retrospect they overlooked him as irrelevant.

Now the writer interrogates them in an effort to spur them to repentance for their ingratitude. "For in what respect were you treated as inferior to the rest of the churches . . . ?" (v. 13). In what respect do you find your church handicapped for not having been founded by one of the other apostles (cf. 1 Cor. 1:6-7)? If Paul was angry about where this has taken him in this chapter, he had every right to be. He has made a fool of himself in order to answer fools on their own terms. What did they expect? Was their only complaint that he did not send them a bill for services rendered? Was that it? Was it "that I myself did not become a burden to you?" (v. 13). Was his only fault that he did not demand an honorarium? Against such ingratitude Paul's irony deals a mortal blow. Then, as though the blade did not penetrate enough, he gives the knife an additional twist with the words "Forgive me this wrong!" (v. 13). Next time, perhaps, he will bill them for his hotel and time. Actually, no, he does not go this far. He will not appeal to the "dark side" and retaliate out of bitterness or hate. This would ultimately defeat his purpose.

In the remainder of the chapter, Paul is making plans for his upcoming visit to them, but he still has two concerns. He is worried that there are many who still have misunderstandings about *his behavior*, especially in regard to financial matters (vv. 14–18). His second concern has to do with persistent reports about *their behavior*, especially in regard to lifestyle issues that he has already addressed several times in these letters (vv. 19–21).

"Here for this third time I am ready to come to you, and I will not be a burden to you" (v. 14). *Idou*, "here," denotes a solemn announcement. Garland translates it with "Behold."[35] It formally begins his stated plans for the upcoming visit. It will be his third (on the chronology, cf. 13:1 and the introductions to both 1 and 2 Corinthians). He still expects nothing in terms of personal remuneration from them. "For I do not seek what is yours, but you" (v. 14). He wants neither their consent nor their wealth. He wants their hearts. "Paul wants his readers to know that it is the gift of their lives to Christ, not of their money to himself that he covets. Because his apostleship is devoted exclusively to building them up in Christ (note v. 19c; 10:8; 13:10), its legitimacy is demonstrated only as their obedience and faith are demonstrated (cf. 10:6; 12:20–21; 13:5, 7, 9b), not by his ability to extract material favors from them."[36]

This point is once again reinforced with Paul's allusion to his parental role in their spiritual development. We all know, he says, that "children are not responsible to save up for their parents" (v. 14). His point is that in the natural course of events, it is the parents' responsibility to look after the welfare of their children, not the other way around. Paul as the spiritual father sees himself as the responsible adult in this relationship. The Corinthian assembly is viewed as dependent children. His parental oversight compels him to protect and nurture this "family." Just as a father or mother will work long hours, sometimes multiple jobs for no other reason than to provide for their children at home, Paul declares, "I will most gladly spend and be expended" (v. 15). "The point is the same one he makes in Philippians 2:17, using different imagery (he is 'poured as a libation on the sacrificial offering of [the Philippians'] faith' [RSV]), and is consistent with his remark in 2 Corinthians 11:28–29 about the constant pressure he is under because of his 'anxiety for all the churches.'"[37] He considered himself utterly expendable in the interests of the Corinthian assembly. This must have been viewed in stark contrast with the hireling impostors in their midst.

Paul then asks a poignant question: "If I love you the more, am I to be loved the less?" (v.15). Despite his feigned naiveté, in the next verse we suspect that the writer drops his guard just a bit. One can almost see the pain in his eyes as he acknowledges, in his question, that despite his physical, spiritual, and emotional investment in them, they have treated him with disdain. Why indeed would they put him through this ordeal? Why would they remain silent when his character was being assassinated? Why are his motives being questioned now? Because he loves them (unconditionally, we might add, as only a parent loves), he cannot simply let it go.

Paul regains his composure and adds, "But be that as it may, I did not burden you" (v. 16; to paraphrase, "It must be admitted that I posed no financial burden upon your church."). An important distinction should be noted in this regard. Paul is not afraid to ask for money from this congregation. Chapters 8 and 9 were dedicated to just that end. What he refused to do was to ask for a "love offering" for *himself*. This he assiduously refused to do (1 Cor. 9:12, 15, 18; 2 Cor. 11:7 9; 12:13). His reasons for this policy are not clear since we know that he received support from other churches (especially those in the poverty-stricken outposts of Macedonia). So it is a mistake to draw from this an unwarranted inference that love offerings are, in principle, wrong. There was something about this particular situation that prompted him to do so. In retrospect, it is evident that this was a wise decision. Had he not done so, his enemies would have had further cause to question his motives. As it is they can only suggest that his actions in managing without their material help were a tacit insult to them. Such an *ad hominem* argument is presumptuous because it reflects on impure motives that they would have no reason to know.

Flashing his fool's mask one last time, Paul adds, "Nevertheless, crafty fellow that I am, I took you in by deceit" (v. 16). The comment is intended as irony. However, the words are likely taken from the mouths of his accusers. As to the reference to "deceit," Garland's insight is likely correct:

> Possibly, someone claimed that the collection was all a ruse by which Paul would have associates gather up the money and he would covertly skim a portion off the top without them being any the wiser and without incurring any social debt to them. It is also possible that no one has accused him of defrauding them at all and that Paul is making a preemptive strike, nipping any such conspiracy theories in the bud before they blossom and sow further seeds of discontent.[38]

To such rumors and innuendo he asks, "Certainly I have not taken advantage of you through any of those whom I have sent to you, have I?" The implied answer to the question is "no." Neither he nor Titus nor the other brother (v. 18; cf. 7:6–7, 13–15; 8:18–19, 22)[39] could be considered to be anything but scrupulously honest. No devious tactics could be seen in Paul or any of his companions. The two verbs *parakalesa* and *sunapesteila*, "I urged" and "sent," while both in the aorist, do not necessarily suggest a past event—that is, a visit from Titus and the brother about which we do not know. Rather, as many commentaries observe, they are to be taken as "epistolary aorists" to designate time in reference to the recipients of the letter—when in fact, they will have seen these men whom Paul will have sent. They can check things out for themselves if they wish to investigate them. The point is important to the unity of the book. Chapter 12 was not written before chapter 8. See comments on 2:1–3 and 7:8 concerning the previous letter that caused sorrow and regret. The comment here occurs in the section sometimes designated as the "sorrowful letter." Unless one speculates regarding a different visit by Titus (not this one), these chapters (chaps. 10–13) cannot be considered the letter about which Paul spoke earlier.

## Paul's Greatest Fears (12:19–21)

"All this time you have been thinking that we are defending ourselves to you" (v. 19). If they are under the delusion that the writer has gone through all of this only to submit to their judgment, he answers: "Actually, it is in the sight of God that we have been speaking in Christ" (v. 19). The apostle was not accountable to the Corinthians—only to God. As for them his consummate concern was their "upbuilding" (v. 19). It was not necessary for Paul to defend himself before anyone—much less qualify his apostolic authority. On the other hand, it was imperative that the Corinthian believers be brought back into line and into submission to their father in the faith.

While it is necessary to distinguish between Paul *qua* apostle and Paul *qua* pastor,[40] there is once again an important principle at stake in regard to both circumstances. As we have noted several times in our comments on this letter, in many churches there is the sense that the pastor serves at the discretion of the people—either as expressed directly by the congregation or indirectly through a board. In fact, such thinking arrogates to the people a position only God occupies. In a world of excessive individualism and franco-style democracy, many churches fail to recognize that ultimate authority derives from God. This includes "rights" that are inalienable only insofar as they are delegated by the Almighty. While Paul's apostolic authority (as delegated by God) is not to be confused with that of a contemporary pastor, it is nonetheless true that both assignments are delegated by God. When the people challenged his integrity, they also (whether inadvertently or not) challenged Paul's authority. He will answer their allegations and concerns. But he will never for one moment relinquish his ultimate obligation to God—nor should any pastor who has been wrongly accused by unscrupulous church members or community leaders. If the leader is God-called and Spirit-led and his life is unimpeachable, no power in heaven or earth may step between him and God's directives. Those who try do so to their own peril.

In the remaining two verses, Paul expresses two concerns. The first is relating to the state of the Corinthians' corporate church life (v. 20). The second is relating to the possibility that immoral behavior continues (v. 21). Barrett explains that the first list suggests "new sinners," that is, people who are following the opposition leaders cited so frequently in this letter. The second list is for "old sinners." These were the libertine "gnosis" referenced in 1 Corinthians 4:13.[41] "For I am afraid that perhaps when I come I may find you to be not what I wish and may be found by you to be not what you wish" (v. 20). His fear is that when he arrives in Corinth, he will discover, still neglected, all the same problems that he has been addressing in these two letters. In speaking as he does of himself, he is not so concerned that he will in some way fail to measure up to their expectations. Indeed, he has already made his point in that regard in the previous verse. Rather, he is saying that if he finds things in disarray when he comes, they will see a side of him that they will not like. The vices he enumerates in the first list are social evils, "strife, jealousy, angry tempers, disputes, slanders, gossip, arrogance, disturbances" (v. 20). These are similar to other lists in the New Testament, but given the manner in which the apostle has experienced some of this firsthand, it takes on more of a personal nuance here. He has been on the receiving end of nearly every one of these vices.

The second list is relating to the incidence of sexual behavior, "impurity, immorality and sensuality which they have practiced" (v. 21). This is the only time he brings this matter up in this epistle. The reader might have hoped that it would not be necessary, but apparently Paul has heard otherwise. He does not mention specifics, he just wants them to know that he is aware that there are some matters that need to be resolved. He is not necessarily referring here to sins practiced before people were saved. Upon their conversion it would have been understood that they had repented of these. See 1 Corinthians 6:9–11, especially verse 11, "And such were some of you, but you were washed, but you were sanctified, but you were justified in the name of the Lord Jesus Christ." "The theme[s] of gnosis, and that of sexual immorality, have dropped out of 2 Corinthians; new troubles, doctrinal and moral, have taken their place. Yet not entirely; Paul fears that when he revisits Corinth he may find both new sinners, who in accepting the intruding false apostles have fallen into strife, envy and so forth, and old sinners (*proēmartēkotōn*) of the Gnostic libertine kind, who have not repented of their fornication."[42]

"I am afraid that when I come again my God may humiliate me before you, and I may mourn over many of those who have sinned in the past and not repented" (v. 21). Paul has so poured out his heart on behalf of these people—to them in person and again in a letter. He has agonized before God for their souls. He has suffered at the hands of satanic forces without and sedition within. His heart's cry is that when he comes he will have nothing but rejoicing to share with them. But his great fear is that it won't go this way. God will humiliate him and he will "lose it" when he stands before them. His fear is related to his personal application of the principle stated in 1 Corinthians 3:10–15 together with the bema judgment in 2 Corinthians 5:10–11. The Corinthian church is Paul's work. It was he who laid the foundation. And he continues to accept responsibility for their spiritual health. He will answer before God for its success or failure. In his mind, if they fail, he also fails (see Rom. 14:12; cf. Heb. 13:17).

## Study Questions

1. Why is Paul so averse to discussing his "credentials"? Why is this "fool's mask" strategy more suited to the situation?

2. In contrast to his enemies at Corinth, what are the more convincing evidences in Paul's life that qualify him as a true follower and apostle of Jesus Christ?

3. How many times was Paul shipwrecked? Where are these documented? Explain.

4. Discuss "Aretas the king." Who was this person? Why is he important to the historical background to the New Testament? You may wish to utilize a Bible dictionary for this.

5. Is Paul's "vision" a parody or an account of a real event in his life? Explain the issue involved here. Why is this important to understanding this passage?

6. What is the meaning of "the third heaven?" You may wish to use a Bible dictionary for this.

7. What are some of the theories regarding Paul's "thorn"? What do you think this was? Suggest some ways Paul's attitude toward this is applicable to most believers even today.

8. What are the "signs of an apostle"? What is the theological significance of this reference?

9. Is it wrong to ask for "love offerings"? Why was it that Paul refused to ask for one when he was at Corinth? Did he ever do this? Where?

10. On the matter of "sexual" sins, does Paul still have concerns, or have they been resolved? Explain.

# CHAPTER 17

# Examine Yourselves
# 2 Corinthians 13:1–10

## Preview:

*As the great apostle Paul prepares for his impending visit to Corinth, he offers a final challenge in his letter for them to do some serious soul searching of their own relationship to Christ. Rather than questioning his credentials, what are their credentials that manifest that they are in the faith? If they answer correctly, they will also recognize who it was that introduced them to that faith in the first place. When Paul comes he is hopeful that all will be well.*

"This is the third time I am coming to you" (13:1; cf. 12:14). On the "third visit" see Acts 18:1; 2 Cor. 2:1; Acts 20:2–3; and the introduction. "To make it fit certain chronological theories, some have tried to interpret this phrase to mean 'the third time I have *planned* to come to you.' But the plain sense of the text is that Paul's next visit to Corinth will be his third, and his reference in the next verse to when he came was with them a second time confirms this reading."[1] "Every fact is to be confirmed by the testimony of two or three witnesses" (v. 1; cf. Num. 35:30; Deut. 17:6; 19:15; Matt. 18:16; John 8:17; 1 Tim. 5:19). Paul would leave no stone unturned upon his arrival. As he promised the last time he visited them, if he had to come again, he "will not spare" (v. 2). Should there be evidence of disobedience and sin in the assembly, Paul's authority as an apostle would be witnessed, not by "signs" but in the exercise of discipline. The reference to "two or three witnesses" is not intended as a metaphorical allusion to his previous visits or warnings. It is rather another repudiation of the vices listed in 12:20 and a declaration that when he comes there will be formal inquiries made and due process followed.

If there are disciplinary matters to adjudicate, he will do so, and it will be done decently and in order (cf. 1 Cor. 14:33). If formal action is warranted, it will not be based on gossip, slander, jealousy, or personal animosities. It will be according to the testimony of "two or three witnesses." We take this further (in keeping with the principle of Matthew 18) that this involves matters that are appropriate to be taken "before the church."

"Since you are seeking for proof of the Christ who speaks in me" (v. 3). They seek a proof that the apostle spoke with divine authority. "For indeed He was crucified because of weakness, yet He lives because of the power of God" (v. 4). Paul's experience was much like that of our Lord, not only in that "he came to his own, and those who were His own did not receive Him" (John 1:11). Christ also endured suffering and weakness, thereby demonstrating the power of God and the wisdom of God. Even so, the weakness of the apostle would serve as a catalyst to demonstrate "the power of God directed toward you" (v. 4). He turns the tables on them. They require proof from him. The proof is in the mirror.

Thus Paul charges his readers, "Test yourselves to see if you are in the faith; examine yourselves!" (v. 5). The pronoun here is in the emphatic position[2] (*eautous peirazete*). This places the emphasis on "yourselves," putting it first in the sentence. In effect, the writer "turns the tables"[3] on them. Paul's critics were prepared to examine *him*, to see if he was rightly related to Christ. He asks them to subject *themselves* to the same scrutiny. Determine if you are "in the faith." This is best understood in connection with 1 Corinthians 2:9 in terms of obedience. "Do you not recognize this about yourselves, that Jesus Christ is in you—unless indeed you fail the test?" (v. 5; "unless you are counterfeits"). Notice the play on the term *dokimēn*, "evidence," in verse 3 and *dokimos* and *adokimos*, "counterfeit," here in verse 5. The expression *ei mēti*, "unless indeed," used with "a verb in the indicative mood is used in conditional statements that are contrary to fact."[4] Paul is neither stating, nor implying, that there is a chance that these people had lost their salvation. He is asking them to test the reality of it. He has already expressed a sincere confidence that they are in the faith (1:24). "The rhetorical question here is therefore not only formally, but also materially and functionally parallel with the one in 1 Corinthians 3:16 about the indwelling presence of God's Spirit. In each case the intent is to secure the Corinthians' acknowledgment that they belong (as a community of faith, and individually) to Another, in whom they have their life and by whom their walk is to be guided. The interrogation, then, conveys an 'indicative' which incorporates an 'imperative.'"[5] "But I trust that you will realize that we ourselves do not fail the test" (v. 6). Regardless of how the Corinthians come out in the test, they are to be assured that the apostle is genuine.

These verses have been used by many (sometimes in conjunction with 1 Cor. 11:28) to teach that Christians should submit to regular examination of their salvation experience. Often this creates anxiety and ambivalence in the hearts of those who struggle with personal and/or habitual sin. Frequently this leads to multiple "salvation experiences" with sincere believers who are so led to doubt whether God really saved them the "first" time. John MacArthur Jr. is illustrative of those who argue this way.

> Doubts about one's salvation are not wrong so long as they are not nursed and allowed to become an obsession. Scripture encourages self-examination. Doubts must be confronted and dealt with honestly and biblically. In 2 Corinthians 13:5, Paul wrote, "Test yourselves to see if you are in the faith; examine yourselves! Or do you not recognize this about yourselves, that Jesus Christ is in you—unless indeed you fail the test?" That admonition is largely ignored—and often explained away—in the contemporary church.[6]

However, this fails to understand the import of Paul's challenge in its context. The "best arguments for his apostolic authority were the Corinthian believers who had been transformed by his ministry."[7] This includes, especially, those who were presently challenging him and expressing doubts about his apostolic credentials. Paul was not asking them to examine themselves with respect to their relationship to Christ in the strict sense. He was asking them to examine themselves in regard to their *shared* relationship with Christ. That is to say, "The proof they seek of Christ speaking in him (v. 3) they will find in their own saving relationship to Christ."[8] Brown adds:

> Might the Corinthians have found themselves disqualified if they examined themselves too closely? Not at all! Paul knew they were Christians, and the Corinthians knew it too. Why then did Paul make such probing remarks? He made them because of the absurdity of questioning his motives and authority in the first place. The Corinthians were Christians; there can be no doubt about it from the way Paul structured his remarks. His ministry had introduced them to Christ; there is no doubt about that either. So when the Corinthians looked at themselves and realized they were who they were because of God's power and authority working in Paul, then the apostle could close his argument by saying, "But I trust that you will realize that we ourselves [*hēmeis*, emphatic in Greek] do not fail the test" (v. 6). If the Corinthians considered themselves to be "in Christ" (and they did), it was pure foolishness to scrutinize the authority of the man who had introduced them to Christ! The Corinthian believers needed only to look in the mirror to find proof that Christ was working in Paul.[9]

At the end of the day, Paul did not appeal to his power, rhetorical skill, status, or the superiority of his ministry to that of someone else. His ultimate appeal was the fruit of his work in people who were now following the Lord and who were experiencing for themselves the power of His presence in their lives. While some may still question his authority as an apostle or the sincerity of his motives, they could never question the reality of Christ in their own experience. And, more to the point, it was Paul they had to thank for bringing the saving message of the gospel to them in the first place.

So to bring this to a conclusion, it is a mistake to use this text to teach that one may "believe," but to do so in such a faulty way that they are not truly saved—or worse, to suggest that one could be saved and then "cease to be a Christian."[10] It is also a mistake to use this text as others do to suggest that it should be used as a litmus test of the sanctifying work of the Holy Spirit. While this is used by the "free grace" proponents[11] in response to the Reformed position expressed in MacArthur and others, it really has the same theological edge on it that brings the questioning Arminian saint to a place of doubt and despair. Paul is teaching neither. He is simply saying to those who were challenging his own integrity that the proof of *his* ministry is in the reality of *their* own salvation—a work that only God can do and which he prays to God (v. 7) they will open their eyes to see for what it really is. If this is a "sobering reminder,"[12] it is not to the doubting believer, but to those who would stand in the pulpit and speak for God. The real evidence of the reality one preaches is in the results—in the lives of people who are transformed by His saving work. Paul has been saying this at least since 1 Corinthians 3 and repeated the argument again in 2 Corinthians 3.

"Now we pray to God that you do no wrong" (v. 7). He is not encouraging them to give occasion to show evidence of his authority through continued disobedience. When Paul says, "though we should appear unapproved" (v. 7), he means "even though it means you will still look on us as reprobates." It was more important that the Corinthian believers do that which was right in the eyes of God than that they should be provided with an opportunity to see the "evidence" of Paul's apostolic authority in terms of discipline. Indeed, such evidence would not be forthcoming, because "we can do nothing against the truth, but only for the truth" (v. 8). Hering notes that this maxim was "undoubtedly not framed *ad hoc.* . . . The apostle is not free to act against it because it is fixed by God."[13] Perhaps he inserts this here because he wants the Corinthians to understand that true apostles bow to the truth—they do not manage it, massage it, or violate it.

"For we rejoice" (v. 9). The confirmation of Paul's joy is that "when we ourselves are weak" and are afforded no opportunity to display apostolic authority through punishment, then "you are strong" (v. 9). By virtue of their spiritual maturity they do not need such a demonstration of his authority. "This we also pray for, that you be made complete" (v. 9). Their spiritual well-being was, of course, Paul's paramount interest.

The comment, "For this reason I am writing these things while absent, in order that when present I may not use severity" is taken by some (e.g., Furnish)[14] as an argument for one of the "partition theories." It is argued that this sums up the purpose for a separate letter constituting chapters 10–13. The arguments for this are less than convincing. It is asserted in the first place that this verse intends to summarize the contents of the entire epistle. On that basis, it is questioned why there is no reference to the contents of chapters 1–9. And furthermore, how could one imagine that he would neglect to remind them of the offering? The argument is patently circular. If we remove the original assumption that this verse is intended as a summary of the entire epistle, the argument falls like a house of cards.[15]

Paul communicates with the Corinthians in writing "while absent" so that when he comes in person he "may not use severity" (v. 10). His intent under the Lord is for "building up and not for tearing down" (v. 10). If in his absence they can be induced to obedience, so much the better.

## Study Questions

1. Discuss what is to be learned regarding church discipline in 1 and 2 Corinthians. What is especially noteworthy about this chapter in this regard?

2. What is the point of Paul's exhortation to "examine themselves"? How does this exhortation relate to his immediate defense of his own apostolic authority?

# CHAPTER 18

# Peace, the Gift of God's Love
# 2 Corinthians 13:11–14

## Preview:

*In Paul's farewell we once again see the warm side of the apostle as he turns his attention back to those "brethren" of the assembly who have manifested their support for him and their readiness to take up the challenges of obedience—both to Christ and to His chosen vessel, Paul. We may safely assume that these whom he greets at the close represent a majority in the church—certainly the leadership. The greeting is intended to initiate a process of reconciliation with the corporate members of this assembly and with the wider circle of believers throughout the region. Thus, as it began, the letter ends on a positive note.*

In the first nine chapters Paul addressed the majority of the faithful brethren in the Corinthian assembly. In 10:1–13:10 his words have been directed primarily to those who questioned his integrity. Paul is not even certain if these are true believers. In his farewell greetings he turns his attention once again to those who really love and appreciate him. Thus, he calls them "brethren" (v. 11). See the comments above on verse 10 regarding those who argue that these last four chapters constitute a separate letter from that in the first nine chapters. These closing verses, it is sometimes argued, belong to the closing of chapter 9 and do not belong here after the severe and sustained rebuke of the church in the immediate context. Plummer indicates that the change in tone is not unusual for Paul and is reflected elsewhere, for example, 2 Thessalonians 3:10–15 and 3:16–18.[1] I would add that the more amicable tone in these verses, understood properly as the closing of the book, in fact, functions to bookend the previous section. He began on a positive note in the first nine chapters. He inserted his challenge to his adversaries in chapters 10–13, and now in the closing verses he returns once again to end with a warm and positive greeting.

## Final Greeting

Paul exhorts his readers, "Rejoice, be made complete, be comforted, be like-minded, live in peace; and the God of love and peace shall be with you" (v. 11). In response to those who see no connection with the Corinthian situation, it is evident that the maturity, contentment, unity, and harmony, reflected in these terms, answer to the immaturity, unrest, division, and quarreling so evident in the Corinthian assembly.

The NASB text understands *chairete* correctly.[2] While the term was used commonly in the ancient world as a farewell greeting—that is, "Grace be with you," Paul frequently uses it in the sense given here: "Rejoice" (cf. v. 9 above; 1:24; 2:4; 1 Thess. 5:16). In an attempt to articulate the force of the idiomatic middle, Barrett translates *katartizesthe*, "be made complete," as "pull yourselves together." For *parakaleisthe*, "be comforted," "exhort," compare Hebrews 13:22. On *to auto phroneite*, "be of the same mind," see Romans 12:16; 15:5; Philippians 2:2; 4:2. On the term *eirēneuete*, "live in peace," see Romans 12:18; 1 Thessalonians 5:13; cf. Mark 9:50. The expression, *ho theos tēs agapēs*, "God of love," occurs only here in the New Testament. The expression, *ho theos tēs . . . eirēnes*, "God of peace," occurs frequently (Rom. 15:33; 16:20; 1 Cor. 14:33; Phil. 4:9; 1 Thess. 5:23). This final admonition and blessing echoes the command of the Lord in Luke 10:5–6; cf. Matt. 10:12–13.

## The Kiss

"Greet one another with a holy kiss" (v. 12; cf. Rom. 16:16; 1 Cor. 16:20; 1 Thess. 5:26; 1 Pet. 5:14). Many to this day practice the kiss as a casual greeting in Eastern as well as European cultures. It can also be observed in regions influenced by significant immigration, such as the ethic communities surrounding New York City. In most of the United States it is not commonplace.

With Garland it is important to note that "[a] kiss appears in the New Testament as a sign of respect and greeting (Luke 7:45), of love and reverence (Luke 7:38, 45), and of reconciliation and family fellowship (Luke 15:20). We find a parting kiss in Acts 20:37. But a '*holy* kiss' represents something more than a social custom. It is a sign of mutual fellowship among persons of mixed social background, nationality, race, and gender who are joined together as a new family in Christ."[3] In the church, master and slave greeted one another without partiality or discrimination. In ancient Greek custom, kissing the ground (in prostration) was a token of reverence and as such is associated with (pagan) worship. In the context of worship, there is evidence that the "holy kiss" was associated with the celebration of the Eucharist and in connection with the liturgy in the ancient church although it is not evident that it predates Justin.[4] Tertullian considered the kiss necessary to the completion of public prayer and was sensitive to the concerns of pagan husbands who did not appreciate that their wives might be kissing other men in public.[5] I agree with Hodge that the concern raised by Tertullian is especially applicable in a highly sexualized culture, such as our own, where what is "holy" could be construed or practiced in an unholy manner. It is better, in this matter, to consider other ways to demonstrate this spiritual, Christian reality in a public way, than to dutifully follow the letter to the detriment of one's soul or the testimony of Christ in the community.[6] In this instance it would seem that Paul is calling upon the assembly, after reading the letter, to then exchange a holy kiss. "In calling upon the Corinthians to exchange a holy kiss, Paul is reinforcing his exhortation to reconciliation, since the holy kiss was undoubtedly an expression of peace and reconciliation among those who exchange it."[7]

## All the Saints

"All the saints greet you" (v. 13; cf. Rom. 16:16; 1 Cor. 16:20). In some texts this phrase does not appear as a separate verse but forms the last clause of verse 12. This was "first introduced into the Greek and Latin texts by Robert Estienne (in 1551 and 1555 respectively), whereby this sentence is still part of verse 12. The renumbering to obtain fourteen verses, which is peculiar to the English version traditions, appears to have originated with the second folio edition of the so-called 'Bishop's Bible,' published in 1572, for the first edition of 1568 has the older division of 2 Corinthians 13 into thirteen verses."[8] This should be properly restricted to Paul's companions at the time. However, the more general truth also finds appropriate emphasis in the apostle. That is, all the saints everywhere enjoy a common fellowship and therefore a mutual interest in the spiritual welfare of one another. The term "saints" is equated with "brothers" and is understood to mean "Christians." It does not signify, as is sometimes taught, those who have predeceased, been elevated to heaven, who are now ruling and reigning with Christ, and performing miracles which have been attested by the careful examination of the church.

For Paul, sainthood was not an honorific title bestowed on the faithful, but a designation given to all those who are believers in Christ. It is a synonym for "believers" (see comments on 1:1; cf. also, Rom. 1:7; 8:27; 12:13;16:2, 15;

1 Cor. 1:2; 2 Cor. 1:1; Eph. 1:1; Phil. 1:1; Col. 1:2, 4; Philem. 1:5, 7). Perhaps, more importantly, this greeting indicates that the writer is identifying with the larger community of saints represented in all the churches (cf. Rom. 8:18; 11:28; 1 Cor. 7:17; 14:33). His travels included ministry throughout Galatia, Macedonia, and Asia. As he made his way south to eventually winter there in Corinth, we imagine Paul had faces of real people from Macedonia in mind. Though poor they were exemplary of those whose faith was unvarnished and evident in their actions. He recalls them fondly as he concludes his painful challenge to this wayward church. Harris is also likely correct when he says, "Paul is probably conveying to the Corinthians the hearty Christian greetings of the whole church as he knew it, thereby reminding them of a wider Christian community who had a vested interest in the healthiness of the church in Corinth. He was not alone in seeking their welfare, and there were others to whom they were accountable."[9]

## Benediction

"The grace of the Lord Jesus Christ, and the love of God, and the fellowship of the Holy Spirit, be with you all" (v. 14).

> This blessing is the most elaborate concluding blessing of the . . . Pauline letters, all of which employ the simpler form "the grace of the Lord Jesus Christ" (Rom. 16:20; 1 Cor. 16:23; Gal. 6:18; Phil. 4:23; 1 Thess. 5:28; Philem. 1:25). In this text, however, we have the only explicit reference to the Father and the Spirit, together with the Son in one Trinitarian formulation. "Without embarrassment Paul has conjoined the Lord Jesus Christ and the Holy Spirit with God in a benediction, just as God the Father and Christ are presented in 1:1 as forming a single source of divine grace and peace.[10]

> Several questions need to be resolved. The first is exegetical. The first two genitives ("of the Lord Jesus," "of God,") are generally agreed to be subjective. That is, they refer to the grace that comes from the Lord Jesus Christ and the love that comes from God. The third is disputed. Taken as a subjective genitive, the last one would refer to the "fellowship that comes from the Holy Spirit. Many such as Barrett argue that it is an objective genitive. This would have reference then to their mutual "participation in the Holy Spirit."[11] Matera suggests that perhaps the writer has both in view, "the fellowship whereby believers are united both with each other and the Holy Spirit."[12]

> Another question we confront is why Paul mentions Christ first in this triadic formula. Several suggestions have been offered, but the most satisfying is

that Paul understands Christ in this instance to be the "means by which God's love reaches the believer. . . . It was through the grace of Christ exhibited in the cross that God demonstrated his love (Rom. 5:8) and that believers came to participate in the Spirit's life and so form the community of the new age."[13] This, of course, understands all three genitives to be objective.[14]

Of further interest is the historical and theological significance of this verse. It has become "an integral part of the majority of liturgies of the Christian Church."[15] The reason for this is the high Christology reflected in the text. It is perhaps the final irony of this sometimes convoluted letter that after all the mundane and often contemptuous issues to which the writer has had to address himself, he concludes with one of the noblest christological benedictions found anywhere in the New Testament. Here, "the parity of status between Christ and God is implied by the juxtaposition, for it would be blasphemous for a monotheistic Jew to associate a mere mortal with God in a formal, religious salutation or benediction."[16] It would be a mistake, nevertheless, to imagine that this is the only place where Paul affirms his belief in the full deity of Christ. Harris offers the following summary of other passages in which his high Christology is evidenced.

> That Paul believed in the deity of Christ is also indicated by his description of Christ as sharing the divine nature (Rom. 9:5; Phil. 2:6; Tit. 3:13) and attributes (Eph. 4:10; Col. 1:19; 2:9), as being the object of saving faith (Rom. 10:8–13) and of human and angelic worship (Phil. 2:9–11), as being the addressee in petitionary prayer (1 Cor. 1:2; 16:22; 2 Cor. 12:8), and as exercising exclusively divine functions, such as creational agency (1 Cor. 8:6; Col. 1:16), the forgiveness of sins (Col. 3:13), and final judgment (1 Cor. 4:4–5; 2 Cor. 5:10; 2 Thess. 1:7–9).[17]

And so Paul invokes God's blessing upon all. Perhaps unintentionally, in so doing he induces what will become a historic liturgical tradition in the churches even as he finalizes his last known letter to this factious church. This fact in itself offers silent testimony to the success of his work. Had he been rebuffed, it is not likely his memory would have been ensconced in such a tradition.[18] We may well assume that they did indeed read the letter, kiss one another with a holy kiss, and celebrate the *koinōnia* of God's grace together. They also took up an offering and had it ready before Paul arrived. Of that we may be assured (see Rom. 15:26–27). Luke reports that Paul spent three months in Greece (Acts 20:2–3). We may reasonably assume much of this time was in the city of Corinth. The letter written to the Romans was likely written from here shortly before his departure for Jerusalem with the collection—including a significant contribution from these faithful and repentant saints.

## Study Questions

1.  How do you understand the change, once again, in the emotional tone of the letter? How do you answer those who suggest this is just another indication of a "composite" work?

2.  Explain how the terms used in the final greeting relate to the various issues confronted by the apostle throughout this letter and his previous one?

3.  Relate the "holy kiss" to worship practices in the ancient church. How was this misunderstood by pagans in the surrounding culture? Is this a problem in our own culture? Why?

4.  From a *theological* perspective, what is most significant about Paul's benediction? What is its *historical* significance? Why is this so ironic, given the nature of this letter?

5.  Who are "saints"? How is this term characteristically used in Pauline letters? You may wish to use a Bible dictionary or a concordance for this.

# Bibliography

Barrett, C. K. *The Second Epistle to the Corinthians*. Harpers New Testament Commentaries. New York: Harper and Row, 1973.

Erdman, C. R. *The Second Epistle of Paul to the Corinthians*. Philadelphia: Westminster, 1929.

Furnish, Victor. *II Corinthians*. The Anchor Bible. Vol. 32A. Garden City, NY: Doubleday, 1984.

Garland, David E. *2 Corinthians*. The New American Commentary. Vol. 29. Nashville: Broadman & Holman, 1999.

Harris, Murray J. *The Second Epistle to the Corinthians*. NIGTC. Grand Rapids: Eerdmans, 2005.

Hodge, C. *Commentary on the Second Epistle to the Corinthians*. Grand Rapids: Eerdmans, n.d.

Hughes, P. E. *Paul's Second Epistle to the Corinthians*. NICNT. Grand Rapids: Eerdmans, 1975.

Ironside, H. A. *Addresses on the Second Epistle to the Corinthians*. New York: Loizeaux, 1939.

Lenski, R. C. H. *The Interpretation of St. Paul's First and Second Epistle to the Corinthians*. Columbus, OH: Wartburg, 1946.

Morgan, G. C. *The Corinthian Letters of Paul*. Old Tappan, NJ: Revell, 1966.

Naylor, Peter. *2 Corinthians*. 2 vols. Darlington, Eng.: Evangelical, 2002.

Plummer, A. "The Second Epistle of St. Paul to the Corinthians." *International Critical Commentary*. Edinburgh: T. & T. Clark, 1915.

Strachan, R. H. "The Second Epistle of Paul to the Corinthians." *Moffatt Commentary*. London: Hodder and Stoughton, 1935.

Tasker, R. V. G. "The Second Epistle of Paul to the Corinthians." *Tyndale New Testament Commentaries*. Grand Rapids: Eerdmans, 1975.

# Notes

## Introduction: Background of 2 Corinthians

1.  See my introduction to the first epistle, *1 Corinthians: Christianity in a Hostile Culture* (Chattanooga, TN: AMG, 2004), 1–11.

2.  For further background on the city and its illustrious history, see David E. Garland, *2 Corinthians*, The New American Commentary, ed. E. Ray Clendenen (Nashville: Broadman and Holman, 1999); Victor Furnish, *II Corinthians*, The Anchor Bible, vol. 6 (Garden City, NY: Doubleday, 1984); Frank J. Matera, *II Corinthians: A Commentary*, The New Testament Library (Louisville: Westminster John Knox, 2003); Murray J. Harris, *The Second Epistle to the Corinthians*, NIGTC (Grand Rapids: Eerdmans, 2005). For the decline and rebirth of rhetorical approaches, particularly as they impact the interpretation and understanding of the Pauline corpus, see Anthony C. Thiselton, *The First Epistle to the Corinthians* (Grand Rapids: Eerdmans, 2000), 46–52. See also Ben Witherington III, *Conflict and Community in Corinth: A Socio-Rhetorical Commentary on 1 and 2 Corinthians* (Grand Rapids: Eerdmans, 1995); and G. W. Peterman's comments on the use and limitations of attempting to unpack Paul's rhetorical skill with his explicit rejection of the use of "eloquence and persuasive words (I Cor. 2:1, 4)" in "Conflict and Community," *Journal of the Evangelical Theological Society* 41 (March 1998): 146–47.

3.  Garland, *2 Corinthians*, 33.

4.  For more exhaustive discussion beyond the scope of this present study, see Harris, *Second Epistle to the Corinthians*, 1–114; Garland, *2 Corinthians*, 33–44; Furnish, *II Corinthians*, 27–57. Some texts compress this to 13 verses rather than 14, as in most English translations. See discussion on 13:12–13.

5.  Garland, *2 Corinthians*, 39.

6.    Ibid., see also Harold J. Ockenga, *The Comfort of God: Preaching in Second Corinthians* (New York: Revell, 1944), 51.

7.    See, e.g., Hans Dieter Betz, *2 Corinthians 8 and 9*, Hermeneia (Philadelphia: Fortress, 1985), and Furnish, *II Corinthians*, 290; Helmut Koester, *Introduction to the New Testament*, vol. 2 (Berlin: de Gruyter, 1987), 53–54; Steven L. Davies, *New Testament Fundamentals* (Sonoma, CA: Polebridge, 1994), 89. For a careful rebuttal of this thesis, see J. D. H. Amador, "Revisiting 2nd Corinthians: Rhetoric and the Case for Unity," *New Testament Studies* 46 (2000): 92–111.

8.    But see Furnish, *II Corinthians*, 290.

9.    Henry C. Thiessen, *Introduction to the New Testament* (Grand Rapids: Eerdmans, 1987), 210.

10.   I am using the term *apocalyptic* here in the sense of genre and imagery drawn from a worldview (common to New Testament biblical writers) in which natural and supernatural realities interface in present reality to bring about God's ultimate purpose.

11.   See, e.g., Edith M. Humphrey, "Ambivalent Apocalypse: Apocalyptic Rhetoric and Intertextuality in 2 Corinthians," *The Intertexture of Apocalyptic Discourse in the New Testament*, ed. Duane F. Watson, SBL-Symposium series, vol. 14 (Leiden, Netherlands: Brill Academic Publishing, 2002), 113–35, 243–63. While I cannot accept her approach to the book, it is evident that she has put her finger on a vital theme of the epistle. In the New Testament there is a "real" interface between God's purposes and intervention in human affairs. Many, such as Humphrey, attribute this to the use of the "apocalyptic genre" common in the first century, in which the real world of space-time is "reconfigured . . . in light of God's future intervening judgment—but also *in the light of past, present, and future salvation and in view of the impinging reality of other mysterious worlds, both heavenly and infernal*" (emphasis is Humphrey's). Evangelicals especially (including myself) recognize that in the New Testament this is due particularly to the promises of Christ concerning His imminent return to bring reward and judgment (e.g. Matthew 24–25; Acts 1:4–11). In the Pauline letters the immediacy of this promise bleeds through repeatedly (cf. esp. 1 and 2 Thessalonians).

12.   Ibid., 115.

13.   Peter Toon, *Heaven and Hell* (Nashville: Nelson, 1986), xiii.

14.   For a helpful synthesis of the prophetic implications of these letters, see also Tim LaHaye and Ed Hindson, eds., *The Popular Bible Prophecy Commentary* (Eugene, OR: Harvest House, 2006), 404–18.

15.   Ibid.

16.   Victor Furnish "Paul and the Corinthians: The Letters, the Challenges of Ministry, the Gospel" *Interpretation* 52, no. 3 (July 1998): 229–45.

17.   Ibid., 229.

18. For more elaborate discussion of the historical, social, and personal factors regarding the founding and development of the church at Corinth, again see my introduction to the first letter, *First Corinthians*, 1–11.

19. Alfred Plummer, *A Critical and Exegetical Commentary on the Second Epistle of St. Paul to the Corinthians* (New York: Scribner, 1915), xviii–xxxvi. See also Furnish, *II Corinthians*, 30–48.

20. It should be noted that this does not call in question the canon of Scripture. It merely argues that there were letters written by the apostle that, by virtue of their having been lost, do not meet the normal criteria for inspired Scripture.

21. *Scofield Reference Bible*, 1,252.

22. See, e.g., R. Bultmann, *The Second Letter to the Corinthians*, trans. Roy A. Harrisville (Minneapolis: Augsburg, 1985), 146–47 (Gnostic view); Dieter Georgi, *The Opponents of Paul in Second Corinthians* (Philadelphia: Fortress, 1986), 5 (Hellenistic Jews); C. K. Barrett, *The Second Epistle to the Corinthians* (New York: Harper and Row, 1973), 30 (Judaizers). This latter view is variously thought to be in opposition to the Twelve (Plummer) or under the authority of the Twelve (Baur). See Randall C. Gleason, "Paul's Covenantal Contrasts in 2 Corinthians 3:1–11," *Bibliotheca Sacra* 154 (January–March 1997): 64–65n15.

23. Gleason, "Paul's Covenantal Contrasts," 65–66.

24. Peter Naylor, *2 Corinthians*, vol. 1, chaps. *1–7* (Darlington, Eng.: Evangelical, 2002), 38.

## Chapter 1—Greetings from Paul and Timothy

1. See J. C. Lambert, "Apostle," in *ISBE*. Concerning the tendency to restrict the term *apostle* to a peculiar inner circle, Lambert notes: "If any such tendency existed, Paul effectually broke it down by vindicating for himself the right to the name. His claim appears in his assumption of the apostolic title in the opening words of most of his epistles. And when his right to it was challenged, he defended that right with passion, and especially on these grounds: that he had seen Jesus, and so was qualified to bear witness to His resurrection (1 Cor. 9:1; compare Acts 22:6ff.); that he had received a call to the work of an apostle (Rom. 1:1; 1 Cor. 1:1, etc.; Gal. 2:7; compare Acts 13:2ff.; 22:21); but, above all, that he could point to the signs and seals of his apostleship furnished by his missionary labors and their fruits (1 Cor. 9:2; 2 Cor. 12:12; Gal. 2:8). It was by this last ground of appeal that Paul convinced the original apostles of the justice of his claim . . . (Gal. 2:8)."

2. See, e.g., Alexandra R. Brown, "The Gospel Takes Place: Paul's Theology of Power-in-Weakness in 2 Corinthians," *Interpretation* 52, no. 3 (July 1998): 271–85.

3. E.g., Elizabeth Castelli, *Imitating Paul: A Discourse of Power* (Louisville: Westminster John Knox, 1997), 89–119.

4. Robert Jamieson, A. R. Faussett, and David Brown, *A Commentary, Critical and Explanatory, on the Old and New Testaments,* Vol. 2 (Harford: S. S. Scranton, 1872), 299.

5. G. E. Ladd, *A Theology of the New Testament,* rev. ed. (Grand Rapids: Eerdmans, 1993), 582. See also K. L. Schmidt, "*ekklēsia,*" in *TDNT* 3:506; Murray J. Harris, *The Second Epistle to the Corinthians,* NIGTC (Grand Rapids: Eerdmans, 2005), 133.

6. C. K. Barrett, *The Second Epistle to the Corinthians* (New York: Harper and Row, 1973), 55.

7. Leopold Sabourin, *The Names and Titles of Jesus,* trans. Maurice Carroll (New York: Macmillan, 1967), 300.

8. Peter Naylor, *2 Corinthians,* vol. 1, chaps. *1–7* (Darlington, Eng.: Evangelical, 2002), 50.

9. Anthony C. Thiselton, *The First Epistle to the Corinthians* (Grand Rapids: Eerdmans, 2000), 63.

10. Ibid.

## Chapter 2—Comfort in Conflict

1. Anthony C. Thiselton, *The First Epistle to the Corinthians* (Grand Rapids: Eerdmans, 2000), 85. Much is made of the Greek epistolary influence evident in Paul's letters. Thiselton cites Schubert, "Form and Function of the Pauline Thanksgivings," *BZNW* 20 (Berlin: Topelmann, 1939), 39–122, 156–73, to show the characteristically Jewish tone of his writing here. See also C. K. Barrett, *The Second Epistle to the Corinthians* (New York: Harper and Row, 1973), 57–58, where he argues for the association with the "Eighteen Benedictions" of the synagogue service—all of which began with "Blessed art thou [*baruk 'attah*], O Lord our God and God of our fathers. . . ." From this association he considers the question whether the opening statement is indicative or optative is decisively answered with the former—against our text which has the optative "blessed be God. . . ." I think Barrett is correct. Hence the reading should be "Blessed is the God and Father of our Lord Jesus Christ. As he adds, "It is more probable that we have here a Christian version of a Jewish blessing: Blessed is God; but the God of the Old Testament, the God of our fathers, is now known to us as also the Father of the Son whom he sent into the world (Gal. 4:4), Jesus Christ."

2. J. C. Lambert, "Praise," in *ISBE.*

3. Ibid.

4. Barrett, *Second Epistle to the Corinthians,* 58–59.

5. Ibid., 59, 60. "It is in the plural, probably because it is so used in the Septuagint as the translation of a Hebrew plural *rahamim).* Paul evokes this Old Testament background in the description of his own circumstances and the deliverance (see verses 8ff.) that God has wrought for him; cf., e.g., Ps.

xxxix (xl).12 (with verse 14, the verb *hruesthai*, used in 2 Cor. 1:10); lxviii (lxix.17 (with *thlibesthai*, used in 2 Cor. 1:6) lxxvii (lxxix).8 (again with *hruesthai* in the next verse)."

6.  Ibid., 61.

7.  As I have noted elsewhere (cf. my commentary *First Corinthians: Christianity in a Hostile Culture* [Chattanooga, TN: AMG, 2004] and n. 2 on the introduction), Paul's rhetorical skills should not be discounted. See Christopher D. Stanley, *Paul and the Language of Scripture: Citation Technique in the Pauline Epistles and Contemporary Literature*, SNTSMS 74 (Cambridge: Cambridge University Press, 1992).

8.  Murray J. Harris, *The Second Epistle to the Corinthians*, NIGTC (Grand Rapids: Eerdmans, 2005), 164–82. In his "Excursus: Paul's Affliction in Asia (2 Cor. 1:8–11): The Personal Background to 2 Corinthians," Harris, with a few modifications, follows W. M. Alexander, "St. Paul's Infirmity," *ExpT* 10 (1904): 469–73, 545–48, to relate this to his "thorn in the flesh" (2 Cor. 12:7). It is argued that it is for this reason the writer is so preoccupied with the subject of death and dying and his own mortality and "weakness" throughout the letter.

9.  John Piper, *Future Grace* (Sisters, OR: Multnomah, 1995), 31ff.

# Chapter 3–Answering Critics

1.  Peter Naylor, *2 Corinthians*, vol. 1, chaps. *1–7* (Darlington, Eng.: Evangelical, 2002), 78.

2.  John G. Stackhouse, Jr., *Can God Be Trusted* (New York: Oxford, 1998), 149–50.

3.  Dan Mitchell, *1 Corinthians: Christianity in a Hostile Culture* (Chattanooga, TN: AMG, 2004), 125ff.

4.  Harold J. Ockenga, *The Comfort of God: Preaching in Second Corinthians* (New York: Revell, 1944), 53.

5.  Augustine, *Confessions* 1.10.16, trans. J. G. Pilkington, in *A Select Library of the Nicene and Post-Nicene Fathers of the Christian Church*, ed. Philip Schaff, series 1, vol. 1 (Edinburgh: T. & T. Clark, 1882).

6.  Ibid., 1.15.24.

7.  Despite Lenski's eloquent protestations to the contrary against this "theory" (R. C. H. Lenski, *The Interpretation of 1 and 2 Corinthians* (Columbus, OH: Wartburg, 1946), 796–804; 876ff.), it is preferred here inasmuch as it makes the most sense of the data. See Mitchell, *1 Corinthians*, 6ff.

8.  Ockenga, *Comfort of God*, 51.

9.  Gene Getz, "Personal Notes," Dallas Theological Seminary, 1973.

10. Ockenga, *Comfort of God*, 54. Brackets are the author's.

11.   Ibid., 50.

12.   See, e.g., Stephen Covey, *Principle-Centered Leadership* (New York: Simon & Schuster, 1992), 42.

## Chapter 4—Restoring a Brother

1.   C. K. Barrett, *The Second Epistle to the Corinthians* (New York: Harper and Row, 1973), 94, suggests the possibility that this came from a traveling preacher who visited the city. In any event, he believes Paul's troubles at Corinth have been "overdrawn."

2.   R. V. G. Tasker, *The Second Epistle of Paul to the Corinthians*, Tyndale New Testament Commentary (Grand Rapids: Eerdmans, 1962), 52.

## Chapter 5—The Smell of Victory

1.   Scott Hafemann, "Paul's Use of the Old Testament in 2 Corinthians" *Interpretation* 52, no. 3 (July 1998): 246.

2.   Ibid.

3.   Ibid., 247.

4.   C. K. Barrett, *The Second Epistle to the Corinthians* (New York: Harper and Row, 1973), 96, 97. Barrett, of course, has his own theory of how the "severe letter" came to be inserted.

5.   Gerhard Delling, "θριαμβεύω," in *TDNT*, ed. Gerhard Friedrich, Ronald Pitkin, and G. Kittel; trans. G. W. Bromiley and G. Friedrich (Grand Rapids: Eerdmans, 1964–1976), 3:160.

6.   Barrett, *Second Epistle to the Corinthians*, 99.

7.   Ibid.

8.   Harold J. Ockenga, *The Comfort of God: Preaching in Second Corinthians* (New York: Revell, 1944), 79.

9.   See Charles R. Erdman, *The Second Epistle of Paul to the Corinthians* (Philadelphia: Westminster, 1929), 36.

10.   Ibid.

11.   R. V. G. Tasker, *The Second Epistle of Paul to the Corinthians*, Tyndale New Testament Commentary (Grand Rapids: Eerdmans, 1962), 58.

12.   G. Campbell Morgan, *The Corinthian Letters of Paul* (Old Tappan, NJ: Revell, 1966), 235.

13.   Barrett, *Second Epistle to the Corinthians*, 105. Emphasis mine.

14.   Ibid.

15.   H. A. Ironside, *II Corinthians* (Neptune, NJ: Loizeaux, 1964), 63, 64.

## Chapter 6—Ministers of the New Covenant

1.   Robert M. Grant, *Gods and the One God*, Wayne A. Meeks, ed. (Philadelphia: Westminster, 1986), 112.

2.   E.g., see Brian McLaren, *A Generous Orthodoxy* (Grand Rapids: Zondervan, 2004).

3.   Ibid., 66.

4.   The language is from the account of Augustine's conversion given in his *Confessions* 8.12, trans. J. G. Pilkington, in *A Select Library of the Nicene and Post-Nicene Fathers of the Christian Church*, ed. Philip Schaff, series 1, vol. 1 (Edinburgh: T. & T. Clark, 1882).

5.   Randall C. Gleason, "Paul's Covenantal Contrasts in 2 Corinthians 3:1–11," *Bibliotheca Sacra* 154 (January–March 1997): 70–77.

6.   Ibid. Gleason cites Barth here saying: "For in 2 Cor. 3 everything depends on the fact that without this work of the Spirit Scripture is veiled, however great its glory may be and whatever its origin." Karl Barth, *Church Dogmatics*, 1.2., ed. G. W. Bromiley and T. F. Torrance (New York: Scribner, 1956), 515. Peter Richardson, "Spirit and Letter: A Foundation for Hermeneutics," *EvQ* 45 (1973): 208–9, also follows this approach to the text.

7.   Ibid., Gleason citing Thomas E. Provence, "'Who Is Sufficient for These Things?' An Exegesis of 2 Corinthians 2:15–3:18" *NovT* 24 (1982): 61, adds, "in addition to the failure to account for the radical antithesis between letter and spirit, by portraying them not as opposites but related to one another positively as text and interpreter." Second, though "Paul does claim that a veil lies upon the reading of the Old Covenant," it is "a veil of hard-heartedness which hides not the meaning of the Bible, but the glory of God." It seems preferable to say that the veil does not hide the meaning of the text but rather obscures its effective application to one's life and the willingness to accept it (1 Cor. 2:14). This is confirmed by the fact that once the veil is lifted, personal transformation results from the believer beholding the glory of the Lord (2 Cor. 3:18). Third, this interpretation fails to relate this passage to Paul's argument against the Judaizers.

8.   Ibid.

9.   C. K. Barrett, *The Second Epistle to the Corinthians* (New York: Harper and Row, 1973), 113.

10.  Stephen Westerholm, "Letter and Spirit: The foundation of Pauline Ethics," *New Testament Studies* 30 (1984): 234–35, cited in Gleason, "'Who Is Sufficient for These Things?'" 73–74.

11.  Gleason, "'Who Is Sufficient for These Things?'" 73–74.

12.  Ibid., 74.

13.  Ibid., 75.

14. Ibid., 76.

15. Ibid., 76–77.

16. Scott Hafemann, "Paul's Use of the Old Testament in 2 Corinthians" *Interpretation* 52, no. 3 (July 1998): 247.

17. Ibid.

18. R. C. H. Lenski, *The Interpretation of 1 and 2 Corinthians* (Columbus, OH: Wartburg, 1946), 947–48.

## Chapter 7—Treasure in Earthen Vessels

1. Charles Hodge, *An Exposition of the Second Epistle to the Corinthians* (Grand Rapids: Eerdmans, 1864), 82.

2. Miroslav Volf, *Exclusion and Embrace* (Nashville: Abingdon, 1996), 258.

3. Alfred Jepsen, "Aman," in *Theological Dictionary of the Old Testament*, ed. G. J. Botterweck and H. Ringgren (Grand Rapids: Eerdmans, 1974), 1:313.

4. Volf, *Exclusion and Embrace*, 260.

5. Ibid., emphasis his.

6. Ibid., 262, emphasis his.

7. Ibid., 263, emphasis his.

8. Ibid.

9. Douglas J. Wilson, "Foundations of Exhaustive Knowledge," in *Bound Only Once*, ed. Douglas Wilson (Moscow, ID: Canon, 2001), 138–39.

10. Harold J. Ockenga, *The Comfort of God: Preaching in Second Corinthians* (New York: Revell, 1944), 121, 122. Coming from the late pastor of Park Street Congregational Church in Boston, his words are breathtaking. "The choice determines whether a man shall live in darkness or light. The god of this world cannot blind the eyes of any except those who will not believe the gospel, our Scripture says. . . . There is a time in life when man arrives at the maturity and point of responsibility where he may choose for himself the God of his life. Hence man is the arena of conflict."

11. G. Campbell Morgan, *The Corinthian Letters of Paul* (Old Tappan, NJ: Revell, 1966), 237.

12. John Smyth, *The Bright Morning Starre* (Cambridge: John Legat, Printer to the Universitie of Cambridge, 1603), 172.

13. J. Oswald Sanders, *Spiritual Leadership*, 2nd ed. (Chicago: Moody, 1994), 116.

14. Author unknown.

15. Morgan, *Corinthian Letters of Paul*, 238.

16. Christian Maurer, "σκεῦος," *TDNT*, 7:358ff.

17. As noted in my commentary on 1 Corinthians, much has [been] made of the analysis of power relations in Pauline thought in the interest, e.g., of contemporary gender issues. In such ideological analysis, the interpreter attempts to critique Paul's real motives as a first-century companion might. What is of primary interest in such an analysis is what Paul is "up to" rather than what he writes. One then attempts to exegete the subtext rather than the text of Paul's letter. In so doing, the interpreter stands over and above the text as a modern-day psychotherapist might a client. The authority is shifted away from the text to the exegete. This interpreter accepts the authoritative voice of Paul as given in the text and—to use Robbins' categories—understands the text as representational, rather than generative of the situation in Corinth. The text correctly reports on the historical and social issues rather than creates a historical and social reality in service to an ideological objective. Having said that, much attention has been given in the last decade to the sociological and rhetorical analysis of 1 and 2 Corinthians. While I appreciate this work and agree that it has brought new insights into our understanding of these letters, I agree with Graham Tomlin who says, "In fairness to earlier scholarship, these more recent approaches do not answer all the questions either. Specifically, there is a danger that a purely sociological or rhetorical approach can tend to ignore what earlier studies saw, namely, the existence of a real ideological divergence from Paul in Corinth." "Christians and Epicureans in I Corinthians," *JSNT* 68 (1997): 51–72. As seen here, there is a real danger in reducing Paul's writings to an exercise in pragmatics and to lose sight of the apostolic authority implicit in his letters—to say nothing of their authority as inspired Scripture.

18. Morgan, *Corinthian Letters of Paul*, 239.

19. Randy Alcorn, *Safely Home* (Carol Stream, Ill: Tyndale House, 2001), 274.

20. Ibid., 277.

## Chapter 8—Walk by Faith, Not by Sight

1. Ibid., 7.

2. The list is not intended to be exhaustive. Certainly much more was accomplished at Calvary, but these are the major themes generally developed in relation to Christ's work on the cross for humankind's salvation.

3. Cf. George N. H. Peters, *The Theocratic Kingdom* II (Grand Rapids: Kregel, 1972), 240–41, 394–403.

4. Murray J. Harris, *The Second Epistle to the Corinthians*, NIGTC (Grand Rapids: Eerdmans, 2005), 175–77.

5. John A. T. Robinson, *The Body: A Study in Pauline Theology*, Studies in Biblical Theology, no. 5 (London: SCM, 1952), 11–33. The definitive answer to this is generally taken to be James Barr, *The Semantics of Biblical Language* (London: Oxford University Press, 1961), 34–38. See also Millard Erickson, *Christian Theology*, 2nd ed. (Grand Rapids: Baker, 1998), 537–57. Erickson

offers a kind of middle ground between the classic approach that borders on bifurcating the soul and spirit and Robinson's misreading of Scripture to craft a psychophysical monism of human nature that looks more like contemporary philosophical personalism than biblical teaching. Erickson and others rightly note that Scripture (and Paul in particular) does not divide nor collapse the two. A better approach, as Leo Garrett suggests, must consider that "the Christian hope is not properly expressed in terms of the immortality of the soul *per se*, but needs to embrace and center in the resurrection of the body, indeed the "spiritual body." Christian redemption encompasses the whole person." J. L. Garrett Jr., *Systematic Theology*, 2d ed (North Richland Hills, TX: BIBAL, 2000), 1:519. It is in relation to the matter of the resurrection of the body that monism falls. The Bible student needs to be very careful here to avoid suggesting that Paul teaches "soul sleep," which is, in fact, the logical extension of Robinson's view. Dualistic views are not without their problems either, but at least they do not require a rewrite of New Testament anthropology. See also Harris, *Second Epistle to the Corinthians*, 124–25.

6.    Garrett, *Systematic Theology*, 1:518–19.

7.    The reader is also referred to Geisler's discussion of this text as well as others used by Arminian interpreters to try to establish that Christians may lose their salvation. See Norman Geisler, *Chosen but Free*, 2nd ed. (Minneapolis: Bethany House, 2001), 129–33.

## Chapter 9—The New Creation

1.    Robert Brow, "Evangelical Megashift," *Christianity Today* (February 19, 1990), 12–14.

2.    John MacArthur Jr. "Open Theism's Attack on the Atonement," *Bound Only Once*, ed. Douglas Wilson (Moscow, ID: Canon, 2001), 138, 95–108.

3.    Ibid., 97–8. MacArthur reacts to the article by Brow cited above.

4.    David F. Wells, *God in the Wasteland* (Grand Rapids: Eerdmans, 1994), 88.

5.    Ibid., 92–93.

6.    Ibid., 30.

7.    Norman Geisler, *Chosen but Free*, 2nd ed. (Minneapolis: Bethany House, 2001), 207.

8.    C. K. Barrett, *The Second Epistle to the Corinthians* (New York: Harper and Row, 1973), 173.

9.    Ibid.

10.   Ibid.

11.   Miroslav Volf, *Exclusion and Embrace* (Nashville: Abingdon, 1996), 51.

12.   Ibid. This is what Volf calls a "catholic personality," (with a small *c*), which is understood as "a personality enriched by otherness, a personality which

is what it is only because multiple others have been reflected in it in a particular way. The distance from my own culture that results from being born by the Spirit creates a fissure in me through which others can come in. The Spirit unlatches the doors of my heart, saying: 'You are not only you; others belong to you too.'"

13. Ibid., 294.

14. Ibid., 51.

15. MacArthur, "Open Theism's Attack on the Atonement," 102.

16. Ibid.

17. Tom Holland, *Contours of Pauline Theology* (Ferne, Ross-shire, Scotland: Christian Focus/Mentor, 2004), 76.

18. Ibid.

19. Ibid., 77.

20. The last word in the Greek text of the book of Acts is *akōlutōs*, "unhindered."

21. Statistics from David Aikman, *Jesus in Beijing: How Christianity Is Transforming China and Changing the Global Balance of Power* (Washington, DC: Regnary, 2006). The statistic is made even more astounding when one realizes that during the Cultural Revolution of 1966–76 every single church building was closed in China. See the interview by Kathryn Jean Lopez with David Aikman at NationalReviewonline.com.

22. H. A. Ironside, *II Corinthians* (Neptune, NJ: Loizeaux, 1964), 159.

# Chapter 10—Perfecting Holiness in the Fear of God

1. C. K. Barrett, *The Second Epistle to the Corinthians* (New York: Harper and Row, 1973), 191.

2. Ibid.

3. Stanley B. Marrow, *Paul, His Letters and His Theology* (New York: Paulist, 1986), 182.

4. Miroslav Volf, *Exclusion and Embrace* (Nashville: Abingdon, 1996), 262.

5. The question of the unity of this passage has long been debated. William O. Walker offers a summary of different views on this question. "The verses have variously been viewed as (a) composed by Paul specifically for inclusion at their present location, (b) composed by Paul for some other occasion but subsequently included at their present location either by Paul or by someone else, (c) composed by someone other than Paul but included at their present location by Paul, or (d) both composed by someone other than Paul and included at their present location by someone other than Paul (not necessarily the same person)." "2 Cor. 6.14–7.1 and the Chiastic Structure of 6.11–13; 2.2–3" *New Testament Studies* 48 (2002): 142–44.

While Walker does not argue the case for or against the unity of the passage, he offers impressive evidence for a chiasmus to be found in the immediate context preceding and following the text. The chiasmus would be seen as follows:

A. Assurance of affection (6:11)

B. Disclaimer of responsibility for alienation 6:12

C. Appeal for affection 6:13

C. Appeal for affection (7:2a)

B. Disclaimer of responsibility for alienation (7:2b)

A. Assurance of affection (7:3)

Walker suggests that the presence of such a chiasmus would present a further argument against the unity of the passage in its present form. While we agree that this is an interesting "new wrinkle," we prefer to follow Barrett in his support for a Pauline intent to craft the material in precisely the manner in which it is found in the traditional text without appeal to redaction either from Paul or an unknown hand. See also Margaret E. Thrall, *A Critical and Exegetical Commentary on the Second Epistle to the Corinthians. Vol I: Introduction and Commentary on II Corinthians 1–7*, ICC (Edinburgh: T. & T. Clark, 1994), who offers a more recent discussion and support of the Pauline authorship of this difficult passage. See also Murray J. Harris, *The Second Epistle to the Corinthians*, NIGTC (Grand Rapids: Eerdmans, 2005), 14–25. While he refrains from dogmatism on the question of the time of its authorship in relation to its immediate context, Harris concludes that "notwithstanding the prima-facie non-Pauline features of the paragraph, its incontestable Pauline characteristics and the very presence of the paragraph in a genuine Pauline letter and in such an expected place suggest that it stems *in toto* from Paul's own hand."

6. Barrett, *Second Epistle to the Corinthians*, 193–204. Barrett engages in a lengthy excursus to answer the charge of many that this text (6:14–7:1) disrupts the continuity of Paul's thought and is likely an interpolation. Barrett offers extensive data to show that it is not only consistent with all that Paul teaches elsewhere on this subject, but that it is consistent with his style. "Paul not infrequently allows himself to wander from his point and then brings himself back to it with something of a jerk." Barrett offers multiple examples of this tendency in the present writer. Furnish, who argues for a non-Pauline authorship, but nevertheless inserted by the apostle, acknowledges that there are legitimate ways to "trace logical connections between the content of the passage and its context in 2 Cor, all of which must necessarily fall short of actually "proving" the case for integrity" (Victor Furnish, *II Corinthians*, The Anchor Bible, vol. 6 [Garden City, NY: Doubleday, 1984], 382–83). I acknowledge that he has a valid point, but his argument is a two-edged sword. If one cannot be certain regarding which theory of logical connection is most likely correct, the denial of any such connection is equally tenuous. Of course, this is not the position Furnish favors. Rather, he under-

stands the inclusion to be similar to the hymn in Philippians 2:6–11, which "is not just inserted into the letter but carefully integrated into the argument and very specifically applied to the appeal the apostle is making (see Phil. 1:27–2:5 and 2:12–18)." For this writer, the burden of proof is on the denial of such connection, not its affirmation. If we apply the principle of the "hard reading" to this text, the weight of probability is decidedly in the direction of our position here since the reference to his enemies as non-Christians is shocking in the very least. Suffice it to say that there is insufficient warrant to question the legitimacy of the placement of this admonition in this context. There is certainly no warrant to suggest that it was added by a subsequent editor of the text. See also Donald G. McDougall, "Unequally Yoked—A Re-examination of 2 Corinthians 6:11–7:4," *The Master's Seminary Journal* 10, no.1 (Spring 1999): 113–37.

7.    Barrett, *Second Epistle to the Corinthians*, 195.

8.    See Thrall's comments on 3:7–11 in *Second Epistle to the Corinthians*.

# Chapter 11—Repentance without Regret

1.    Victor Furnish, *II Corinthians*, The Anchor Bible, vol. 6 (Garden City, NY: Doubleday, 1984), 391–92, gives special attention to the "function" of this passage. While most commentators tend to see chapter 7 as the conclusion of the appeal in chapter 6 (i.e., that they appear to have been reconciled to him, and for that he is joyful), following Stanley N. Olson, "Confidence Expressions in Paul: Epistolary Conventions and the Purpose of 2 Corinthians" (Ph.D. diss., Yale University, 1976), 201, Furnish sees it as introducing the two chapters to follow where the writer makes an appeal for the collection for the saints in Jerusalem. "In conformity with a familiar Hellenistic literary pattern, Paul emphasizes his confidence in those of whom he is about to make a substantial request." Otherwise, Furnish arranges the subsections much as we have them here. We wonder why it cannot be taken as both—that is, his confidence in their participation in the collection is due to the fact that they have dealt with the issues in the church as Paul instructed. See also Stanley N. Olson, "Epistolary Uses of Expressions of Self-Confidence," *JBL* 103 (1984): 585–97, and "Pauline Expressions of Confidence in His Addressees," *CBQ* 47 (1985): 282–95.

2.    Miroslav Volf, *Exclusion and Embrace* (Nashville: Abingdon, 1996), 120.

3.    Ibid., 125. Many will no doubt take issue with Volf's Anabaptist arguments for nonviolence, but his insight here is profound with respect to the import of Jesus' offer of forgiveness and its relation to His sacrifice for sin.

4.    Second Corinthians 7:5–16 together with 1:1–2:13 has been examined with special attention to Paul's use of the "pathetic proofs, or appeals to the emotions in the creation of persuasive discourse." L. L. Welborn examines pity, anger, and zeal in these passages "in light of the treatment of these emotions by ancient rhetorical theorists." He argues that "a survey of ancient letters demonstrates that appeals to these three emotions were deemed appropri-

ate to the function of the conciliatory style. A concluding section reflects upon Paul's attempt to bring about a christophoric transformation of the emotions aroused by his letter." "Paul's Appeal to the Emotions in 2 Corinthians 1:1–2:13; 7:5–16," *JSNT* 82 (2001): 31–60.

5. J. Oswald Sanders, *Spiritual Leadership*, 2nd ed. (Chicago: Moody, 1994), 60.

6. Murray J. Harris, *The Second Epistle to the Corinthians*, NIGTC (Grand Rapids: Eerdmans, 2005), 540–41.

7. Ibid., 543.

8. Compare Olson, "Confidence Expressions in Paul," 196.

9. Victor Furnish, *II Corinthians*, The Anchor Bible, vol. 6 (Garden City, NY: Doubleday, 1984), 398.

## Chapter 12—We Are in This Together

1. Murray J. Harris, *The Second Epistle to the Corinthians*, NIGTC (Grand Rapids: Eerdmans, 2005), 553.

2. Peter Naylor, *2 Corinthians*, vol. 2, chaps. *8–13* (Darlington, Eng.: Evangelical, 2002), 12–13. Nevertheless, while this was certainly Paul's fervent hope (9:13–14), Matera is probably correct in his suggestion that while the "the collection was immensely important to Paul, it may not have had the impact upon the Jerusalem church for which he so fervently hoped" Frank J. Matera, *II Corinthians: A Commentary*, The New Testament Library (Louisville: Westminster John Knox, 2003), 183. Victor Furnish, *II Corinthians*, The Anchor Bible, vol. 6 (Garden City, NY: Doubleday, 1984), 412–13, cites Johannes Munck, *Paul and the Salvation of Mankind*, trans. F. Clarke (Richmond: Knox, 1959), 302–3, who argued that the collection for the Jews in Jerusalem is to be interpreted in light of Romans 11:25–26. Paul is provoking his "kinsmen" to jealousy in hopes perhaps of fulfilling Old Testament prophecy concerning Gentiles bringing gifts to Zion in the last days (Isa. 2:2, 3; 60:5–6; Mic. 4:1, 2). Others have noted correctly that such speculations (however ingenious) are beside the point. Paul was asked to take this project on, and he promised that he would do it. He is merely carrying out his obligation in the matter. We also dismiss suggestions that the gift-giver relationship between the Gentiles and the Jerusalem church has political significance.

3. Ibid., 9.

4. Harris, *Second Epistle to the Corinthians*, 88–89.

5. Harris notes: "When a harvest failed, the normal prices—already inflated—could multiply up to sixteen times. . . . And Josephus mentions a house tax that was levied in Jerusalem (*Antiquities* 19.299)," *Second Epistle to the Corinthians*, 89.

6. For further reading, see ibid.

7.  There are reports of a great earthquake on March 23, AD 37, in the reign of Caligula, followed by another in the reign of Claudius, accompanied by widespread crop failures. Concerning this Hering's comment is worth noting. "We may wonder whether Macedonia had been especially tested by the earthquakes which, in the time of Claudius, shook certain provinces. But we have not found any information on this point in Pliny the Elder or in Tacitus." Jean Hering, *The Second Epistle of Saint Paul to the Corinthians* (London: Epworth, 1967), 58n2.

8.  Harris, *Second Epistle to the Corinthians*, 554–55, offers a fairly exhaustive list of expressions in Paul relating to the offering. He lists thirty-three passages citing terms such as "contribution," "service," "gift," "remembering the poor," "gift of blessing," "grace," "privilege," etc., throughout his New Testament letters.

9.  Ibid., 555–56. Harris adds, "Also, the abrupt way in which the apostle introduces the theme of 'the collection for God's people' at 1 Cor. 16:1, with no reference to the collection's destination (but see 1 Cor. 16:3) and purpose or to any motivation for contributing, presupposes the Corinthians' acquaintance with the project. We cannot be sure when they first heard of the venture, but it may have been in Paul's 'previous letter' (cf. 1 Cor. 5:9, 11), written perhaps in AD 53, or by news from the Galatian churches referred to in 1 Corinthians 16:1."

10. Ibid., 559–60. Barrett agrees. He says, "This word is used in these chapters in a bewildering variety of ways." C. K. Barrett, *The Second Epistle to the Corinthians* (New York: Harper and Row, 1973), 218.

11. Furnish, *II Corinthians*, 413.

12. Naylor, *2 Corinthians*, 2:16.

13. Matera, *II Corinthians*, 187.

14. Dan Mitchell, *1 Corinthians: Christianity in a Hostile Culture* (Chattanooga, TN: AMG, 2004), 21.

15. Barrett, *Second Epistle to the Corinthians*, 221.

16. See Harris, *Second Epistle to the Corinthians*, 569–72.

17. Naylor, *2 Corinthians*, 2:21.

18. Hering, *Second Epistle of Saint Paul to the Corinthians*, 59. For further discussion of the textual variant here, see David E. Garland, *2 Corinthians*, The New American Commentary, ed. E. Ray Clendenen (Nashville: Broadman and Holman, 1999), 373–74.

19. Garland, *2 Corinthians*, 375.

20. Ibid., 376.

21. Ibid., 378.

22. Furnish, *II Corinthians*, 418.

23.   Ibid.

24.   Barrett, *Second Epistle to the Corinthians*, 224–25.

25.   Garland, *2 Corinthians*, 380.

26.   Naylor, *2 Corinthians*, 2:35–36.

27.   Charles Hodge, *An Exposition of the Second Epistle to the Corinthians* (Grand Rapids: Eerdmans, 1864), 206.

28.   Naylor, *2 Corinthians*, 2:34.

29.   Matera, *II Corinthians*, 193.

# Chapter 13—Seek Ye First the Kingdom

1.   Dan Mitchell, *1 Corinthians: Christianity in a Hostile Culture* (Chattanooga, TN: AMG, 2004), 78. See Philip Edgcumbe Hughes, *Paul's Second Epistle to the Corinthians*, NICNT (Grand Rapids: Eerdmans, 1962), 3:267.

2.   I am indebted here to the list cited from E. Clowney in D. A. Carson, "Worship under the Word," in *Worship by the Book*, ed. D. A. Carson (Grand Rapids: Zondervan, 2002), 48.

3.   For an extensive discussion of a number of alternative candidates, see P. E. Hughes, "1 Corinthians," *The Biblical Expositor*, Carl F. H. Henry, consulting ed. (Philadelphia: A. J. Holman, 1973), 3:312–16.

4.   AUT Victor Furnish, *II Corinthians*, The Anchor Bible, vol. 6 (Garden City, NY: Doubleday, 1984), 434.

5.   Peter Naylor, *2 Corinthians*, vol. 2, chaps. *8–13* (Darlington, Eng.: Evangelical, 2002), 47.

6.   For further discussion, see Victor Furnish, *II Corinthians*, The Anchor Bible, vol. 6 (Garden City, NY: Doubleday, 1984), 437–38.

7.   H. A. Ironside, *II Corinthians* (Neptune, NJ: Loizeaux, 1964), 195–96.

8.   Frank J. Matera, *II Corinthians: A Commentary*, The New Testament Library (Louisville: Westminster John Knox, 2003), 204.

9.   Furnish, *II Corinthians*, 446.

10.   E.g., Alfred Plummer, *A Critical and Exegetical Commentary on the Second Epistle of St. Paul to the Corinthians* (New York: Scribner, 1915), 258.

11.   Murray J. Harris, *The Second Epistle to the Corinthians*, NIGTC (Grand Rapids: Eerdmans, 2005), 635.

12.   Naylor, *2 Corinthians*, 2:64.

13.   "A similar emphasis on giving in accordance with the promptings of the heart is found in the accounts of the monetary or material offerings made for the construction of the tabernacle (e.g., Exod. 25:2, 'You are to receive the offering for me from all whose hearts prompt them to give'; Exod. 35:21,

'all who were willing and whose hearts moved them came and brought an offering to the Lord to be used for the Tent of Meeting'). But in 2 Corinthians 9:7 a decision about the amount to be given is involved." Ibid., 635n13.

14. Matera, *II Corinthians*, 206. He adds, "The sufficiency of which Paul speaks here is not inner self-sufficiency, a favorite virtue among the Cynic and Stoic philosophers. Rather, Paul views *autarkeia* as a sufficiency of material wealth, supplied by God, which believers can disperse to those in need. Thus God provides believers with the sufficiency necessary to do 'every good work.'"

15. David E. Garland, *2 Corinthians*, The New American Commentary, ed. E. Ray Clendenen (Nashville: Broadman and Holman, 1999), 411. He goes on to say, "The principle Paul lays out is similar to the crass economic principle that the rich get richer and the poor get poorer. The generous get richer; the miserly grow poorer. . . . Martin Luther said: 'I have had many things in my hands that I lost; the things that I placed in the hands of God I still possess.'"

16. Ibid., 412.

17. The enlightenment philosophers from D. Hume forward bifurcated "is" from "ought." What is does not lead to conclusions regarding what ought to be. The problem with this is seen in ethical concerns of character. If one is a leader in the community, Aristotle reasoned, such a role entails ethical behavior. In this sense, if one is a police officer, one ought to be courageous. If one is a craftsman, one ought to be skilled in the craft. In this passage, Paul seems to be arguing that if one is of proven character (in this sense), that person will be giving to the poor.

18. Andrew Fuller, *Gospel Worthy of All Acceptation*, in Joseph Belcher, ed., *The Complete Works of the Rev. Andrew Fuller*, vol. 2 (1845; repr. 1988), 328–42. Document provided by David Oldfield, Post Falls, ID http://www.geocities.com/baptist_documents/fuller.gospel.worthy.2.html.

19. John McRay, *Archaeology and the New Testament* (Grand Rapids: Baker, 1999), 247. John Knox, "Philemon," *The Interpreter's Bible*, vol. 11 (Nashville: Abingdon, 1955), 557–60, notes interesting parallels between Ignatius, *Letter to the Ephesians*, chapters 2 and 3, and phrases in Philemon. Knox also reports that a later bishop at Ephesus was named Onesimus and that he was responsible for collecting and maintaining Paul's works. See John E. Stambaugh and David L Balch, *The New Testament in Its Social Environment* (Philadelphia: Westminster, 1984), 152.

## Chapter 14—Weapons of Our Warfare

1. Manuel A. Bagalawis, "Ministry as Warfare: An Exegesis of 2 Corinthians 10:2B–6" *AJPS* 3, no. 1 (2000): 5–18.

2. Ibid, 5.

3. David E. Garland, *2 Corinthians*, The New American Commentary, ed. E. Ray Clendenen (Nashville: Broadman and Holman, 1999), 418.

4. Ibid.

5. C. K. Barrett, *The Second Epistle to the Corinthians* (New York: Harper and Row, 1973), 244–45.

6. See ibid. Barrett argues that chapters 1–9 constitute one letter (mostly addressed to the believers) that was sent on and could not be retrieved—even if the writer had wanted to do so. Shortly thereafter, he had further disturbing news that the false teachers had scored another win and these fickle believers had once again turned their backs on Paul. Armed with that information, Barrett suggests, Paul sits down and fires off chapters 10–13. This is addressed primarily against the false teachers. In effect, the two documents become two parts of the same communication. While this is one of the more conservative of the partition theories, we nevertheless must reject it because, despite the internal evidence, there is no external evidence whatever for such a scenario.

7. Peter Naylor, *2 Corinthians*, vol. 2, chaps. *8–13* (Darlington, Eng.: Evangelical, 2002), 2:82.

8. Randy Alcorn, *Safely Home* (Carol Stream, Ill: Tyndale House, 2001), 149.

9. Evan S. Connell, *Son of the Morning Star: Custer and Little Bighorn* (San Francisco: North Point, 1984), 112.

10. Ibid.

11. Douglas J. Wilson, "Foundations of Exhaustive Knowledge," in *Bound Only Once*, ed. Douglas Wilson (Moscow, ID: Canon, 2001), 139–40.

12. Augustine, *Confessions 1.1*, trans. J. G. Pilkington, in *A Select Library of the Nicene and Post-Nicene Fathers of the Christian Church*, ed. Philip Schaff, series 1, vol. 1 (Edinburgh: T. & T. Clark, 1882).

13. Augustine, *On Christian Doctrine* 1.18.28. It is this comment in Augustine that was likely an adaptation of the Pythagorean maxim "all is number," which inspired the famous maxim derived from Miguel de Cervantes in *Don Quixote*, "All truth is God's truth." We would neither agree with what the man of La Mancha made of this nor with what many wish to make of it today—in Cervantes it seems to indicate a web of fatalism in which the main character is caught. Many today use the expression to suggest that anything dubbed "true" (e.g., from science or psychology) must be considered to be such all the way up to the mind of God. The problem with this thinking is that it equates what is known contingently with what only God knows absolutely. With Augustine and with Paul we would say that only that which is validated by revelation can be known with certainty. These truths are those out of which we fashion our "weapons of warfare" and which are "divinely powerful for the destruction of fortresses." Whether drawn from the text of Scripture or from the text of nature, ideas are true only insofar as they are "captive to the obedience of Christ."

14.  For discussion on five options regarding identity of these people, see Murray J. Harris, *The Second Epistle to the Corinthians*, NIGTC (Grand Rapids: Eerdmans, 2005), 688–90. I think it is most likely that these people were masquerading as the true disciples of Jesus but were in fact "false apostles" (cf. 11:13, 23).

15.  Ibid., 700.

16.  Naylor, *2 Corinthians*, 2:117.

17.  Ibid., 118.

18.  See Matera, *II Corinthians*, 234–35.

19.  Wolfhart Pannenberg, *Systematic Theology*, trans. Geoffrey W. Bromiley (Grand Rapids: Eerdmans, 1998), 3:377–82.

20.  Matera, *II Corinthians*, 237.

## Chapter 15—Fools Talk

1.  Murray J. Harris, *The Second Epistle to the Corinthians*, NIGTC (Grand Rapids: Eerdmans, 2005), 729. See also my introduction to the first epistle, *1 Corinthians: Christianity in a Hostile Culture* (Chattanooga, TN: AMG, 2004), 1–11.

2.  Ibid., 730.

3.  *Ophelon*, in connection with an unattainable wish used, as here, with the imperfect expresses present time and with the aorist indicative to denote past time (1 Cor. 4:8). With the future indicative it may signify an attainable wish—although not seriously so. In either instance, it signifies a proposition that is absurd on its face and unlikely even when seriously attempted. In this text, the writer is saying that he does not expect anything to come of this, but he will nonetheless give it his best.

4.  Harris, *Second Epistle to the Corinthians*, 733. See also C. K. Barrett, *The Second Epistle to the Corinthians* (New York: Harper and Row, 1973), 270–72.

5.  Peter Naylor, *2 Corinthians*, vol. 2, chaps. *8–13* (Darlington, Eng.: Evangelical, 2002), 124.

6.  Victor Furnish, *II Corinthians*, The Anchor Bible, vol. 6 (Garden City, NY: Doubleday, 1984), 499.

7.  Harris, *Second Epistle to the Corinthians*, 734–38, Of special note is his discussion of the question of Paul's role in relation to the "virgin" *qua* "bride." Four suggestions have been made, (1) the friend of the groom or the groomsman, (2) the friend of the bride, (3) the Father's agent, (4) the father of the bride. Of these, the last is his preferred sense.

8.  It is not possible, or necessary, to go into this issue here, but the reader should take note, for example, of Charlotte Caron, *To Make and Make Again: Feminist Ritual Thealogy* (New York: Crossroad, 1993); Carol Christ, *Rebirth of the Goddess: Finding Meaning in Feminist Spirituality* (New York: Routledge,

1997); Mary Daly, *Pure Lust: Elemental Feminist Philosophy* (Boston: Beacon, 1984); et al. See also Leon Podles, *The Church Impotent: The Feminization of Christianity* (Dallas, TX: Spence, 1999); Mary Kassian, *The Feminist Mistake: The Radical Impact of Feminism on Church and Culture* (Wheaton: Crossway, 2005). Radical feminists of the last century have created an anachronistic and idealized neo-pagan form of personal spirituality attractive to those who have little or no understanding of ancient history or practice. Contemporary Wiccans and others have been influenced by this association. We ignore this to our peril.

9.   Frank J. Matera, *II Corinthians: A Commentary*, The New Testament Library (Louisville: Westminster John Knox, 2003), 243–44, argues that it is going too far to say that the reference to "another Jesus" means that the intruders held to a "heretical" Christology. It is difficult to imagine that Paul would have been so exercised on the matter if the error was, as Matera suggests, little more than a matter of approach. What makes it difficult here is that Paul uses *allos*, rather than *heteros* (as he does, e.g., in Gal. 1:6–7). There are clues in 2 Corinthians 4:5 and 5:16. It is probably not possible to be entirely dogmatic on the question based on what can be known for certain in this text. The real issue is that (regardless of what they were preaching) they, in fact, gave them a hearing—whereas they have not given Paul the same courtesy. See Barrett, *Second Epistle to the Corinthians*, 275–80. See also David E. Garland, *2 Corinthians*, The New American Commentary, ed. E. Ray Clendenen (Nashville: Broadman and Holman, 1999), 462–64; J. Murphy-O'Connor, "Another Jesus (2 Cor. 11:4)," *RB* 97 (1990): 248.

10.  See also the discussion in Furnish, *II Corinthians*, 500–501.

11.  Douglas J. Wilson, "Foundations of Exhaustive Knowledge," in *Bound Only Once*, ed. Douglas Wilson (Moscow, ID: Canon, 2001), 166.

12.  Ibid. Wilson, in context, is discussing the Open Theists who use the same names for God but imbue Him with a different set of attributes. Perhaps this is a good analogy here since it is still to be determined whether they, in fact, worship the God of Abraham, Isaac, and Jacob. Obviously, this is not an issue we can resolve here, let alone in a footnote!

13.  Furnish, *II Corinthians*, 505, citing from G. Mussies, *Dio Chrysostom and the New Testament*, SCHNT 2 (1972): 179, and H. Windisch, *Der zweite Korintherbrief*, MeyerK 6 (Gottingen: Vandenhoeck und Ruprecht, 1924), 332, also cites *Dio Chrysostom* (32.39); and Josephus (*Antiquities* 14.1.1; 20.12.1; and *Against Apion* 27) points out that Jews "do not favour those persons who have mastered the speech of many nations or who adorn their style with smoothness of diction," but rather those who show their true wisdom by having "an exact knowledge of the law."

14.  For a summary of the best arguments in favor of this position, see Barrett, *Second Epistle to the Corinthians*, 242–53.

15. R. V. G. Tasker, *The Second Epistle of Paul to the Corinthians*, Tyndale New Testament Commentary (Grand Rapids: Eerdmans, 1962), 149, suggests that Paul may well have coined the term as it is used here and in 12:11.

16. Ibid. For an excellent summary and review of the options and essential arguments in support of them, see Furnish, *II Corinthians*, 502–5.

17. Harris, *Second Epistle to the Corinthians*, 751.

18. Ibid., 762.

19. Tasker, *Second Epistle of Paul to the Corinthians*, 151–52.

20. John M. Frame, "Open Theism and Divine Foreknowledge," in *Bound Only Once*, ed. Douglas Wilson (Moscow, ID: Canon, 2001), 94. While I do not wish to engage in an extended debate with the Open Theists on this point, it is vital to recognize that a biblical worldview, contra that of the pagans, was distinctive precisely on this point—i.e., that God's knowledge is inexhaustible.

21. Garland, *2 Corinthians*, 484, cites R. H. Strachan, *The Second Epistle of Paul to the Corinthians*, MNTC (London: Hodder and Stoughton, 1935), 24–24.

22. Matera, *II Corinthians*, 253.

23. Ibid., 254. He remains reluctant on this account to suggest that the actual "teachings" of these miscreants are heretical, only that they are nonsupportive of the ministry of the apostle and on that account will have to give an account to God for their actions. The judgment voiced against them in this text is too severe, however, to be limited merely to persons whose style and method are incompatible with Paul's. See Garland, *2 Corinthians*, 484.

24. Harris, *Second Epistle to the Corinthians*, 773.

25. Furnish, *II Corinthians*, 495.

26. Garland, *2 Corinthians*, 485.

27. Ibid.

28. Ibid.

29. Ibid.

## Chapter 16—Playing the Fool for Jesus' Sake

1. Victor Furnish, *II Corinthians*, The Anchor Bible, vol. 6 (Garden City, NY: Doubleday, 1984), 532.

2. Jean Hering, *The Second Epistle of Saint Paul to the Corinthians* (London: Epworth, 1967), 82.

3. Ibid.

4. Stephen Arterburn and Jack Felton, *Toxic Faith* (Nashville: Nelson, 1991), 19–46.

5.   Furnish, *II Corinthians*, 514.

6.   Hering, *Second Epistle of Saint Paul to the Corinthians*, 83.

7.   Furnish, *II Corinthians*, 516.

8.   Peter Naylor, *2 Corinthians*, vol. 2, chaps. *8–13* (Darlington, Eng.: Evangelical, 2002), 196. See also n. 171.

9.   Hering, *Second Epistle of Saint Paul to the Corinthians*, 87. See also discussions in Furnish, *II Corinthians*, 521–23; C. K. Barrett, *The Second Epistle to the Corinthians* (New York: Harper and Row, 1973), 303, 304; R. V. G. Tasker, *The Second Epistle of Paul to the Corinthians*, Tyndale New Testament Commentary (Grand Rapids: Eerdmans, 1962), 167–68.

10.  Hering, *Second Epistle of Saint Paul to the Corinthians*, 87.

11.  Ibid., 88.

12.  Hering's comment, 88n49, is both anachronistic and strange. He comments, "In itself this stratagem has nothing humiliating about it. Some eastern monasteries, like the convent of St. Catherine at Sinai, normally welcome visitors by hoisting them up in a basket." Later Christian monastic practices in the tradition, e.g., of St. Anthony, could not have had any relation to practices that might have occurred centuries before. Beyond this, the seriousness of the situation is clearly demonstrated by the context.

13.  Betz is cited in his attempt to find parallels with one of the many ascension narratives in the ancient world. Barrett (*Second Epistle to the Corinthians*, 307) and Harris (*Second Epistle to the Corinthians*, 831), argue against this on the basis of the internal force of the text.

14.  Harris, *Second Epistle to the Corinthians*, 830–32.

15.  Barrett, *Second Epistle to the Corinthians*, 308.

16.  Henry Alford, *The Greek Testament* (Chicago: Moody, 1968) vol. 2, 710.

17.  For discussion see Furnish, *II Corinthians*, 525–26.

18.  I assert this despite Hering's warning, "It is useless then to seek the content of these revelations in the apostle's letters!" 91.

19.  Harris, *Second Epistle to the Corinthians*, 854.

20.  Ibid., 857, 858.

21.  Naylor, *2 Corinthians*, 2:210.

22.  Harris, *Second Epistle to the Corinthians*, 858, offers a fairly comprehensive and helpful catalog of views identified with adherents. In n. 160 he also cites several surveys of interpretive options, including those of Lightfoot, Plummer, Allo, Hughes, and Thrall.

23.  Adapted from ibid., 857.

24.  Ibid., 713.

25. Tasker, *Second Epistle of Paul to the Corinthians*, 175.

26. Ibid.

27. Naylor, *2 Corinthians*, 2:215.

28. Barrett, *Second Epistle to the Corinthians*, 319.

29. Furnish, *II Corinthians*, 553.

30. Ibid.

31. Ibid.

32. Barrett, *Second Epistle to the Corinthians*, 321. Emphasis his.

33. Calvin, cited in Tasker, *Second Epistle of Paul to the Corinthians*, 180.

34. Naylor, *2 Corinthians*, 2:212.

35. Garland, *2 Corinthians*, 531.

36. Furnish, *II Corinthians*, 564.

37. Ibid., 565.

38. Garland, *2 Corinthians*, 533.

39. The reference to the "brother" could either be the one sent by the churches or the other individual identified by Paul as "our brother." Regardless, his point is the same. All the people appointed by Paul to represent him at Corinth were trustworthy and godly men.

40. See my comments on 1:5; 2:17; and 10:1.

41. Barrett, *Second Epistle to the Corinthians*, 332.

42. Ibid.

## Chapter 17—Examine Yourselves

1. David E. Garland, *2 Corinthians*, The New American Commentary, ed. E. Ray Clendenen (Nashville: Broadman and Holman, 1999), 539 and n. 475, adds that this is further confirmation that these chapters cannot be the "sorrowful letter" referenced earlier.

2. Ibid., 337.

3. The expression is Perry C. Brown's. See "What Is the Meaning of 'Examine Yourselves' in 2 Corinthians 13:5?" *BibSac* 154 (April–June): 177.

4. Ibid., 185. Cf. also C. K. Barrett, *The Second Epistle to the Corinthians* (New York: Harper and Row, 1973), 338, *passim*.

5. Victor Furnish, *II Corinthians*, The Anchor Bible, vol. 6 (Garden City, NY: Doubleday, 1984), 577.

6. John F. MacArthur, Jr., *The Gospel According to Jesus* (Grand Rapids: Zondervan, 1988), 23, 190, 197.

7. Philip Edgcumbe Hughes, *Paul's Second Epistle to the Corinthians*, NICNT (Grand Rapids: Eerdmans, 1962), 3:481, also cited in Brown, "What Is the Meaning of 'Examine Yourselves'. . . ?" 181.

8. Ibid.

9. Ibid., 187.

10. W. G. Kummel, in Hans Lietzmann, *An die Korinther I, II*, Handbuch zum Neuen Testament 9, 5th ed with supplements by W. G. Kummel (1969), cited with approval in Barrett, *Second Epistle to the Corinthians*, 337.

11. E.g., Z. C. Hodges, *The Gospel under Siege* (Dallas: Viva, 1992), 112.

12. Again, Brown's term here. "What Is the Meaning of 'Examine Yourselves'. . . ?" 188.

13. Jean Hering, *The Second Epistle of Saint Paul to the Corinthians* (London: Epworth, 1967), 101–2.

14. Furnish, *II Corinthians*, 580. He argues, "While this statement of purpose is admirably suited to the material found in chaps. 10–13, it is ill-suited as a description of the purpose of chaps 1–9. Nothing in chaps. 1–9 suggests that Paul is planning a visit to Corinth in the near future, and nothing there suggests that he would find it necessary to deal harshly with the congregation if he were to come. Moreover, it is unthinkable that Paul would sum up the purpose of any letter which included the kind of appeal found in chaps. 8, 9 (on behalf of the collection for Jerusalem) without the slightest further reference to that request. These problems are solved if, as seems probable for a variety of reasons, chaps. 10–13 constitute a separate letter.

15. For discussion, see also Garland, *2 Corinthians*, 581.

## Chapter 18—Peace, the Gift of God's Love

1. Alfred Plummer, *A Critical and Exegetical Commentary on the Second Epistle of St. Paul to the Corinthians* (New York: Scribner, 1915), 379–80; see also David E. Garland, *2 Corinthians*, The New American Commentary, ed. E. Ray Clendenen (Nashville: Broadman and Holman, 1999), 552. For the opposing view, see Victor Furnish, *II Corinthians*, The Anchor Bible, vol. 6 (Garden City, NY: Doubleday, 1984), 580, cited above; C. K. Barrett, *The Second Epistle to the Corinthians* (New York: Harper and Row, 1973), 341.

2. My understanding is opposed to Barrett, *Second Epistle*, 342, who also supports a partition theory and is loathe here to necessarily see anything unique to the Corinthian situation. In support he cites the use of the term elsewhere in the New Testament in Philippians 4:4; Acts 15:23; 23:26; James 1:1.

3. Garland, *2 Corinthians*, 554–55.

4. Barrett, *Second Epistle to the Corinthians*, 343.

5.  Tertullian, *De Oratione* , trans. S. Thelwall, 1869 (The Tertullian Project) Chap. 18, http://www.tertullian.org/anf/anf03/anf03-51.htm#P11920_3330472 (accessed May 11, 2009).

6.  Charles Hodge, *An Exposition of the Second Epistle to the Corinthians* (Grand Rapids: Eerdmans, 1864), 312. See also my *1 Corinthians: Christianity in a Hostile Culture* (Chattanooga, TN: AMG, 2004), 157–65, where I argue for a similar approach to the "head covering" seemingly prescribed by the apostle.

7.  Frank J. Matera, *II Corinthians: A Commentary*, The New Testament Library (Louisville: Westminster John Knox, 2003), 313. See also Furnish, *II Corinthians*, 582, 583.

8.  Furnish, *II Corinthians*, 583.

9.  Murray J. Harris, *The Second Epistle to the Corinthians*, NIGTC (Grand Rapids: Eerdmans, 2005), 937.

10. Ibid.

11. Barrett, *Second Epistle to the Corinthians*, 344, which see for fuller discussion of this issue, including suggested reading.

12. Matera, *II Corinthians*, 314. Dan Wallace includes a "plenary genitive" that would allow for this, although he does not include this verse as an example. See D. B. Wallace, *Greek Grammar beyond the Basics* (Grand Rapids: Zondervan, 1996), 119–21.

13. Harris, *Second Epistle to the Corinthians*, 938.

14. See ibid., 938–41, for a discussion of the arguments on each side of this fairly even debate. At the end of the day, Harris agrees with Barrett, Meyer, Lietzmann, Windisch, Seeseman, Kummel, Hauk, Goodspeed, Moule, Hermann, Furnish, Wolff, Martin, and Thrall that the decisive weight is with the objective genitive. With this I also concur.

15. Jean Hering, *The Second Epistle of Saint Paul to the Corinthians* (London: Epworth, 1967), 103.

16. Harris, *Second Epistle to the Corinthians*, 938.

17. Ibid.

18. Nor would we have expected Clement to have praised Paul as an example in his letter to the believers in Corinth a generation later (1 *Clement* 5:5–7).

# About the Author

Dr. Daniel R. Mitchell is the academic dean of Liberty Theological Seminary and professor of Theological Studies. Dan has been in full-time ministry since 1964, serving as a chaplain, pastor, and seminary professor. He has been with Liberty since 1976. He is a graduate of Washington Bible College (B.A.), Capital Bible Seminary (Th.M.), and Dallas Theological Seminary (S.T.M.; Th.D.). In addition to many published articles, he was general editor of the *King James Study Bible* (Nelson) and consulting editor of the recently published *KJV Study Bible* (Zondervan). He has pastored two churches in Virginia, during which time he preached through 1 Corinthians in anticipation of writing the previous volume on the first epistle to the Corinthians. This volume on Paul's second letter was written in anticipation of teaching the course "The Corinthian Correspondence" at LTS. He has also taught at Western Seminary, and seminaries in Holland and Brazil. Dan lives with his wife, Nancy, in Forest, Virginia. They have four grown children and ten grandchildren.

## About the General Editors

Mal Couch is founder and former president of Tyndale Theological Seminary and Biblical Institute in Fort Worth, Texas. He previously taught at Philadelphia College of the Bible, Moody Bible Institute, and Dallas Theological Seminary. His other publications include *The Hope of Christ's Return: A Premillennial Commentary on 1 and 2 Thessalonians, A Bible Handbook to Revelation*, and *Dictionary of Premillennial Theology*.

Edward Hindson is professor of religion, dean of the Institute of Biblical Studies, and assistant to the chancellor at Liberty University in Lynchburg, Virginia. He has authored more than thirty books, served as coeditor of several Bible projects, and was one of the translators for the New King James Version of the Bible. Dr. Hindson has served as a visiting lecturer at Oxford University and Harvard Divinity School as well as numerous evangelical seminaries. He has taught more than fifty thousand students in the past twenty-five years.